Straight Talk about Bonds and Bond Funds

Other *Straight Talk* Books from McGraw-Hill

John Slatter
STRAIGHT TALK ABOUT STOCK INVESTING

Dian Vujovich
STRAIGHT TALK ABOUT MUTUAL FUNDS, revised edition

Dian Vujovich
STRAIGHT TALK ABOUT INVESTING FOR YOUR RETIREMENT

Straight Talk about Bonds and Bond Funds

Hildy Richelson

Stan Richelson

McGraw-Hill

New York   San Francisco   Washington, D.C.   Auckland   Bogotá
Caracas   Lisbon   London   Madrid   Mexico City   Milan
Montreal   New Delhi   San Juan   Singapore
Sydney   Tokyo   Toronto

Library of Congress Cataloging-in-Publication Data

Richelson, Hildy.
    Straight talk about bonds and bond funds / Hildy Richelson and
Stan Richelson.
            p.   cm.
    Includes index.
    ISBN 0-07-052303-7
    1. Bonds.   2. Investment analysis.   3. Bond market.   I. Title.
HG4651.R53   1996
332.63'23—dc20   96-12420
                                                          CIP

McGraw-Hill

A Division of The McGraw-Hill Companies

1 2 3 4 5 6 7 8 9 0   DOC/DOC   9 0 1 0 9 8 7 6

ISBN 0-07-052303-7

*The sponsoring editor for this book was David Conti, the editing supervisor
was Patricia V. Amoroso, and the production supervisor was Pamela Pelton. It
was set in Palatino by Victoria Khavkina of McGraw-Hill's Professional Book
Group composition unit.*

Printed and bound by R. R. Donnelley & Sons Company.

This publication is designed to provide accurate and authoritative information in regard to the subject matter covered. It is sold with the understanding that the publisher is not engaged in rendering legal, accounting, or other
professional service. If legal advice or other expert assistance is required,
the services of a competent professional person should be sought.

*—From a declaration of principles jointly adopted by a committee
of the American Bar Association and a committee of publishers.*

   This book is printed on recycled, acid-free paper containing a
minimum of 50% recycled de-inked fiber.

To our mothers and children with love
Elsie and Beatrice
Jolie and Scott

Contents

Preface

Bonds are an essential part of all financial programs. This book will arm you with a tool kit of simple but powerful strategies that will enable you to determine successfully how bonds fit into your portfolio and how to invest in bonds. We will provide you with the knowledge that is used by the wealthiest investors to structure their bond portfolios. We designed this book for investors of all means who want to take responsibility for their financial lives by putting themselves in a position to make their own decisions and actively contribute to their own success. Through practical tips and financial alternatives, we will guide you to build your own portfolio. The bond market lingo is explained in the text and further clarified in a long glossary.

All investors walk the line between greed and fear. Investing in stock was all the rage as the bull market continued on in 1995. Lost in the media coverage was the other half of the investment world, the world of bonds and bond funds. Bonds are important for the typical investor who is adverse to risk and who cannot afford to lose capital reserves. Bonds have a secure place in the world of investments because of their usefulness in solving financial problems. In today's market, bonds are like Rodney Dangerfield: They don't get enough respect. This book makes the case for bonds and bond funds.

This is not a textbook. It is a how-to book. An emphasis is placed on real problems and practical advice. We have drawn upon our many years of advising clients about bonds and financial planning to put together a handbook about bonds and bond funds. Based on our work with our clients, we are very familiar with the kinds of questions an intelligent investor might ask. Often a client might start out saying, "You might think this is a dumb question but..." There are no dumb questions, only good questions posed by inexperienced investors.

We have posed a few questions of our own. These are not questions to trick you, but rather questions you can use to gather information about bonds and bond funds long after you have forgotten many of the particular details of this book. By knowing the right questions to ask, you will be able to gather information about bond investments. This book will give you the tools to evaluate the information that you receive.

It will also give you the tools to think about how bonds might be useful to you in dealing with your financial life cycle. Though all our lives may be varied, we share more in common than birth, death, and taxes. We must plan for catastrophes, retirement, and the costly pleasures of family life, including weddings and college education for our kids. That takes advance planning. When we are involved in our busy lives, it is difficult to reflect on a long-term plan for our lives. Seven case studies of individuals are provided to help you think about your own situation. They provide practical examples of how people in different walks of life solved their financial problems with bonds and bond funds.

In order to know how to use bonds, it is important to understand the special attributes of bonds. If you understand how a bond works, then you will also have a better understanding of bond funds and other products that package bonds. Understanding bonds will also enable you to evaluate products that produce income like a bond but are not bonds.

Bonds can be dressed up so that the basic bond is barely recognizable. Bond imitators abound because the basic bond is a very safe and secure investment.

In Part 1 we describe in summary terms the advantages and risks associated with bonds, together with an outline of all the different kinds of bond investments. We describe how bonds began and explain the nitty-gritty of what they are. You are introduced to the language of bonds so that you can speak with authority when you deal with your broker and other advisers.

All investments have risks. Doing nothing with your money has different risks. If the risks are known, then they can be evaluated and dealt with. We describe all the different kinds of risks that you might encounter when buying bonds and explain how to deal with these risks practically and minimize them.

One source of confusion in buying bonds is how to evaluate a bond offering. There are many yield concepts applied to bonds and to bond funds. We simply review all the yield concepts and describe in words, with a very few numbers, the mathematical concepts that you need to know to be a savvy bond or bond-fund buyer.

There are many different kinds of bonds. Some are triple tax-exempt from federal, state, and local taxes. Others are fully taxable. Some are backed by mortgages, and others by corporations or the federal government. Each type of bond has a practical place in the portfolio of the intelligent investor. Part 2 of this book describes the major categories of bonds and bond funds and the procedures that will guide you in how to buy each category.

We discuss certificates of deposit and U.S. savings bonds because they are widely used. We point out the positive aspects of these investments and discuss safe alternatives for short-term investments. Other bond categories for short- or long-term investments described in Part 2 include U.S. Treasury bonds, U.S. federal agency bonds, municipal bonds, and corporate bonds (including junk bonds). Each category of bond has its own advantages, uses, and risks. Bonds can be purchased individually or as part of a short- or long-term bond fund. Understanding their advantages and pitfalls will guide you in selecting the right category of bond to solve your financial problems.

Both individual bonds and bond funds serve different functions within a portfolio and have different strengths and weaknesses. You must decide what is right for you. We advise that, where possible, buying individual bonds makes sense for most people who gain an understanding of bonds. Purchasing individual bonds will minimize your fees, maximize your return, and give you the power to customize your bond portfolio to your own needs. However, we explain why bond funds should be used if you want to purchase money-market funds, junk bonds, or mortgage pass-through securities. Funds are also very valuable if you have only small amounts to invest or you have the need for ready liquidity.

Part 3 of this book compares the advantages and disadvantages of open-ended bond funds, closed-end bond funds, and unit investment trusts. While each of the three entities has theoretical advantages, for practical reasons, open-ended bond funds are the preferred investment vehicle. We focus on the open-ended bond mutual funds in great detail, including a discussion of fees and liquidity. Some types of bonds are easier to deal with and safer when purchased as part of a fund. Others are not.

Both bonds and bond funds must compete with stock for attention. The media pours forth a huge volume of material daily, weekly, monthly, and annually. We review the presentation styles of information about bonds and discuss how to sort through the information. We talk about how and where to find the information that you need to make good investment decisions and how to evaluate the noise and glut of useless information being provided by the media. We deal with what to do if you know that you don't know.

Knowing about bonds and bond funds is not enough. You must also learn how to purchase them. In Part 4 we describe how to find and work with a broker when you buy and sell bonds. Brokers have a conflict of interest because they must sell the bonds and other bond products that the brokerage house owns. They have a difficult job. To be a successful investor you have to know how to work cooperatively with them. We explain how to use your broker to your best advantage when you buy and sell bonds.

Part of your job is to know the basics of buying a bond or bond fund. We give you a step-by-step approach to buying individual bonds, from preparation to investigation to the mechanics of the completion of the trade. We present a standard by which you can measure bond funds and choose a fund family. Specific bond fund families are recommended, and we provide addresses and phone numbers. We also present a list of questions that the intelligent investor can use to measure products that imitate bonds. When interest rates sink to what seems to be an impossibly low level, bond imitators are plentiful.

The world of bonds is wide and deep. This book will not drown you in detail. We try to give our advice and conclusions clearly. We tell you where we stand on a question. You might not agree with all of our conclusions, but you will know what we recommend and why. We do not list a multitude of considerations and tell you to weigh them. Our goal is to provide *Straight Talk about Bonds and Bond Funds*.

If you have any questions while you read our book, feel free to call or write us.

Hildy Richelson, Ph.D.
President, Scarsdale Investment
  Group, Ltd.
Box 858
Ambler, PA 19002-0858
215-646-7693

Stan Richelson, J.D., LL.M.
  (in taxation)
Investment Counsel and Attorney
Box 858
Ambler, PA 19002-0858
215-646-8768

Acknowledgments

We draw our strength from the critical thinking and writing of many authors. We have absorbed their philosophy and insights and have made them part of our lives. We wish to acknowledge their work and their influence on this book.

John C. Bogle is chairman, The Vanguard Group of Investment Companies. He is the conscience of the mutual fund industry. He has set a standard in the fund industry for all to follow, particularly regarding bonds and index funds. At Vanguard, the shareholders and their funds own the management company. This unique structure accounts for Vanguard's low fees, which set the standard for the entire industry. Mr. Bogle has written an outstanding book on funds entitled *Bogle on Mutual Funds*.

Joe Dominguez and Vicki Robin are among the leaders in the philosophy of downshifting, combining personal needs with economic and financial endeavors. Their book *Your Money or Your Life* teaches how to lead a life that reflects personal needs and preferences. It is one of our favorite personal finance books. We aspire to the same level of practicality.

Burton G. Malkiel, a professor at Princeton University, has written a book entitled *A Random Walk Down Wall Street*. This is a classic book about how stocks and bonds work in the real world. It is without hype or conflict of interest. We aspire to the same standard.

Jacob Needleman has written a book entitled *Money and the Meaning of Life*. The title tells the story. Needleman is a professor of comparative religion.

Financial Passages by Benjamin J. Stein introduced us to the concept of financial passages, giving the concept of financial planning a new twist.

Andrew Tobias's book entitled *The Only Investment Guide You'll Ever Need* is a great introduction to investments, written with style and humor. We aspire to his clarity.

We have learned a great deal about the practical world of bonds from *The Bond Buyer*, a daily publication to the trade that reports on the nuances of the municipal bond market.

We owe thanks to those people who are on the front lines, the bond brokers who assist us and our clients in buying and selling bonds every day. We would like to mention a few who have been advising us for many years: George Connerat at Merrill Lynch; Frank Ackerman at Bear, Stearns; and Debbie Weiner at Gruntal & Co. There are other brokers who have contributed to our understanding of bond investments and the financial markets: Fred Uhde at Hutchinson, Shockey, Erley; Peter Cristus at Gabriele, Hueglin & Cashman; Dan Quigley at Mellon Financial; Peggy O'Neill at W. H. Newbold's; Charles Ryan and Barry DeWitt at William R. Hough; Peter Mangin at Barr Brothers; Peter Appuzzo at Wheat First Butcher Singer; Hal Grodzins at Stoever, Glass; and Lucia Bertea at Monarch Financial.

Sid Aronson, Carole Haas, Sam Kirschner, and George Robinson have mentored us over the years. They have helped to raise our consciousness and emotional intelligence. They have enabled us to be better people and to be of greater service to our clients.

Finally, we learn about life and investments every day from our clients who provide the real-life context to our study and work. By asking questions, they have helped us sharpen our skills.

PART 1

Understanding and Using Bonds to Solve Financial Problems

1
Why Invest in Bonds?

Anyone who stops learning is old, whether at twenty or eighty. Anyone who keeps learning stays young. The greatest thing in life is to keep your mind young.

HENRY FORD

Introduction

Stocks and bonds are suitable investments for most individuals. Exotic investments in commodities, collectibles, and gold are too risky and illiquid to form the basis of a serious investment program.

For the last 70 years stocks have outperformed bonds. Why not invest all of your money in stocks? There are many good reasons for not putting all of your investment eggs in the stock basket.

- An investment in stocks puts your principal more at risk than an investment in bonds. Preserving principal is a high priority with most investors. Our first investment rule has always been, "Don't lose money." Preserving your principal becomes more important as you get older.

- Your financial goals and personal situation should drive your choice of investments. The temptation to reallocate your money into different "hot" investments and "hot" stocks every six months can be costly and your investments may lag behind the successes of a market sector.

- Stocks are much more volatile and unpredictable than bonds. Thus, stocks are not suitable investments to use for short-term goals such as a rainy-day fund or saving for a house, car, or boat. The value of stocks may fall dramatically. Stocks do not come due at a fixed date. By contrast, you will receive the face value of your bonds at a fixed date.

- Stock dividends are not as predictable as the income produced by bonds. Company policy may reduce or terminate dividends. The dividend income from old standbys such as electric utilities and the telephone companies is not what it was in the past.

Bonds are a premier investment. All individuals should have at least some of their money invested in bonds. Take a tour of the world of bonds. See the Income Selector at the end of this chapter. There are many different kinds of bonds, and many ways to own them. We will advise you how to take advantage of the opportunities available to you and warn you of the many pitfalls. Knowing what not to do is at least as important as understanding the investment opportunities brokers offer you.

Buying a bond for the first time can feel a little scary. There you are with your hard-earned cash sitting safely in a bank. Although your principal is safe, you are not happy with the interest rate you are being paid. You want a higher return. You know there are other investment alternatives that pay higher returns. However, you also know that investing in something about which you know little might result in the loss of your money. What to do?

Tip_____

The return on an investment is always proportional to the degree of risk. There is no free lunch. If you want a higher return, be prepared to step up to more risk. We will provide you with the information you need to evaluate the risks so that you can make good decisions about your money.

You have heard about bonds. They come in many different varieties. What you have read or heard about bonds might seem somewhat confusing. Learning about bonds will take your time and energy, and you have lots of things to do. You will have to evaluate the advice of others and make a decision about how to invest your money. Not taking action is also making a decision that the current placement of your funds is satisfactory.

The goal of *Straight Talk about Bonds and Bond Funds* is to help you understand the world of bonds well enough for you to make your own decisions and to work with brokers and advisers. More specifically, we will help you find answers to some questions you have about investing. We will introduce you to the following subjects:

- What is a bond? What are the advantages and the pitfalls of investing in bonds?
- How can bonds and bond funds fit into your financial planning?
- What are the mathematical concepts related to bonds that you should know?
- What are the different kinds of bonds? When is it appropriate to buy Treasury bonds, EE bonds, mortgage pass-through securities, corporate bonds, and municipal bonds?
- How do you know when to buy bond funds instead of bonds?
- Where do you find information about bonds and bond funds?
- How do you deal with a broker in order to get the best bonds at good prices?
- Are there any special techniques to know when buying bonds?

Why Learn about Bonds?

Bonds can provide a substitute for the allowance money you got from your parents when you were young. Bonds provide a regular stream of income every six months. For this reason, many people buy bonds even when bonds are not in the "hot" sector of the investment market. They would rather have a predictable second income than a potential for greater upside gain.

Bonds can provide you with a predictable cashflow based upon regular payments of interest and a return of your principal when the bond comes due. Wouldn't it be nice to plan on an extra sum of money coming in each month?

Bonds and their close relations are embedded in your financial life. Bonds are the foundation blocks of bond funds, money-market funds, and balanced funds. A pass-through security might contain the mortgage from your home or your student loan. Your pension plan is probably partly dependent on bond investments. Insurance companies meet their obligations partly through bond investments. Money borrowed through bond issues build your schools, sewers, water systems, electricity, municipal buildings, roads, and new corporate parks.

Individual bonds:

are simple to understand,

have provided a predictable steady stream of interest income for hundreds of years,

are relatively safe,

return your full investment when the loan comes due,

can mature in one month or thirty years, as you desire,

can be purchased individually or as part of a bond fund,

are part of a highly regulated industry overseen by the Municipal Securities Rulemaking Board (MSRB), the Securities and Exchange Commission (SEC), the Public Securities Association (PSA), the rating agencies (Moody's Investors Service, Standard & Poor's Corporation, Fitch Investors Service Inc., Duff & Phelps), the financial press, and the general public.

Personal Responsibility

Learning about investments sometimes seems like an overwhelming task. Even the most sophisticated investors often follow someone else's advice without doing their own investigation. You can acquire enough financial knowledge to tell your broker and your adviser what returns you want and what risks you are prepared to take. It is your money! You are ultimately responsible for the outcome.

The Foundation for New Era Philanthropy began in 1989 with a promise to double investors' money in six months. George G. Bennett Jr., chief executive, was able to convince large foundations and big donors to deposit their funds with New Era in an unsecured brokerage account. In the philanthropic community, everyone knew of a foundation that had deposited money with New Era and received back twice as much. John Templeton Sr., the wealthy founder of a large family of mutual funds, was one of Bennett's big supporters and on New Era's board of directors. What would you have done if you were offered the deal of double your money in six months?

The temptation is overwhelming, but you can guess the outcome. In 1995 an Australian accountant working at a small midwestern religious college uncovered the fraud. However, he was unable to prevent his own college from joining the investment herd. His colleagues would not accept his suspicions that there were no anonymous donors matching the deposits at New Era as everyone thought. With the funds collected from later donors, New Era paid the first donors in what turned out reportedly to be a giant Ponzi scheme. In Philadelphia, many of the large foundations deposited funds with New Era. The director of the Philadelphia Museum of Art, Robert Montgomery Scott, said that he wasn't "smart enough" to have invested in New Era.

Are You Smart Enough?

Your investment needs are different from the investment needs of others. There is no ideal investment for everyone. What investment to choose depends upon your individual circumstances and objectives. How do you visualize your situation in five years or ten years? Let your financial goals and personal situation drive your choice of investments, rather than trying to find the next hot investment area that will double your money in a year or two.

Bonds won't make you rich overnight. They won't provide you with great windfalls unless you speculate on interest-rate fluctuations. What bonds will do is provide you with a good, regular return on your money, often matching stock market returns without the associated risk to your principal. Bonds can provide a basis of security leading to personal freedom. The income from your bonds will enable you to pay the rent if your job disappears.

There are always pitfalls in any investment. In order to help you make, not lose, money, we have to have straight talk about bonds and bond funds.

The Risks of Investing

The risks of investing lie within us as well as in a given investment and market environment. While examining the risks of a particular investment, it is important to examine your own personal attitudes toward investing and be clear about your objectives. If you do not have clear goals and objectives, you might be more easily swayed by a convincing salesperson or the anticipation of extraordinary returns.

Fire Company X, for example, was very dissatisfied with the 2 percent to 4 percent returns it was making on its bank certificates of deposits. Its finance committee members read that other investors had been making a 15 percent return on stocks. Perhaps they were being derelict in their duty, they thought. They anticipated purchasing a costly new fire engine and also needed money available for emergency repairs. They knew that they did not want to put the fire company's money at risk and that they needed to maintain liquidity in case of emergency needs.

At the urging of some members of Fire Company X, the finance committee explored other investment alternatives. They contacted an outside adviser and stipulated that they only wanted investments that were safe and liquid. A liquid investment is one that can be sold easily without high transaction costs of sale. The outside adviser recommended that Treasury bills and notes, which could range in maturity between three months and seven years, would pay more interest than CDs. The adviser also said that corporate bonds of similar maturities would pay more than Treasury bills and notes. However, the corporate bonds would be less liquid than the Treasury bonds.

Then from out of the ranks of the fire company came a young broker who said that he could recommend investments that would yield a lot more than Treasury and corporate bonds. He recommended buying a mutual fund which invested in foreign stocks. He also recommended an annuity. At this moment, the hope for higher returns caused the fire company to disregard its objectives of safety and liquidity and the advice of its outside adviser who recommended investments that were in accord with the stated objectives. The fire company purchased a foreign stock fund despite the fact that it was very risky and had high initial fees and even higher yearly fees. The fire company also purchased the annuity despite the fact that it locks the money away by imposing high exit fees. The *teaser rate*, or initial high interest rate used to attract the investor, is lowered to lusterless returns after a short period of time.

All too often the individual investor heeds the refrain of "Trust me! I will double your money in no time!" The investor loses sight of the story that ends with the question: "And where are the customers' yachts?" The question was asked by a customer in response to seeing all the yachts owned by a broker and his associates.

One of the best defenses against unintentionally making a high-risk investment is to ask for a *prospectus,* a document required by the SEC in which all the risks must be disclosed. Believe that! Then if you decide to proceed, it will be with your eyes open. Do not be hurried into an investment without reviewing the prospectus. There is always another deal coming down the pike. If a current prospectus is not available for the current offering, ask to see one for a prior deal. Bond prospectuses are generally not available unless it is a new issue, and then usually are not available until after the deal is sold. However, there are many questions which can be raised and answered which should give you comfort.

If there are losses, only the investor suffers them. Brokers, having made their fee, move on. You are ultimately responsible for your choices. A loss of your principal is very hard to recoup. For example, if you had $100 and lost 50 percent of your investment, you would be left with $50. If you then were to make 50 percent, you would only have $75. You would need to make 100 percent on your money to break even. If you had the same $100 and made 50 percent on your investment, you would have $150. If you then lost 50 percent, you would have $75. *Losses to your capital cannot be easily recouped!*

The Continuum of Risk and Reward

Your job, your family, the activities you like to do keep you busy. Money is something which is supposed to be there when you need it. Who has time to think about it? Somehow, at the end of the month when the bills come in there never seems to be quite enough. Yet you have to save for the biggies—children's education and retirement, not to mention that special vacation about which you always dreamed.

Plan ahead to save what you know you will need, rather than saving whatever is left over at the end of the month. If you know you have a purpose for saving, that extra pair of shoes, the new billfold, that extra dinner out are not so important. What you need is a plan.

Part of the plan is making your money work as hard for you as you work to get it. That means that at the end of the month you evaluate your money's performance. Lazy money is money which is costing you money. Unpaid credit card bills with an annual percentage rate of 18 percent may be a cost you can avoid. Are you working for the credit card company or for yourself? You can find a credit card company with a cheaper rate and pay off that debt! Got any cash around? Where is it sitting? How much is it earning in the account where it is? Can you do better? How much more risk is there to make it work harder?

Risks can be thought of as a continuum, with the investments which represent the lowest risk on one end and the highest-risk investments on the other end. Investments secured by the federal government, such as U.S. savings bonds, certificates of deposit, three-month and six-month Treasury issues, and bank deposits backed by the Federal Deposit Insurance Corporation (FDIC) are considered the safest of all investments. Safe is good, but where is the yield? Interest rates on long-term Treasury bonds collapsed from over 14 percent in 1981 to below 6 percent in 1993. In 1989, the average yield on interest-bearing checking accounts was 5.15 percent. By 1993 it was 1.65 percent, a decline of 68 percent. In an effort to stave off inflationary pressures, the Federal Open Market Committee raised the federal funds target rate seven times from 3 percent to 6 percent between February 4, 1994, and February 1, 1995. The rates on bank checking accounts and savings accounts were slow to change.

Do you still allow your money to collect in checking accounts, or are you insisting on higher returns? You could explore other states' banks that pay higher interest on their checking accounts. Alternatively you could make sure that your idle cash is popped into a certificate of deposit, a money-market fund, or a Treasury bill for three months or six months.

Stepping up the continuum of risk are individual bonds with maturities of less than five years. These can be of very high credit quality with minimal market volatility. Nothing is guaranteed, but you will get your principal back from your bond investment in five years. Given changes in the tax structure and changes in the investment environment, you will be able to make a new investment decision at the end of that time. By locking up your money for a longer period of time you may get more yield or you may get only a guarantee of the same yield for a longer period. At times of low inflationary expectations, such as existed in 1995, you may not get much yield pickup between one year and five years. If the Federal Reserve decides to lower short-term interest rates to put more money into the economy, then you will be glad of your decision.

Short-term bond funds do not fall into the same category as short-term bonds because the principal invested in funds is not returned at a fixed due date. If you put your money into the fund when interest rates are low and the Federal Reserve raises short-term interest rates, you will lose principal if you have to sell your fund. Bond funds with 10-year maturities suffer from the same problem. In addition, many bond funds have special types of investments that bolster yields but make them particularly sensitive to interest-rate fluctuations and, hence, loss of principal. See Chaps. 11 and 12 on bond funds.

Stock index funds, 30-year bonds, and long-term bond funds are another step up the risk ladder. The price of these investments fluctuates with the movement of long-term interest rates. Investments in stocks and long-term bonds were very profitable from 1981 to 1993 because of the steep decline in interest rates over that period of time. But speculating on long-term interest rates and the stock market takes you on a roller coaster ride. Everyone is ecstatic on the uphill pull, but the downward collapse of the stock market and the rise in long-term interest rates can be dizzying. The time you need the money may be when your stocks and long-term bonds have declined substantially.

International bonds and international bond funds, high-yield bonds and high-yield bond funds take another step into the altitude of high yield and high risk. When you invest in international funds you take on both interest-rate risks and currency risks. Though the international invest-

ments that are priced in foreign currency are touted because they are supposed to be a hedge against dollar investments, recent research concludes
that it is questionable whether they go up in value when dollar-denomi-
nated investments decline. Rather, international investments and U.S.
investments appear to move in the same direction. Thus, international
investments may not provide a hedge like they are advertised to do.

High-yield bonds, also known as junk bonds, provide high interest
rates but put your capital at risk. Perhaps you will be able to distinguish,
or find a fund that can distinguish, between higher-quality low-rated
bonds and those teetering on default. Junk bonds fall into the same category as low-grade real estate. You may never get all your principal back.

Continuing in the category of high yield and high risk are premium
mortgage bonds. They are risky despite the fact that they have a triple-A
credit rating. (See Chap. 4 and Table 4-1 for an explanation of bond ratings.) This is because you might pay more than the redemption price at a
time when interest rates are dropping. People refinance their mortgages
to get the lower rates. That means money flows back to the issuer of the
bonds who then calls in the bonds at the face value of the bonds. The calls
are unpredictable. If you paid $1030 for a bond, it could be called next
month for $1000. This is a conservative investment, however, if it is pur-
chased through a large Government National Mortgage Association
(GNMA) bond fund. The size of the fund cushions the movement of interest rates.

Penny stock, commodities, and collectibles are all grouped together at
the riskiest extreme of the continuum. The value of all investments is
based on supply and demand. If there is too much supply or not enough
demand, you will not be able to get your money out. There is no way of
predicting that, when you need or want your money, you will be able to
exit gracefully and happily.

It is often assumed that riskier investments will necessarily result in
higher returns. At least the investor is promised much higher returns if
she will put her money at risk. The problem with this scenario is that
because of the higher risk, the money invested may be lost. The promised
returns may never materialize. If this is the case, then the lower-yielding,
safer investment would have been the better choice.

The Income Selector

A portfolio of bonds would be invaluable if you wish to plan for your
retirement, pay for your child's education, self-insure part of your
insurance coverage, or reduce your income in order to take a less

demanding or more fulfilling job (i.e., "downshift"). The predictable income generated by a bond portfolio would supplement your income and might enable you to succeed at or at least try a new lifestyle.

The Income Selector is a laundry list of possible different sources of income. It is a useful overview of the major possible income-producing investments. Each of these investments is explained in more detail in Part 2 of this book.

Tax-Free Municipal Bonds

Municipal bonds provide income which is free of federal income tax and possibly state and local taxes. The maturity range of municipal bonds is from 1 year to 30 years on new issues. Credit quality can vary greatly. See Chap. 9.

Taxable Municipal Bonds

Taxable municipal bonds are issued by state and local governments and their agencies. These bonds are subject to federal income taxes. They pay a yield similar to corporate bonds. Taxable municipals are appropriate for a pension plan. Taxable municipal bonds may be more desirable than corporate bonds if the municipal bond issuer is a better credit.

Treasury Bonds

Treasury bonds, bills, and notes are subject to federal income tax but are free of state and local taxes. They are backed by the full faith and credit of the U.S. government. New bills have a 30-day maturity, and bonds have a maximum maturity of 30 years. These bonds do not have credit risk. See Chap. 6.

Federal Agency Bonds

Federal agency bonds are issued by the agencies of the federal government. They have slightly lower credit quality than Treasuries and, therefore, yield a bit more than Treasuries do. Treasuries are easier to trade than agency bonds and the costs of trading Treasuries are lower.

GNMAs are popular federal agency bonds that are backed by the full faith and credit of the U.S. government. They have a high cashflow.

Their yields are not directly comparable to bond yields because their cashflow is not predictable. The yield is generally higher than other triple-A credits, which compensates for the unknown factors. GNMA income is subject to federal, state, and local income tax. See Chap. 8.

U.S. Savings Bonds

Otherwise known as E, EE, or HH bonds, they are issued by the federal government. These are zero-coupon bonds sold in small denominations to the retail investor through banks or directly from the Federal Reserve Bank. See Chap. 7.

Certificates of Deposit

Banks offer certificates of deposit. Brokerage houses sell CDs issued by banks. These CDs are FDIC-insured if you invest less than $100,000 in a CD issued by a particular bank. There may be a minimum investment in a CD if it is sold through a brokerage house. See Chap. 7.

Corporate Bonds

Bonds issued by major corporations have a maturity range similar to other bonds of 1 to 30 years, though a few bonds have a maturity of 100 years. These bonds are fully taxable by the federal, state, and local governments. Quality ranges from junk-bond status of single-C to triple-A. The higher the yield, the lower the quality. Corporate bonds will provide a higher return than Treasury bonds and agency bonds because corporate bonds have a greater credit risk. This is a nice way of saying that corporate bonds might default and you might lose some or all of your investment. A default is more likely for high-yield (junk) bonds than investment-grade bonds. See Chap. 10.

Money-Market Funds

Money-market funds come in many flavors. There are taxable money-market funds that invest in a wide range of debt obligations; treasury money-market funds, which are exempt from state and local taxes; municipal bond money-market funds, which may be triple tax-exempt; or general market municipal bond money-market funds, which hold municipal paper from around the country. See Chap. 12.

Open-Ended Bond Funds

Bond mutual funds pool the money of many investors to achieve good investment returns. Shares in open-ended mutual funds can be redeemed upon request at the end-of-the-day share price. Bond funds can invest in Treasury bonds, corporate bonds, and mortgage pass-through securities. The credit quality and maturity range for the funds will vary. They can pay monthly income. They are very useful in a retirement plan at the time of life when some of the principal as well as the income is being consumed. Money-market funds are a kind of mutual fund. See Chaps. 11 and 12.

Closed-End Funds and Unit Investment Trusts

Like their open-ended cousin, closed-end funds and unit investment trusts pool investors' resources. However, these two investments cannot be redeemed on request but must be sold at the current market price, on the stock exchange for closed-end funds and to the fund sponsors for unit investment trusts. For a comparison of open-ended and closed-end bond funds and unit investment trusts, see Chap. 11.

2
What Is a Bond?

In the Beginning

Since the beginnings of time people were always running out of resources (including money) to do the things they wanted to do. The solution to this problem was to borrow resources from someone else. Going into debt is an old story. If the borrower and lender knew each other well, they might settle the deal with a handshake. If not, the borrower might agree to sign a piece of paper that said "I Owe You (IOU) so many dollars, and I agree to pay it back in the following way." The lender holds the IOU as evidence of the debt. As part of the agreement, there would generally be an understanding that the lender would receive something extra for lending. It might be a payment in kind, such as a bushel of wheat, a goat, or some extra money worth more than the original loan. This something extra is *interest*.

If all went well there was a "win-win" situation. The borrower was happy because he had the goods or the money. The lender got back his money with the something extra.

Some borrowers are more reliable than others. One person might repay a loan on time, but another might not be so prompt in repaying the loan. In a small community, the lender and the borrower would probably know each other. If the lender did not know the borrower, he would inquire around to find out about the character of the person and his family to ascertain how risky it would be to make the loan. The lender would ask where the borrower hoped to get the funds to pay back the loan. The lender would then determine for himself whether there was a good likelihood of the loan being repaid on time. The amount of interest charged by the lender was based on this determination. If the lender believed that the borrower was not a good risk, he would ask for more interest than he might from someone else borrowing the same amount. The borrower might pay more interest if this were his first loan because there was no history of his reliability.

Once the lender decided to make the loan, he would establish the terms of repayment. "I want you to pay me interest in the winter and the summer, on the money that I lent to you. In addition, you must repay the principal amount after the fall harvest." The lender might agree to no payments for four years, and at the end of that time, all the money would be repaid with interest.

The *principal* is the original amount of the money loaned and repaid. The "interest" is the amount of money that is paid by the borrower for the use of the principal.

The Bond Market

The bond market rests upon the simple principles of borrowing and lending which were established in the community. A bond is the same as the IOU. Both are evidence of the debt, the promise to pay that the borrower makes to the lender. In the bond market, the borrower is also called *the issuer*. The issuer agrees to pay interest on the loan at specified times. The financial community brings together the borrowers and the lenders. Examples of borrowers include large corporations and the federal and state governments and their agencies. Borrowers pay the rating agencies to evaluate their financial health. The rating agencies take the place of the members of the community and inform would-be lenders about the reliability of the borrower. As further protection for the lender, every bond has a legal opinion imprinted on it written by lawyers who have reviewed the legal documents and verified their accuracy. There is also a *prospectus,* which clarifies the economic strengths and weaknesses of the borrower and the terms of the deal. Some bonds are insured, guaranteeing the repayment of the principal and interest when due.

In a small community, if a borrower failed to meet his financial obligations, he would develop a bad reputation and no one would lend to him anymore. The financial community functions the same way in the bond market. For example, Brevard County, Florida, issued some "certificates of participation" (COPs). These come with contingencies. In this case, payments of principal and interest were not legally due unless the county legislature made annual appropriations. In 1994, the county legislature decided it had borrowed money and constructed a new municipal building that no one wanted. The legislature resolved not to appropriate money to pay the interest and principal due on the COPs. The rating agencies, the insurers of other county debt, and the brokerage houses demanded that the county change its attitude and make the agreed upon payments of principal and interest. After some wrangling, Brevard County got the message and appropriated money to pay for the COPs. The county issued new bonds and used the funds to pay off the COPs. The exchange of one bond issue for another is a *refunding*. The new bonds obliged the county to draw upon all of its many resources to meet its obligation in all events. There were no preconditions to payment of principal or interest. It issued a *general obligation bond* or *GO*.

The bottom line is that an issuer risks being ostracized from sources of capital if it does not abide by the letter and the spirit of the loan. At best, the cost of borrowing funds will rise if the lenders fear that the issuer will not abide by the terms of the agreement.

Bond Practicalities: Understanding the Market

Unlike the stock market, where most trading takes place on three primary exchanges, bonds sell on a dealer-to-dealer basis. The bond market is more comparable to the market in Oriental rugs and antiques than it is to the stock market. Stocks sell on the New York Stock Exchange, the American Stock Exchange, or the NASDAQ. Traders track the changes in value on a minute-to-minute basis. Corporate bonds might trade on the New York exchanges. However, most trade off the exchange in a dealer-to-dealer market. Treasury bonds have a core of primary dealers who sell to many other dealers. Municipal bonds are not listed at all on an exchange. All sell in a dealer-to-dealer market.

The Marketplace for Bonds

It is a mistake to assume that just because you purchase stocks from a particular broker it is wise to also purchase your bonds from the same broker. Many stockbrokers do not know much about bonds. Many stock buyers who use discount brokers believe that they can also purchase bonds at a discount from the same source as well. This is not the case. There are no discount bond brokers.

The bond market is a dealer-to-dealer market. Large brokerage houses and banks hire traders to deal in specific types of bonds. They might have a Treasury bond desk, a corporate bond desk, and a municipal bond desk. A *desk* means that the firm hired traders who specialize and trade a particular portfolio. Each trader specializes in a particular type of corporate bond or a particular region in municipal bonds. There are also small specialty houses called *boutiques* that deal in a narrow range of bonds.

Even among very large brokers, there are many who do not deal in all kinds of bonds. In 1995, major brokers such as Dean Witter and CS First Boston decided that the underwriting of municipal bonds was not profitable, and they stopped being market makers. Though they may have been a good source of municipal bonds for the retail buyer at one time, they no longer underwrite new issues. In order to purchase bonds for their retail clients, Dean Witter and CS First Boston now have to purchase them from other dealers and, thus, might not be the lowest-cost seller of municipal bonds.

The marketplace further subdivides itself into a wholesale and a retail market. In the wholesale market, corporate bonds trade in million-dollar-block sizes, with $50 and $100 million blocks not infrequent. The prices you see in the newspaper reporting trades and Treasury bond yields are reporting on block trades of at least $1 million. You will get a lower yield on your retail purchases. Municipal bonds trade in $100,000 block sizes. There are many more issuers of municipal bonds than corporate bonds. Thus, the fabric of municipal bond trading is even more complex than the other bond markets.

You need to shop around in order to determine which brokerage house has the kind of inventory you require. There are some brokers whose specialty is the retail municipal market. They deal in smaller lots of bonds and their salespeople are usually quite knowledgeable. Full-service brokers will always say that they inventory all kinds of bonds, but their bond desks have specialties as well. The only way to know who can best serve you is by speaking to brokers at many different houses. Unless the bonds sell as part of a new issue, brokers will be unable to tell you about the same bonds you have seen elsewhere. If the bond issue is recent, more dealers may have it in inventory. However, the greater likelihood is that if you call three brokers, you will get three different lists of bonds to consider.

Some brokers who try to sell you bonds may not understand all of the aspects of the bonds that they are selling, unless bonds form a significant part of their business. For example, the broker must know how to call up the bond information on the various computer screens. If the broker is not sophisticated in these matters, then he will not know where to look for the information. Just because you have a relationship with someone who sells stock, that does not make that person a suitable bond sales representative. You would not consider the person who sells lighting fixtures an expert in paint, even though paint and lighting fixtures are sold in the same store.

Types of Bond Specialties

Some brokers specialize in *story bonds*. Avoid bonds that require a long description and explanation (i.e., a story) of where the money is coming from to pay the debt if it makes you feel uneasy. If you are not offered the kind of bonds you are looking for, be sure to look elsewhere.

A broker might carry an inventory of municipal bonds with a strong regional concentration in high-tax states such as New York, California, Massachusetts, Pennsylvania, and Connecticut. Other brokers might specialize in selling nursing home debt. *Junk* or *high-yield bonds* form another specialty. The types of general market corporate bonds followed by a firm will also differ.

Tip_____

Finding the right person and the right place to sell you bonds may not be easy. However, your efforts will be rewarded by a secure portfolio and better-than-usual rewards. See Chap. 13 on how to work with a broker.

Negotiating the Price of a Bond

Most corporate and all municipal bonds sell in a *principal's market*. This means that the broker who sells you the bonds is in fact the owner of the bonds. By contrast, when a broker sells you stock, he is usually functioning as a broker. A broker brings together a buyer and a seller and earns a fee (called a commission) for his services. Since the broker in a bond trade is the owner of the bonds, you can bargain with him. In order to bargain, you must have some idea as to what kind of yield you could reasonably expect on a similar bond. It is not useful to pick a number out of the hat that has no semblance to actual market prices. Municipal bonds purchased in December 1994 at a 6.5 percent tax-exempt yield did not sell at that yield one month later. If you plan to make a purchase, it would be helpful to follow the general movement of interest rates by checking on Treasury yields. You might call the brokers on a regular basis for a short period so you can get a feel for the rates. You can ask the broker to tell you what were some good offerings he sold that particular day. Then you would have a basis for understanding what the broker thought was an inexpensive offering relative to the market.

Good offerings usually do not sit around very long. You have to prepare yourself to act quickly. The brokers will call their regular customers when a good offering appears in their inventory. In a bond house, all the brokers nationwide are selling the same inventory, and the cheapest items are the first to go. See Chap. 15 on how to buy bonds.

How Bonds Are Priced by the Brokerage Firms

Bond pricing depends on the following factors:

- The price at which the bonds were bought
- How much it costs to complete the paperwork necessary to sell or purchase the bonds
- How long the bonds have been in inventory
- Current and anticipated movement of interest rates

Just as the type of inventory is different from one broker to another, so will be the pricing of the bonds. Except for the bonds traded on the published exchanges, there is little specific information on how individual bonds trade. By comparing bonds of the same market sector, quality, and quantity the price of a bond can be established. Brokers use a bond matrix showing market sector yields to help establish their prices.

In the pricing of a bond, the broker gets a percentage of the price received from the sale, and the trader who represents the brokerage house earns a percentage for the brokerage house. The trader sets the price, but the broker might have some discretion to cut the price based upon how much of a markup the trader has allotted to him. Brokers will not voluntarily disclose what the brokerage house paid for the bond or how much they are making on a trade, though they may tell you if you ask. It is up to you to shop around and decide on the best buy.

One way to decide if you have made a good purchase is to ask what the purchase price of the bond would be if you were to sell it back to the same brokerage house the same day. The sale price of the bond would not be the same as the purchase price because the brokerage house has to make a profit. That would give you an idea of the *spread,* which is the amount of profit that the house makes on the sale of the bond. The brokerage house does not charge a commission on the purchase or sale of a bond. You could ask the broker to give you hypothetical bids on a number of bonds you are considering to discover the differences in the spread.

Corporate bonds are priced in relationship to Treasury bonds of the same maturity. Thus, Citicorp bonds might be selling at 80 basis points over Treasuries. There are 100 basis points in one percent. As the prices of the Treasury bonds fluctuate, so will the corporate bonds. If a five-year Treasury bond is yielding 6 percent, the Citicorp bond will yield 6.8 percent.

Evaluating Your Current Bond Holdings

Bonds purchased and kept in a brokerage house are priced monthly. These prices are estimates. The actual prices at which you can buy and sell might differ greatly. If the bond issue doesn't trade frequently, the bond prices are drawn from a bond matrix.

The use of the matrix does not always accurately reflect the true price of the bond. Disparities can result due to the size of the block, market volatility, and desirability of the issue. There are several hundred thousand distinct municipal bond issues outstanding, and their prices might vary widely from one pricing service to another. If a bond does not trade, the traders might have trouble deciding what they are willing to pay.

Matrix prices differ substantially from an actual price. For example, Bridgeport, Connecticut, Series A bonds with a 7.25 percent coupon due 6/1/2005 were valued at 97.252 or $9725 for a $10,000 bond by one brokerage house. These same bonds were bid at 106 or $10,600 and would have been reoffered for sale at 107.85 or $10,785. At the bottom of the brokerage statement there is a disclaimer that reads: "Most bond prices are derived from a pricing matrix and therefore might deviate from actual market prices. They are provided as a guide for portfolio value. Please check . . . for current market quotations." You better believe it!

Technical Tip_____

The forward rate is the rate that indicates where the market thinks rates are going. The forward rate is the product of the futures market, where traders make bets on the direction of interest rates or hedge the bond positions they are currently holding. Since there are many factors influencing the direction of interest rates, the forward rate may not accurately reflect what will actually happen. Be aware that when you ask about interest rates brokers sometimes quote the forward rate, because that is on their screen, rather than the current rate.

A Bond Description

A bond bid might look like this: "10 Pennsylvania St 6% due 10/1/99 at 102." Let's decode this shorthand.

- 10 refers to the number of bonds being offered for sale. Each is worth $1000. This offering would be for $10,000 face value.

- Pennsylvania State is the name of the issuer. This might not be a complete description of the issuer, and it would be prudent to ask if this

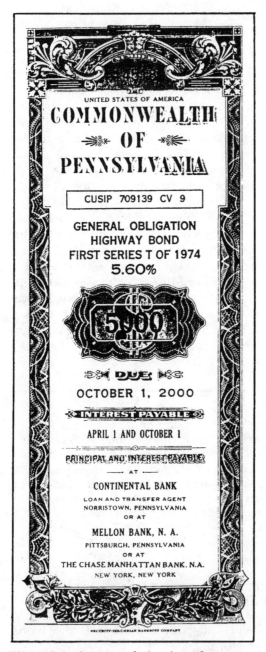

Figure 2-1. One view of a bond certificate.

description is complete. This bond might be issued by an agency of the state of Pennsylvania, or be a general obligation of the state. The credit quality might be different.

- 6 percent is the *rate* or the bond's *coupon*. The coupon is the interest rate at which the bond was originally issued. It determines how much interest is paid semiannually. This amount used to be written on the coupons attached to the bond itself. To find out how much interest the bond will pay, multiply the rate (e.g., 6 percent) by the face amount of the bond (e.g., $10,000). To find the semiannual rate, divide by 2. In this case the interest the bond will pay is $600 annually (6 percent × $10,000) or $300 semiannually.

- 10/1/99 is the date that the bond will mature or come due. At maturity, the issuer will repay the $10,000 principal. The bond seller is telling you about the bond; she will say the date as 10, 1, 99 and expect you to know that she means October first in the year 1999.

- 102 is the unit cost per each $1000 bond quoted in percentage. Thus, 102 percent (1.02) × $1000 equals $1020 per bond. Ten bonds would cost $10,200. For simplicity sake, just add a zero to the unit cost to get the cost of one bond.

Par, Discount, and Premium

Bonds are at *par* when they sell at their face value. Thus, a bond sold at $1000 is at par. If bonds sell for less than par, then they are discount bonds. Thus, a $1000 bond priced at $950 is selling at a discount. In the example in the previous section, the bond was selling at a *premium* ($1020) or for more than the face value or par. The reason for this will become clear in the later discussion of bond yields and bond pricing.

Tip_____

Insist that the broker give you information about bonds in the same order every time. You might make a chart that looks like this on which to write the bond offerings:

Rating	Face Amount	Issuer	Coupon	Maturity	Call Date	Call Price	Cost	Accrued Interest	Yield to Maturity

Figure 2-2. Categories for analyzing bonds.

You would also need a place to put explanatory information about each bond. You could number each bond offering and put the explanatory information on another page keyed by number.

Accrued Interest

A bond previously owned by someone else probably was not sold on the date the bond pays interest. As a result, when the interest is paid, the previous owner is due the interest for the period of time the bond was his. Bond interest is calculated based on a 360-day calendar year. In the earlier example, the bond pays interest on October 1, but assume it was sold on October 15. Thus the seller is due 14 days' interest. The total annual interest for the year is $600 divided by 360 days times 14 days of interest due the seller, which equals $23.33 (600/360 × 14 = $23.33). The buyer pays the $23.33 as *accrued interest* at the time of the purchase. The buyer recoups the accrued interest on the next interest payment date.

Forms of Ownership

The most common form of bond ownership currently is *book-entry only*. With this form of ownership you never receive a bond certificate. Evidence of your ownership of the bond is the confirmation you received when you purchased it and the listing on your monthly brokerage statement. Brokerage houses or banks hold all book-entry bonds. The brokerage house registers the bonds at a depository for further credit to you, the beneficial owner. The trustees forward the interest payments to the brokerage house, which then deposits it into your brokerage account.

Tip_____

Keep your brokerage statements and confirmations in a safe place. This is your only proof of ownership of book-entry only bonds.

Registered bonds are bonds evidenced by a physical certificate. You can receive a piece of specially engraved paper that states that you are the owner. It also outlines the obligations of the issuer, names the trustee bank, and includes a legal opinion about the nature of the representation made by the issuer. The owner receives interest payments in the mail every six months. To redeem the bond at its due date, you return the certificate to the trustee.

Write down the name and address of the trustee of each bond you hold. Keep this list with the check stubs from your interest payments in a safe place. This will be helpful if you move or decide to transfer title and need to contact the trustee.

Bearer bonds consist of a certificate like registered bonds, but they have no bond owner name on them. They come with coupons attached to the bonds that you clip off and deposit in your bank every six months. This type of ownership is being phased out.

Tip_____

If you lose your certificates, you can get them replaced, but it will cost you 2 or 3 percent of the face value of the bonds.

How Form of Ownership Affects the Sale of Bonds

One advantage of holding bonds in certificate form is that you can sell them easily to any broker. When people sell anything, from a house to yard-sale items, they hope a number of people will come to bid. By calling different brokerage houses, you can get them to bid on your bonds. Once you agree on who will purchase the bonds, you mail the bonds to that brokerage house.

If you are holding bonds in a brokerage house account and plan to sell them, it is important to know if they are DTC-eligible. DTC-eligible bonds are electronically transferred through the large bond depositories called the Depository Trust Company (DTC). If they are not DTC-eligible, the brokers send the physical certificates. All book-entry bonds are DTC-eligible. The electronic system used to transfer most bonds is called the ACAT (A Customer Account Transfer) system.

If you sell a bond which is not DTC-eligible and it is held by a brokerage house, it may not be transferred quickly enough to meet the settlement deadline. It can take a long time for a brokerage house to transfer bonds with a physical certificate.

Tip_____

You should be able to buy and sell bonds at different brokerage houses and have the bonds electronically delivered into your primary account.

Through the ACAT system, brokers are able to transfer bonds immediately. This is how the brokers complete the trades they make with other brokerage houses. When you sell your bonds, they must be delivered in three business days. The only way you will be able to do this is by using the ACAT system. If you find that you are unable to sell your bonds to a noncustodial broker (one who is not holding the bonds at the time of the sale), please call or write and let us know of your plight. To maintain a competitive selling market for the retail client, there must be the ability to sell your bonds to whomever gives you the best price.

When to Sell Bonds

Most individuals do not trade their bond portfolios. They consider restructuring their portfolios only under certain special circumstances.

- A change in your federal tax bracket might lead you to sell municipal bonds and purchase taxable bonds, or vice versa. This might be the result of retirement, large losses, or donations.

- A change in your residence—from one high-tax state to another high-tax state or from a low-tax state to a high-tax state.

- Increased cashflow requirements, for a house purchase, a business venture, college expenses, inheritance taxes, or other major obligations.

- Changes in the tax code that might affect your status with regard to the Alternative Minimum Tax, or changes in your own tax situation.

Bond Swapping

If you decide that you need to restructure your portfolio, you might consider swapping your bonds instead of selling them outright. A bond swap occurs when the bond owner buys some bonds and sells other bonds at the same time. Swap season is usually in December as people review their tax situation and decide if it is advantageous to sell.

When the market is very turbulent, it is difficult to do a swap because dealers may be unwilling to purchase bonds for their inventory. In a swap it is important to know if you are getting a better price for your bond because the trader does not have to take as big a markup in a swap. It is best to time a swap when the market is firm for at least several days. When selling any bonds, it is always better to sell "round lots" of 25 bonds or multiples thereof.

Settling Bond Transactions

The ability to transfer bonds electronically assumes greater importance with the new SEC three-day settlement rules. Called *T-Plus 3,* bond trades settle (i.e., are paid for) in three business days after the trade date.

What this means to you is that you may not be able to get a confirmation of the trade by mail before paying for your bonds. Confirmations can be sent by e-mail or faxed to you by the broker generally the day after the sale. Unless you wire money or send it by overnight mail, it may not arrive in time. If it does not arrive in time, there may be penalties. If you want to send a check, get a complete description of the bond, your account number, and total cost. Mail the check the same day that the bond was purchased. You might ask that a printed description of the bond be sent to you from one of the wire services if you wish to verify the description.

Some brokers are telling their clients that the confirmation is merely an advisory of a trade already confirmed in some other way. National Discount Brokers has automated telephone confirmations. The problem with telephone confirmations is that you don't always get a complete description of the bond. For example, you may have thought that you purchased $25,000 face value of a Pennsylvania State General Obligation bond, only to find out that the bond description was for Pennsylvania State Industrial Development bonds. It is always important to review the confirmation and make sure it reads the way you thought it would.

The brokers are encouraging clients to keep their money and securities in their brokerage house accounts. Firms like Merrill Lynch have most of their customers' money in house, so they are unconcerned by the change. The brokers' hope is that if they hold the money and securities, then additional securities transactions will also occur there. However, whether you decide to do all your transactions at one brokerage house is up to you.

There are other considerations in keeping your money in a brokerage house instead of a bank. The FDIC insures bank accounts. If the bank goes bust, you'll get your money back, including the interest it had earned, up to a maximum of $100,000 per account. Brokerage accounts are protected too but with a difference. The Securities Investor Protection Corporation, or SIPC, is an $890-million nonprofit fund supported by the brokerage houses. When a brokerage house fails, SIPC protects up to $500,000 in securities and $100,000 in cash. However, brokerage houses sweep most of your cash into a money-market fund. As such, you would not get back cash, but you would get back shares in the money-market fund. The distribution of your shares and securities may take months.

While your account is frozen, you will be unable to sell any of your securities or receive any interest or dividends until settlement.

Some brokerage houses charge a $50 inactivity fee if there were no trades made in the account over the last 12 months. For bonds not held in safekeeping there might be fees for bond registration ($10 or more), coupon collection ($5), redemption ($5), and odd-lot transaction (up to $50 per trade). If you keep your securities at home or in a bank vault, you can avoid bank redemption fees by mailing your securities to the trustee directly.

What to Do if Securities Are Lost or Stolen

If you hold your own securities and you discover that they have been lost or stolen, you will have to purchase a *surety* or *indemnity bond.* This is an insurance policy to protect the issuer and potential buyers in case the "lost" security is redeemed or sold. The surety bond is obtained through your brokerage house or directly from a surety company. You must fill out an affidavit of loss that must be notarized and returned. The fee is usually 2 percent to 4 percent of the face value of the bond. Thus, a bond certificate with a market value of $10,000 might cost $300 to replace. Replacing a certificate usually takes four weeks to six months. During this time, the security cannot be sold or redeemed.

If you choose to hold your own securities, you should protect them by keeping them in a vault. Photocopy all securities you have and keep the copies with copies of the confirmations separate from your securities. For a very small fee, it is possible to purchase vault insurance for "belt and suspender" protection. You will have to examine your own needs and habits and decide what is best for you.

Pricing Information

Yield-to-maturity is the figure that is the basis for determining the price of the bond. It is the basis for comparing the worth of similar bond issues. The yield-to-maturity figure assumes the reinvestment of the interest from the bond at the same rate as the yield. For example if a bond has a yield-to-maturity of 7 percent, it is assumed for the purpose of this computation, that all the interest payments will be reinvested at the same 7 percent rate. In the event that this does not occur, then the effective yield is actually either higher or lower.

Tip_____

*Yield-to-maturity determines the price! Price does not determine
the yield! Focus on the yield-to-maturity number. Do not lose sight of it.*

Don't confuse the yield-to-maturity with the current yield. The current yield assumes no reinvestment of interest and only tells you how many dollars you will currently receive. If the rate or coupon is high, the current return will also be high, higher than the yield-to-maturity. This often leads to confusion to the unsophisticated buyer, who focuses on the higher current yield while overlooking the more important yield-to-maturity figure. See Chap. 5 for a more detailed explanation of yield-to-maturity.

Yield-to-maturity should also be the determining factor in buying corporate bonds. A broker, however, may focus on prices of corporate bonds traded on the New York Bond Exchange. If the bonds trade on the New York Bond Exchange, then the broker will tell you the last bid and ask price. The *bid* is what the bond buyer offers to pay for the bond. The *ask* (or offer) is what the seller is asking for the bond. For example, X Bank might be 99.50 bid and 99.75 asked. In this case the *spread,* the difference between the bid and the ask price is $2.50 per bond. The spread varies based upon the size of the bond lot, the demand and availability of the bond, and the amount the broker needs to cover the trade. However, to verify for yourself the desirability of the deal, you must focus on the final yield.

Municipal bond sellers usually don't give a bid and ask price, though there is also a spread there. If you asked if there is a commission on bonds, the answer would probably be no. The spread is the way the broker and the brokerage house earns money on bond transactions. Some of the "discount" brokerage houses also charge a fee for buying bonds in addition to the spread they make in the transaction. Banks and brokers charge fees for the purchase of Treasuries on the auction, because they make no spread on those transactions.

One source for pricing information is the Standard & Poor's Corporation's and the Public Securities Association's pilot program for a price information hotline. In an effort to improve pricing transparency, the two agencies have joined together, in conjunction with J. J. Kenny, to provide 25 bond prices for $9.95. A given price may reflect an actual transaction on a particular day, but more likely it will be a price evaluation or an *opinion* of the value of your bond. This is not a market quotation, and your bond may not trade at the price quoted. To access this information, you must know the CUSIP (Committee on Uniform Security Identification

Procedures) number of your bond. A CUSIP number is a nine-digit industry standard securities identification number that uniquely identifies a bond issue. It is on your bond confirmation.

The price evaluations are based upon a block size of $1 million worth of bonds. These prices will not be the same for the odd-lot trades of less than $100,000 or even odder lots of less than $25,000. The Public Securities Association hopes to be able to begin a similar service for smaller bond purchases in 1996. Actual market prices may differ according to the size of the transaction. For more information on this municipal bond service call 1-800-Bond-Info.

Understanding a Bond Confirmation

A bond confirmation is a summary of all the information concerning a trade. Though the confirmations from different brokerage houses might have different appearances, they all must contain the same information. Confirmations contain many abbreviations. Following is a list of the information and abbreviations you will find on confirmations and an explanation of what they mean:

- *SIPC.* Brokerage insurance to protect your account.

- *Account Number.* Your account number at a particular brokerage house. Put this information on your check so the deposit goes to the right place.

- *Trade Date.* The date you bought the bonds. When you report the transaction on your income tax form, use this date.

- *Settlement Date.* The date the money is due at the brokerage house.

- *Quantity.* The face value of the bonds you purchased.

- *CUSIP Number.* This nine-digit number, pronounced "Q-Sip," is a fingerprint of the bond issue. Each new issue has its own identifying CUSIP number.

- *Security Number.* The number of a particular bond certificate within an issue.

- *Security Description.* The complete description of the bond, including the name, series, interest rate, maturity date, and other pertinent information.

- *Yield (YLD).* Sometimes called *basis.* This is the yield-to-maturity of your bonds. Note that only this yield, not the current yield, is on the confirmation. The yield-to-maturity figure guides the sale and purchase of bonds.

- *Dated Date (DTD).* The date the bond was first issued. Some trustees use this date and the bond description, including the series, rather than the CUSIP number, to keep track of the issues they monitor.

- *Trustee.* The institution that is responsible for making the semiannual interest payments and paying the principal amount when due. If you hold registered bonds, you will receive your checks and call notices from the trustee. The trustee will never have to contact you if your bonds are in a brokerage house. If you hold your own bonds, the trustee will mail the interest checks to you.

- *First Coupon (FC).* On a new issue, the first coupon payment is usually not for six months' interest. A *short first* coupon might pay interest after only two or three months. Sometimes bonds are issued with a *long first* coupon, which means that interest is paid after more than six months. It is only necessary to pay attention to this feature if the bond is a new issue or a recent resale of a new issue.

- *Security Format.* There are three formats that were previously described. *Book-Entry Only (BEO).* The bonds must be held at a brokerage house. *Registered (R).* You can receive a certificate or leave them at a brokerage house.

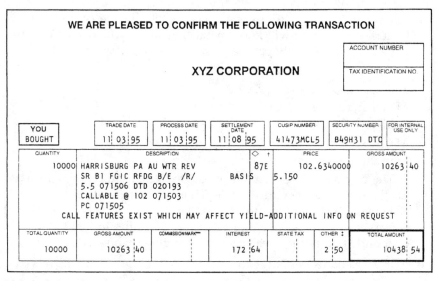

Figure 2-3. A bond confirmation.

Bearer (B). The bonds may be registered as to principal or interest only. They will have coupons attached if you take delivery.

- *Bond Ratings.* S&P (Standard & Poor's); Moody (Moody's Investors Service); Fitch (Fitch Investors Service); and Duff & Phelps. The bond rating is on some confirmations but not all. If a bond is unrated the broker must indicate this on the confirmation.

- *Call.* The first call date. The confirmation will indicate if the bonds are priced to the first call or to a later par call. If the bond has a call, the issuer has the right to redeem the bonds back from you at that particular date. The yield-to-call may be more important than the yield-to-maturity.

- *Price.* The amount you agreed to pay per $100. This is the *unit price.*

Technical Tip_____

To change the unit price into dollars, multiply the unit price by 10. Assume that the unit price is 73.176. In this case, the value of each bond is $731.76.

- *Principal Amount.* The quantity of bonds multiplied by the price of the bond expressed as a decimal.

- *Accrued Interest.* The interest due the seller for the days she owned the bonds since the last interest payment date. The confirmation will state both the number of days' interest and the dollar amount due the seller. Some confirmations specifically spell out the payment dates. Others assume you will know what they are if you know the maturity date. The monthly payment pattern is as follows:

January and July
February and August
March and September
April and October
May and November
June and December

The payment dates remain the same. Usually the payment dates are the same as the maturity date. Thus, if the maturity date is July 1, 2000, then the bond pays interest on January 1 and July 1. Municipal bonds almost always pay interest on the 1st or the 15th of the month. Corporate bonds and Treasury bonds might pay on any date.

- *Post.* Miscellaneous charge for postage, handling, or "other." It is usually between $2.50 and $4.75.

- There are also many abbreviations used in the bond description itself. These abbreviations indicate what entity is responsible for the repayment of the loan, the insurer, and miscellaneous information. Some of the more frequently used abbreviations are: REDEV—redevelopment; AGY—agency; REF—refunding; TAX ALLOC—tax allocation; GO—general obligation bond; REV—revenue bond; INSD—insured; UT—unlimited tax; LT—limited tax; CPN—coupon; CSD—central school district; SCH DIST—school district; WTR & SWR—water & sewer; N/C—noncallable; HFA—Housing Finance Authority; PRF (Pre-Ref)—pre-refunded; CTR—center. Insurance company abbreviations include MBIA, FGIC, AMBAC, FSA, and CAP GTD. LOC is a letter of credit from a bank.

- *Delivery Instructions.* Your directions saying where to deliver the bonds after you pay for them if they are not going to your mailing address. You could be directing them to a brokerage account where you keep your securities if you bought them at some other brokerage house.

3

Using Bonds to Solve Financial Problems

Why Buy Bonds?

Bonds are useful in solving many of our financial problems. Life-cycle problems—those situations which we all face with the passage of our lifetime—are particularly suited to financial planning with bonds because of bonds' two unique features:

- A predictable stream of income
- A fixed date when the bond comes due and the investor receives back the face value of the bond

No other category of investment has these two features. Stocks and real estate are equity investments that never come due. Stocks and real estate may provide a stream of income, but the stream is generally lower and always more unpredictable. Commodities trading, including gold, silver, copper, soybeans, sugar, and the futures and options on these commodities, are pure speculations.

- Bonds and their close relations are embedded in your financial life.
- Bonds are the foundation blocks of bond funds, money-market funds, and balanced funds.
- Mortgage-backed securities might contain the mortgages from your neighbors' and your homes.

- Your pension plan is partly dependent on bond investments.

- Insurance companies meet their obligations partly through bond investments.

- Banks use their bond investments as one source of revenue for their interest payments to you.

- Your schools, sewers, water systems, electricity, municipal buildings, roads, and corporate parks may have been built with borrowed money through a bond issue.

Bonds can be used to diversify a portfolio of stocks and other investments. A portfolio of high-grade bonds that produces a dependable stream of income will provide a strong investment base. A bond portfolio will enable you to take on more risk with other investments and with business ventures. Particularly over relatively short periods of time, such as five years, bonds are much less volatile than stocks. This means that over a five-year period, bonds with a life of seven years or less will fluctuate less in value than a portfolio of stocks. This reduced volatility is important if you are saving for time-specific goals such as a child beginning college in six years or for the purchase of a large item such as a house or car.

Bonds have also proved to be a very lucrative investment vehicle. From the mid-1980s to the mid-1990s, bonds have performed as well as stocks on a risk-adjusted basis. Taking the risk of losing your principal into account, bonds have kept pace with stocks due to high interest rates and capital gains resulting from falling interest rates.

Bonds' unique features make them valuable investment vehicles to solve many of life's problems. For example:

- Assume that you want to buy a home in five years and need $20,000 for a down payment. If you buy bonds with a five-year maturity and a $15,000 face value, the interest income produced by the bonds together with the return of the $15,000 face value will be about $20,000. The same reasoning applies when you want to save money for any large fixed purchase in the future.

- Assume you are retired or wish to supplement the income that you earn from your job. A portfolio of bonds provides a predictable stream of income on which you can depend.

- Assume you own a typical business that provides an uneven and unpredictable stream of earnings. Some years you earn more than budgeted needs, and in other years your expenses exceed your income. A portfolio of high-grade bonds that produces a steady stream of predictable income provides an ideal supplement to your business income. If you add to your portfolio of bonds, as your bond income increases, the income from your business becomes less essential to maintaining your lifestyle and meeting your required expenses.

Why Save Money?

Let's start at the beginning. Why save money? If you have no reason to save money, why do it? It is much more fun to spend money than to save it. While we don't know each reader's financial situation, we do know a lot about people in general.

We save money to deal with life crises and problems that affect our individual financial stability and that of our families. Many of these problems follow a predictable pattern and occur at particular times during our life cycle. The possibility and the predictability of these problems enable us to plan for them. We all will have to deal with some or all of the following issues:

- The risk of premature death
- The possibility of sickness and disability
- Property loss and personal liability (e.g., auto accident)
- The probability of job loss
- The desire for downshifting
- Retirement
- The possibility of marriage and divorce
- The expenses of raising children, including their college costs
- The desire for major purchases such as a house

Since we all have similar issues to face, possible solutions have been developed over the years to deal with these issues. In our financial planning practice, we address these issues. Bonds are extraordinarily useful in solving just the kinds of financial problems that are posed by these life-cycle issues.

Every investor walks the line between fear and greed. When we are propelled to invest by the news of a great bull market instead of investing to meet financial goals, we step onto the roller coaster. When markets are rising, we all want to participate and make a killing. We hang back waiting to see if the rally is real. The result is that we often come in at a market top. When the markets are falling, we are afraid that we will lose everything and often sell at a market bottom. A 1994 survey released by the Federal Reserve Board stated that "the proportion of financial assets held in bank CDs, checking and savings accounts, and in saving bonds fell by one-fifth—from 31.7 percent in 1989 to 25.4 percent in 1992." More troublesome is that the move from the more conservative investments into stocks and long-term bonds took place after a steep rise in both market sectors. People took their carefully guarded money out of the safety of CDs because they saw stocks and the total return on bonds (interest and bond price appreciation) rise dramatically. Without understanding the nature of the markets, they were set up for a fall.

You need a plan of action to avoid riding the roller coaster and making decisions you will regret later. Each sector of the market takes a turn in the spotlight as the place to be. However, no one can predict where the spotlight will shine next. Many investors look to see what market sector is hot and rush to put money there. The result is frequently that by the time the investor has moved his funds, the light has moved on and that sector is in decline. A substantial loss is the result. To avoid making decisions based upon hot sectors, it is helpful to consider what your own personal needs are and how your needs can be met by different investment considerations.

Taking Stock: Your Personal Financial Inventory

Before we look at each of the life-cycle issues, you should take a look at where you are at present. Dig into your personal files and put together all of your financial documents.

The first order of business is to pull together all of your insurance to see whether you are satisfied that you have adequate coverage to protect you and your family in the face of catastrophic events. Do you have adequate life insurance, health and disability insurance, and house and liability insurance?

The next item to review is your pension and retirement plans. How do your retirement plans protect you? Does your employer provide any plans that you are not taking advantage of? Tax-favored plans are your best investments because they shelter your income from tax, allowing it to compound tax-free. View your retirement investments as just one piece of the total investment pie. An overall plan helps you to decide what the appropriate investments are for different pockets of money and helps to centralize and reduce them to a manageable scale.

The first line of defense in dealing with any of life's problems is to have an emergency cache of funds and a line of credit that you establish before there is a need. There is no one way to do this. Some of the alternatives are:

- *A bank or credit card company.* The time to set up your line of credit is before you have a need. After you have a need, the bank or credit card company may not consider you a good enough risk for a loan.

- *Home equity line of credit.* This is the cheapest form of a loan and the most tax-efficient. Set up a home equity line of credit before there is a need. If you borrow on your home equity line of credit, the interest that you pay will be tax deductible up to certain limits. The interest that you pay on a personal loan or a credit card loan is not deductible for tax purposes.

- *Margin loan in a brokerage account.* You can usually borrow money from your broker using your stocks and bonds as collateral for the loan. Since this loan is secured by good collateral, the interest rate (called the broker loan rate) will be relatively low. This is a very convenient way to borrow money. As you get extra cash, you can pay down the loan very conveniently as well. There are no fixed payments required as there are in many other types of loans. You only pay interest on the amount of the loan that is outstanding.

- *Cash savings in a bank or other cash equivalents.* Money-market mutual funds, bank savings accounts, certificates of deposit, and Treasury bills and notes are excellent vehicles for an emergency fund. They have little or no market risk and they can be easily liquidated. You can cash in the CD or sell the Treasury. An alternative is to borrow against the Treasury securities if they are held at a brokerage house.

- *Short-term investments.* To earn a higher yield but have more risk to your principal, you might buy either two- or three-year Treasury notes or buy a short-term bond fund. The most secure are those which only invest in short-term Treasury notes and Treasury bills. As you increase the yield and the maturity of your investments, you will create a greater risk to your principal if you need to sell your bonds or bond funds when interest rates are rising. Since mutual funds never come due, there is always a market risk here. Short-term bonds should, if possible, be held to maturity.

Planning for a Catastrophe

Insurance softens the impact of premature death, sickness and disability, and property loss and liability. To the extent that insurance can cushion a basic problem, it is often an elegant solution to supplement inadequate resources. Advance planning for the prospect of catastrophe takes away some of the fear of the unknown.

We know we will all die sooner or later. Some of us will have continuing obligations that survive our death, particularly if the death is premature. We might have a spouse, parents, or children who depend upon us for financial support. Our savings may not be sufficient to provide the required support after our death. If there are assets, investments in bonds provide a stream of income for your loved ones.

At some point in our lives we may become very sick or even disabled for a period of time so that we can't work at our jobs. Unless our employer is both very rich and understanding, sickness and disability may result in severe financial hardship. Some of us have risky jobs or we do risky things, making the problem worse. Some jobs are so demanding that even a small injury will prevent the continuation of employment. For example, a cardiac surgeon or musician might be unable to work because of an injured finger.

Your home is a major asset. It can disappear in flames from lightning striking your roof or from a cigarette that sets your bed on fire. Your automobile takes you to and from work, exposing you to possible accidents leading to temporary disability or worse prospects.

Though these catastrophes may never affect you, it is prudent to provide yourself and your family with a blanket of protection. Various kinds of insurance have been devised to meet your needs. Payments from life insurance, disability insurance, home owner's policies, and car insurance provide funds to alleviate the pain of crisis situations.

Depending upon your circumstances, you might want to minimize the size of your premiums by increasing your deductibles. In effect, you act as your own insurer for the first $500 or $1000 of loss. You can do this if you have enough invested resources to call upon in times of emergency. Bonds can provide a steady stream of income, thereby evening out your cashflow and providing resources upon which you can rely in times of emergency.

Planning for Job Loss, Job Change, or Retirement

No one keeps a job forever anymore in corporate America. From an optimistic point of view, we might say that the job market has become more fluid. From a pessimistic point of view, we might say that the job market resembles a game of musical chairs, where more and more chairs (i.e., jobs) are being removed faster as we get older. As a result there are more times when employees will find themselves between jobs. This is a life-cycle issue that happens more frequently today.

Some individuals are deciding to trade money for time. These people voluntarily decide to give up their jobs and do other work that is either less demanding or more fulfilling to them. It is called *downshifting*. For many people, downshifting is a choice forced upon them by economic downturns. In the 1980s blue-collar workers faced job reductions as employers exported jobs overseas to employ cheaper unskilled workers. In the late 1980s and the 1990s white-collar middle management employees lost their jobs to technological advances and changes in management theory. These employees must decide if they are going to pursue evaporating jobs or seek completely different employment that provides less compensation. Suan, a chemist for 20 years, is contemplating starting a muffin business and a travel agency business connecting swimmers in Thailand and in the United States. Her income will not be steady and there will be no health or retirement benefits. Though she would like to work as a chemist that is not an alternative today.

Downshifting is a choice for some following the tradition of Ralph Waldo Emerson and Henry David Thoreau. The choice of fewer material goods adds to the value of life by expanding hours devoted to family, friends, hobbies, and other worthwhile pursuits. It is a blueprint for being able to do what you want to do by learning to do with fewer material things. Joe Dominguez and Vicki Robin wrote a handbook for downshifters called *Your Money or Your Life* describing how to manage with less by keeping track of your spending and deciding to spend less. The question we need to ask ourselves, the authors say, is whether we are really enjoying the money we spend, or are we spending money because we are living someone else's dream? Have we absorbed the "good life" as described by the media, while not really enjoying ourselves? The method suggested by Dominguez and Robin is to closely track the money you spend and evaluate whether it is worth expending your life's energy to obtain the material goods. If the answer is no, then they recommend curtailing spending in order to build a nest egg. The nest egg will throw off an income. The income will supplement your living expenses after you take a less lucrative, more satisfying job. The spin-offs include more free time for preferred pursuits. Their book is a wake-up call to people unhappily tied to a job. It shows that there is a subculture of people out there choosing to live in a more purposeful and conscious way. We don't have to wait until retirement to choose another lifestyle.

Most of us won't work forever. We will retire either voluntarily or involuntarily. In either case, this is a life-cycle event that we will be subject to sooner or later. Retirement is a very large event in everyone's life.

In order to retire with enough funds, a great deal of advance planning is necessary. Retirement planning has four pillars of economic support:

- Government support provided by social security and medicare
- Employer-provided pension plans
- Worker-supported pension plans
- Personal savings outside of pension plans

The first two of these pillars of support are now very shaky and can no longer be counted on as completely reliable sources of retirement funds. As a result of the massive federal deficit, we expect that in the future you will have to provide most of the funds for your own retirement. That is not a pretty thought. The federal government is looking to reduce retirement benefits for the elderly as a means of curtailing the massive federal debt. While there will always be some government support and certain employer incentives provided, the amount of support from these two sources will certainly decrease. As a result of the aging of the population, some commentators claim that the medicare trust fund at present government funding levels may go bankrupt in 2002. The benefits of the social security program have only been marginally reduced so far. However, some politicians claim that the only way to save social security is by cutting benefits.

Accumulating enough of a retirement fund is the largest and thus the most difficult financial goal to achieve. In the good old days, about 10 to 15 years ago, employers took care of most of their employees' pension planning. The amount of an employee's pension was determined by a formula based on the employee's salary and number of years with the employer. Using the formula you would be able to calculate the yearly pension you would receive as a lifetime annuity for you and possibly for the life of your spouse.

Compare that with what we have today. Now, more and more pension plans have been converted to 401(k) plans and other so-called *defined contribution* plans. In a defined contribution plan, the employees must take responsibility for how much they will contribute to the plan and how they want to invest the funds. The amount of pension benefits that an employee will have at retirement cannot be predicted. That amount depends upon how much the employee contributes to the plan and the skill he uses to invest the funds. Employees not only have to provide the bulk of the money for the plans, they must also invest the money themselves. Americans are thus being pushed toward reluctant self-reliance and must take responsibility for their own retirement planning.

The federal and state governments have a substantial interest in employees having enough for their own retirement so that the governments will not have to support them. To help individuals successfully deal with their retirement, the government provides incentives in the form of tax deductions for employee contributions and tax-free buildup of funds inside the retirement plans. It is essential for you to use these tax incentives. With the federal government as your partner, your retirement plans will provide the most profitable location for your retirement savings. For employees there are pension, profit-sharing, and 401(k) plans sponsored by the employers. For the self-employed there are Keogh plans and Individual Retirement Accounts (IRAs).

Tip_____

You should take advantage of retirement plans as the most tax-efficient way to save. Utilize these plans first for your long-term savings.

Sometimes these employer plans are so favorable that it might make sense to borrow the money in order to participate in them. An example of this is a 401(k) plan where the employer matches part of your contribution to the plan. If the employer contributes 50 percent of what you contribute, you have an immediate 50 percent gain on your investment. In addition, all the earnings on the money in your plan will accumulate tax-free. You should view these plans as required investments, bearing in mind there is a penalty for early withdrawal.

The classic investments for retirement plans are stocks and bonds. Many advisers believe that the balance between the two should relate to age. They suggest that if you are younger invest more money in stocks, and if you are older invest a greater portion of your funds in bonds. Bonds are an excellent investment vehicle for pension plans. Bonds provide safety of principal and a predictable stream of income. The theory is that bonds are more suitable investments as you get older because the value of your bond investments will not change as much as stock values. The change in investment value is called *volatility*. When you are older, you can withstand less volatility of your principal.

If you are highly dependent on your bond income in your new lifestyle, you would want to invest in only high-grade bonds, i.e., bonds that are rated A or better. Thus, you might choose to invest in Treasury bonds, agency bonds, and better-rated corporate bonds. If you are in the 28 percent tax bracket or higher, then you would also consider tax-free municipal bonds. If you are in the 15 percent tax bracket, you would benefit more from taxable bonds than tax-free bonds. You would not buy municipal bonds for your pension plan.

If you wished to minimize the risk that rising interest rates will devalue your bond holdings, you would invest only in short-term bonds. Minimizing the interest-rate risk is advantageous if you need to sell some of your bonds to support your new lifestyle. To minimize the risk to your capital, you would probably not want to invest in stocks or junk bonds.

If you are in your twenties or thirties, you might have a balance of stocks and bonds in your pension plan. However, as you get older and have less tolerance for volatility and losses from stocks, the percentage of your investments in bonds should grow. While stocks did very well in the 1980s and early 1990s, the return on bonds was high as well. The sky-high interest rates in the 1980s followed by plummeting interest rates into the 1990s caused the prices of bonds to appreciate. The total return on long-term bonds between 1983 and 1993 was a 13.1 percent annual return, while the total return on stocks as measured by the Standard & Poor's 500 Index was 15.6 percent.

Planning for a Family

Most people will get married and about half of those who marry will also divorce. Both place large demands on the couple. Savings are helpful to get over the rough edges. If you are anticipating a divorce, the most liquid, easily valued and divisible investments are most desirable. They facilitate the divorce with the least legal expense. While the divorce proceeding is progressing, you want very conservative investments that don't need your attention. High-grade bonds cushion the economic impact of a divorce by providing a stream of income, and they are easily divisible if that is necessary.

That children and college are expensive is one the great understatements in modern-day America. Four years at a private college costs as much or more than a first home. Saving the required amount of money necessary to accomplish this goal takes a great deal of planning and a long time frame.

There are two distinct strategies for saving for college. The first strategy states that college is so expensive that in order to afford it, you must invest all of your college fund in growth stocks. The theory holds that the only way to ensure sufficient funds is to risk your principal in the hopes of larger-than-average gains. Some major brokerage firms support this strategy. They draw the usual straight-line graph that shows that in 15 years a college education will cost at least $200,000. There are a number of problems with this approach. First, straight-line graphs are generally misleading. (Remember how the price of oil was going to be $100 a barrel in 1980?) Second, 80 percent to 90 percent of college students presently attend public institutions that charge about a third of the cost of private college. In 1995, $37,000 could buy you four years at a public college, including room and board, while a comparable private education cost $80,000. If tuition constantly increases, more students will go to public colleges or the private colleges and government will have to provide more support. Third, if college does cost $200,000, no one but the super-rich will be able to afford college and most of the private colleges will close.

The second strategy suggests that your job is to have some money available for sure. Growth stocks may not be sky-high at the date that your child is ready for college. It is possible that stocks might be in a down cycle. You must decide whether you wish to risk your college nest egg on the prospects of growth stocks or choose the alternative of investing in bonds. If you invest in bonds you may not have a huge amount of money in your college fund, but you will have what you saved plus the income on your savings. To the extent that you need more, your child will borrow it, as most college students do now. Before you go deep in debt to pay for college, remember this: You are nearing the end of your earning ability, while your children are at the beginning of theirs. It is altogether appropriate for your children to bear a significant amount of the burden.

In order to pay for college expenses without financial hardship for the family, the solution is to start saving early. We had a social security number for our daughter Jolie shortly after she had a name. When you start saving early, the magic of compound interest lends a large hand to your effort. A dollar received today has more value than the same dollar received at a later date because it can begin to earn interest sooner. This is referred to as the *time value of money*. The time value of money is the relationship of time, money, and the rate of interest, and their impact on the growth of savings.

Tip

The "Rule of 72" gives an estimate of how long it takes for your money to double given a specified interest rate. You can divide 72 by an interest rate to see how long it will take your money to double. You can divide 72 by a number of years to find the interest rate at which your money would double. For example, if your money is earning 7 percent, it will double in 10 years.

Bonds are particularly valuable to fund college expenses because you can buy them to come due in the first year that your child is scheduled to begin college and in each year thereafter. You could buy Treasury bonds, agency bonds, and highly-rated corporate bonds. If you are in the 28 percent tax bracket or higher, and if you are holding the college fund in your name, you should consider municipal bonds. An interesting investment idea for you if you earn a moderate amount of income is to buy U.S. savings bonds. There is a big tax advantage in buying savings bonds if you use the proceeds from these bonds to fund your child's college education. See Chap. 7.

How Bonds Can Help You Meet Your Financial Goals: Seven Case Studies

There is an adage in the investment field that "bonds are for income and stock is for growth." This statement does not recognize that bonds can meet your needs for both growth and income. Bonds will provide growth if you do not spend the income! Let's see how a number of individuals have used bonds and bond funds to solve their financial problems.

Mr. College Grad

Mr. College Grad, for example, is a recent college graduate who is saving for a boat and a house in the future. He doesn't have much money now, but he has adopted a savings plan which includes purchasing a certificate of deposit each month in order to save for his house. This is the way that his parents saved for their retirement. Though he knows that there are other investments that might pay more, at the moment he is satisfied with the CDs. With CDs he knows that if market interest rates rise, he will not lose principal. He can put in as little or as much as he wants. He knows he has to follow the strategy of paying himself first if he has any hope of achieving his dreams. This means he must put his savings first before he spends any money. After he accumulates $5000, he will purchase a bond paying a higher interest rate.

To save for his boat, Mr. Grad will purchase a bond mutual fund. The fund will be *open-ended,* meaning that he will be able to purchase as many shares as he wants and redeem them for cash at any time from the mutual-fund company. To open an account he will need between $250 and $1000, depending upon the fund family. He decided to open a fund account knowing that he will need ready access to that money to pay for his boat. He realizes that the price he will have to pay for the added flexibility is that the value of his principal will fluctuate with the rise and fall of interest rates.

Tip

Interest rates are perverse: When interest rates rise, the value of your bond declines. When interest rates decline, the value of your bond rises.

Mr. & Mrs. Y. G. Suburban

Mr. & Mrs. Y. G. Suburban live in New York State. They plan to save for the college education of their newborn daughter. They decided to purchase New York municipal zero-coupon bonds coming due in 18 years. These municipal bonds are exempt from federal, New York State, and New York City taxes. They purchased zero-coupon bonds because they pay interest only when the bond matures. Zero-coupon bonds can be purchased for a substantial discount to the face value of the bonds. For example, $50 invested today will be redeemed for $100. So for an outlay of $5000, the Suburbans know, with 8 percent interest, they will have $20,000 in the year their daughter enters college, and they will owe no taxes on the $20,000.

Mr. Early Retiree

Mr. Early Retiree is an accountant who took early retirement from a large corporation at age 56. He had been planning for this retirement from his corporate job for many years. He knew he would continue to work for the rest of his life in his own private practice, but he also knew that his income would not be steady. To supplement his income, he invested his money in municipal bonds. They pay tax-free income every six months on a regular basis. By purchasing bonds that pay income in different months, he has an orderly flow of income to add to his earnings. With the added income supporting him, he is able to ride out the slow business times. If Mr. Retiree were in a low tax bracket, he would buy taxable bonds, such as Treasury bonds or corporate bonds, which pay more interest than municipal bonds.

When Mr. Retiree has cash he does not need, he lets it accumulate in a money-market fund until he has enough saved for another bond. He chose a money-market fund because the *value* of the fund will remain at a dollar per share, unlike stock and bond funds where the share price fluctuates.

Mr. A. Gressive

Mr. A. Gressive, an executive, aged 60, plans to retire in five years. He is earning a high salary, but has always had some trouble saving money. In the past he has invested in stocks and commodities with mixed results. His income will drop substantially when he retires, so he will be in a low tax bracket. He intends to move from New York to Florida after retirement and thus will pay no state or local income tax. His specific financial goal is to accumulate substantial additional capital during the five-year period before his retirement, while he is in a high tax bracket, without taking any further risks.

Mr. Gressive sold his stock and commodities positions and purchased discount municipal bonds coming due in six years. He wanted to avoid any further risks to his irreplaceable capital. The bonds should mature, he thought, in a year when he had no earned income. That way, the taxes due on his capital gain (the difference between what he paid for the bond and its face value) would be very low. Then he would invest in taxable bonds, either Treasuries or corporates, taking advantage of his new low tax bracket. He also might want to use the funds to buy a house, car, or other large item after retirement.

In fact, deciding to invest in bonds has to come after other financial considerations. Each individual or family unit has many issues with which to deal if proper financial decisions are to be the outcome. In order to give you a taste of the possible complexities, we have described three real-life situations in more detail.

Tracy Teacher

Tracy is a 23-year-old woman who graduated from college and then earned a master's degree from Columbia University Teacher's College. Her education left her $20,000 in debt. The interest rate on her college debt is 7 percent. Her first teaching job was at a private school in Pennsylvania that paid her $25,000 a year. The school has a contributory pension plan to which the school makes a contribution for each teacher. The teacher can contribute additional amounts to her own pension account as well.

Tracy needs a car to get from home to work. Buying a used car required a car loan of $5000 at 15 percent interest. She rented an apartment for $500 per month. Tracy has assets of $25,000: $10,000 in a savings bank and $15,000 worth of two individual growth stocks that she received as a gift. The stocks paid no dividends. Tracy had a boyfriend with whom she had a very close relationship.

Table 3-1. Tracy Teacher's Financial Position

Assets	
Bank savings account	$10,000
Two growth stocks	15,000

Liabilities	
College loans	$20,000 at 7% interest
Car loan	5,000 at 15% interest

Tracy knew that the first line of protection was to buy herself certain insurance protection. An insurance salesperson met with Tracy and suggested that everyone, including her, should have a life insurance policy. He told her that the cost of the policy would be very low at her age. Tracy had learned not to sign on the dotted line until she had time to think though any financial proposal. While buying life insurance seemed very responsible, she came to the conclusion that it was unnecessary since no one was relying on her earnings but her. However, she knew that she did need health insurance and disability insurance. Fortunately, her school provided both of these policies on a group basis at a reasonable cost. She rightly signed up for both when she first came to work.

Tracy rented an apartment and thus thought that the landlord had to buy insurance protection, not her. She was partly right. The landlord did need fire protection and liability protection. However, we advised Tracy that she needed a basic renter's insurance policy as well, to insure her furniture and other valuables in case of a fire. She also needed liability protection in case someone sued her for injuries incurred in her apartment. Finally, we advised Tracy to combine her renter's insurance with an umbrella policy, to give her extra automobile insurance protection. A so-called umbrella policy extends your auto insurance policy and gives you other liability protection as well. Tracy has now taken care of all her basic insurance needs at a very reasonable cost.

Tracy expressed concern that she did not have tenure and could lose her job in the next year or two. She also wanted to buy a condo unit. She asked us whether it was a good idea to use $15,000 of her $25,000 in assets as a down payment on the condo unit. We recommended that Tracy not buy the condo unit unless she had reason to believe that the condo would appreciate rapidly. Otherwise, it was too risky. If she lost her job, and she found a different job in another city, the condo would have to be sold. There are substantial expenses in buying and selling real estate. She might also need the down payment as a reserve fund to carry her expenses while she looked for another job. She might get married. In this case the condo might not be suitable because of its location or its size. It was too soon in her very changeable life to get tied down with real estate.

While Tracy was just beginning her career and was not thinking about retiring, we suggested that she take advantage of her school's 403(b) plan. We suggested that she could contribute some of her salary to her plan without paying tax on it. In addition, her contribution would appreciate tax-free until she withdrew the money. This is a very tax-efficient way to save. If she saved very early in her career the magic of compound interest would take care of her retirement planning. Her pension plan allowed her to choose a no-load open-ended mutual fund. We suggested that she invest her pension money half in a GNMA fund and half in a long-term Treasury bond fund since the money would be invested for 40 years.

Finally, we suggested that she sell her two growth stocks because she was not getting enough diversification with just two stocks. We suggested that she pay off her 15 percent car loan since it was unlikely that she would earn more than that from her investments. If she wanted a stock investment, she might buy a stock index fund such as the Vanguard Index Trust-500 Portfolio. This would give her an investment in 500 stocks and guarantee that if the stock market went up, she would have an equivalent capital appreciation. We also suggested that she take most of her money out of the savings account that was yielding 2 percent and invest it in a Treasury money-market fund that was yielding 5.5 percent. This was her immediate backup money that she could transfer into her account with a phone call. She would more than double her return without taking any additional risk. She should not pay off her $20,000 college loan because the 7 percent interest rate was reasonable, and it enabled her to keep emergency money in a money-market account.

Laura Lawyer

Laura Lawyer is a 40-year-old divorced woman. Laura worked as a lawyer for the last 15 years since her graduation from NYU Law School. She would like to consider downshifting or changing careers in 10 years when she is 50. Laura presently has no retirement plan. For the last 10 years, Laura and her law partner have done very well in their specialty practice as environmental lawyers, practicing in midtown Manhattan high above Park Avenue. The long hours that Laura spent developing

Table 3-2. Tracy Teacher's Improved Financial Position

Assets	
Treasury money-market fund	$10,000
Vanguard S&P 500 Index fund	10,000

Liabilities	
College loans	$20,000 at 7%
Car loan	0

Future contributions to her pension plan
50% to a GNMA fund
50% to a long-term Treasury bond fund

Table 3-3. Laura Lawyer's Financial Position

Assets	
Co-op apartment in Manhattan minus mortgage (550,000−300,000)	$250,000
East Hampton beach house	500,000
Checking account	25,000
Total Assets	$775,000

her high-pressure litigation practice resulted in a divorce five years ago from her husband Lenny. Laura and Lenny have two children, ages 8 and 10, who live with Laura. As part of the property settlement, Laura received title to the couple's co-operative apartment in Manhattan. The co-op is worth $550,000 and has a mortgage on it of $300,000. Laura also received title to their beach house in East Hampton. This house is worth $500,000 and has no mortgage on it. Laura thus received assets worth $750,000 from her divorce settlement. She has no other assets except for $25,000 in her checking account. Laura's children both attend an expensive private school in Manhattan that costs $15,000 each or $30,000 for the year in tuition and fees.

Laura consulted us immediately after her divorce to get our advice about her new financial situation. We reviewed with Laura the financial issues presented by her new life.

As a result of her legal training, she was well aware of the liability issues that she faced. She had a large malpractice insurance policy. She also had substantial health and disability policies. Finally, she had a home-owner's policy and an umbrella policy to cover potential liability from auto accidents or other activities that might result in injury to another, such as her erratic golf game.

Laura expressed concern about whether she would have enough to downshift in 10 years and retire in 20 years. She was also concerned whether she would have enough of a college fund for her share of her children's education that she estimated to be $100,000.

After our discussion, Laura came to the conclusion that her earnings from her law firm were enough to pay all of her day-to-day expenses. However, without her former husband's contribution, she would have to change her lifestyle if she wanted to be able to realize her goals. Her largest current expenses were her co-op apartment and her children's private school costs. She also needed cash to fund her retirement plan, develop a college fund, and have substantial savings to enable her to downshift. Laura worked with us to develop the following plan.

One major concern was that all of Laura's assets were in real estate. Her assets were not diversified and did not provide a stream of income. Moreover, when Laura wanted to make lifestyle changes in 10 and 20 years, the real-estate market might be in a down cycle. To deal with these concerns, Laura decided to sell her co-op in Manhattan for $550,000 and buy a house with more space in Scarsdale, a nearby suburb of Manhattan, for $500,000. Although Laura would prefer to live in Manhattan, she would not be able to meet her financial goals if she did. Staying in Manhattan, she would not be able to fund her pension plan or have the opportunity to downshift after 10 years. Although Laura had a large profit from her co-op sale, she was able to shelter all of the gain but $50,000 from current tax because she bought another principal residence within two years. The $50,000 was expended in moving expenses, closing costs, new furniture, fixing-up expenses, and taxes. The house in Scarsdale would provide more space for the children as they got older. More importantly, the Scarsdale public schools were so good that Laura could send her children there and save $30,000 a year.

Laura would use the $30,000 tuition savings to fund her Keogh profit-sharing plan. The $30,000 contribution to her Keogh plan would also result in a $30,000 tax deduction on her income tax return. We recommended that the Keogh plan invest in corporate bonds and a GNMA mutual fund because the income from investments accrues tax-free in the plan. If she invested $30,000 at 8 percent a year for 10 years in her Keogh plan, she would have about $435,000. At the same rate of return, she would have $1,373,000 at the end of 20 years.

Laura also decided to sell her East Hampton house for $500,000 and invest the proceeds after tax and closing costs of $400,000 as follows: $350,000 in a portfolio of tax-free municipal bonds and $50,000 in two-year Treasury bonds. The Treasury bonds would be easy to sell if she needed cash, or she could borrow money from her broker using the bonds as collateral.

Finally, we suggested that Laura transfer most of the $25,000 out of her checking account, which was yielding less than 1 percent interest, and into a tax-free money-market fund.

While she did not like paying the $100,000 tax bill resulting from the sale of her East Hampton house, she would have had to pay tax sooner or later when she sold this property. The bonds would create a stream of income for Laura and her family that she could use to even out the cash-flows from her law practice. Laura's firm had very good years and average years. With her new obligations because of the divorce and higher expenses, the average years might not result in enough income to pay all of her bills. The income from the $30,000 (tuition savings) invested in bonds would supplement her income in those years. If her law practice did well and she was able to save all of her bond income, she would have enough to downshift in 10 years. She did not want to invest in stocks because of their volatility. She had enough volatility in her law practice. Her bonds would smooth out her overall cashflow. She would buy the municipal bonds in such a way that one bond valued at $25,000 came due in each year beginning in eight years from now, when her first child would be going off to college. Laura put $50,000 into two-year Treasury bonds to serve as a cash reserve. She bought a tax-free money-market fund and tax-free municipal bonds because in her high tax bracket the lower tax-free interest rates resulted in more after-tax income than would be generated by taxable bonds.

Table 3-4. Laura Lawyer's Improved Financial Position

Assets	
Scarsdale house value minus mortgage	$200,000
Tax-free municipal bonds	350,000
Two-year Treasury bonds	50,000
Tax-free money-market fund	25,000
Total Assets	$625,000

Had Laura been more emotional and less rational about her situation, she might have made other choices with less beneficial results. Laura really loved living in Manhattan. Life there was a wish fulfilled. Leaving New York, even for a pleasant suburb, felt like exile to Siberia. If she had remained in New York City, however, the school bills would have continued to eat up her excess cash. The deterioration of New York City real-estate prices would have undermined her nest egg. If she had kept her house in the Hamptons, she might have seen it washed away in a hurricane or seen the property value eroded along with the beach front. There may be unforeseen beneficial results through the maintenance of old ties, but those are less tangible than the foreseen deterioration of her financial position.

Jack and Jill

Jack and Jill are both in their mid-thirties. They have been happily married for 10 years and live in Florida. They have two children, ages 6 and 7, and numerous pets. Jack works as a salesperson for a small company. Jill works as a technician for a large publicly held chemical company. Together they earn $60,000 per year. The family needs the income of both Jack and Jill to continue their present modest lifestyle. They own a home that is worth $100,000. It has a mortgage on it of $60,000. Both Jack and Jill each can contribute to 401(k) plans where they work. In addition to their mortgage debt, they also have a $3000 credit card debt charging interest at 18 percent and $5000 in auto loans outstanding charging 15 percent interest. They lead a very frugal lifestyle centered around their family. This has enabled them to save at the rate of $5000 per year.

Table 3-5. Jack and Jill's Financial Position

Assets	
House value minus mortgage	$40,000
Jill's company stock	20,000
Treasury bond mutual fund	10,000
Growth fund	10,000
Total Assets	$80,000
Liabilities	
Credit card debt	$3,000
Auto loans	5,000
Total debts	$8,000

Their objectives are to provide a college fund for their children and a retirement fund. Jill's excellent fringe benefits provide the family with health insurance and provide her with disability insurance and $50,000 of group term life insurance. Because the family needs the income of both Jack and Jill to survive, life insurance is a necessity for both of them. They can buy an additional term life insurance policy on Jill's life from her employer for $150,000 and at least a $200,000 term life insurance on Jack's life. Jack should also buy a disability policy to protect his earnings, particularly when their children are young.

The next level of life-cycle concern for Jack and Jill is to have a rainy-day fund available to draw upon if either one of them loses his of her jobs. The size of the fund that they should be able to draw upon in this emergency should be at least $25,000. When we reviewed their assets with this objective in mind, we advised that Jill should sell the $20,000 of her employer's stock that she owns. We did not make this recommendation because we thought that the company was currently a poor investment. The recommendation reflected the fact that they should not have half of their investments in the company that Jill relies on for her salary income. Jack and Jill's income sources should be more diversified. Jill is most likely to lose her job when her company is doing poorly. It is at just that time that Jill's company stock is likely to decline because of its poor earnings. The growth fund is also not suitable for a rainy-day fund because growth stocks are too volatile. Jack and Jill want stability and predictability for their rainy-day fund. A money-market fund or a $10,000 two-year Treasury bond would be more appropriate. A Treasury bond mutual fund would be acceptable as long as it is a short-term Treasury bond fund. A long-term Treasury bond fund would, like growth stocks, be too volatile for this purpose.

Jack and Jill decided to supplement the rainy-day fund with a line of credit. Since they have equity of $40,000 in their house, there should be no problem in securing a home equity line of credit if they do it now while they are both employed. Another line of credit should be a credit card with a large debt limit. They can set this up now. If they can't get a high debt limit on one card, they can sign up for two or more cards. Neither of these lines of credit should be used unless there is an emergency. If a large loan is needed the home equity loan has two advantages over the credit card. The interest rate is lower on the home equity loan, and it is tax deductible. Credit card interest is no longer tax deductible.

With the rainy-day fund taken care of, the next use of their excess cash should be to build up their 401(k) plans. Jack and Jill should contribute as much as they can to these plans, which are tax-efficient and tailor-designed to encourage savings. First, the contributions to these plans are made with pretax dollars. Second, the employer generally matches part of the contribution. Third, the earnings accumulate tax-free until they are withdrawn. Fourth, if the employee changes jobs, at least the employee contributions together with the earnings in the plan can be transferred tax-free to an IRA or another employer plan. If the employee works long enough at the job, the employer contribution will be transferable as well. In Jill's case her employer's contribution to the 401(k) plan is likely to be in employer stock, another reason to sell her employer stock. Jack and Jill can invest the money in their 401(k) plans in mutual funds specified under their retirement plans.

Jack and Jill's objective is to save money by not spending it. By using extra cash to pay down their 18 percent credit card debt and their high-interest-rate car loan, they are saving money. If they can't spare enough cash to pay down the loans, they might consider putting an equity loan on their house and using that cash to pay down the credit card and car loans. This would save interest charges and make the interest paid tax-deductible.

Finally, Jack and Jill should start making contributions to a college fund for their children. As funds become available, they can buy either zero-coupon Treasury bonds, EE bonds, or municipal bonds as their savings vehicles for this purpose. Jack and Jill can purchase Treasury bonds with a maturity that matches the start of each child's college education.

Table 3-6. Jack and Jill's Improved Financial Position

Assets	
House value minus mortgage	$40,000
Rainy-day fund	
Two-year treasury bonds	
Money-market fund	$25,000 in total
College fund	
Zero-coupon treasury bonds	
EE savings bonds	
Treasury bonds	
Municipal bonds	$8,000 in total
Total assets	$73,000
Liabilities	none

Thus, a bond purchased today should mature in 11 years, when their first child becomes 18. They can also consider zero-coupon U.S. savings bonds. If Jack and Jill put the EE bonds in their own name, use them for college tuition, and the couple's income is not very high, the interest earned on the EE bonds will not be taxable. As Jack and Jill get into a higher tax bracket, they might buy tax-free municipal bonds in their own name if the children are young. When their children are 14 and older, then bonds can be bought in the children's names because at that age the income would be taxed at the children's lower tax rate. For an explanation of tax considerations in buying bonds, see the section on taxable equivalent yields in Chap. 9.

Summary

Each person has very different investment needs, which must be individually considered. There is no ideal investment for everyone. What investment to choose depends upon your individual circumstances and objectives. How do you visualize your situation in 5 years or 10 years? For most investors who have limited resources, we suggest that your financial goals and personal situation should drive your choice of investments, rather than reaching for the sky with risky investments.

Bonds won't automatically make you rich enough to quit working. They won't provide you with great windfalls unless you speculate on interest-rate fluctuations. What bonds will do is provide you with a good, regular return on your money, often matching stock market returns without the associated risk to your principal. Bonds can provide a basis of security leading to personal freedom.

4
Pitfalls and Possibilities

*To get profit without risk, experience without
danger, and reward without work is as
impossible as it is to live without being born.*
A. P. GOUTHEY

*Nothing in life is to be feared. It is only to be
understood.*
MARIE CURIE

Everyone would like to have more money. That is why you are taking
the time to read this book. Many people envisage themselves floating on
a yacht or making large donations to charities and being regarded as a
philanthropist. Perhaps your dream is more modest—getting away
from the current routine, finding a better job, sending your kids to better schools, or taking more vacations.

Within the investment community, the stock market is often the vehicle chosen to try to satisfy those dreams. Lured by stories of great
rewards, money pours into stocks. "Joe Smith bought XYZ Corporation,
and wouldn't you know, the price doubled in six months." That's the
kind of story we hear at cocktail parties, at work, and from the brokers.
We don't hear as much about the losses. It's not party time when you
hear "I invested $1000 in XYZ stock. Its value declined by 50 percent
down to $500. Even if it goes up 50 percent, I will only have $750. I won't
have all my money back." We like to think of the upside, and minimize

the downside. More adventurous souls might try the commodities markets. Investing in gold, silver, and commodities can be alluring. Many commentators have said everyone knows that when the dollar declines against the major currencies, then gold and silver increase in value in anticipation of inflationary pressures. Common knowledge, however, does not always match what actually happens.

Tip_____

Unlike stocks, including preferred stock, bonds will eventually come due at their face value.

Bonds can also be used to speculate, and many times people gamble in bonds without realizing it. In a feature story on bonds in the April 1995 issue of *Smart Money*, a popular personal financial magazine, the sad story of Sharon Prather was described. Prather, a 40-year-old woman, put her nest egg for her dream house in the amount of $75,000 into Dean Witter's Government Income Trust Fund in 1993 and lost 17 percent of her principal in the face of rising interest rates in 1994. Included with the article is a photograph of her looking dejected, with the caption "Sharon Prather bailed out of bonds after losing 17 percent of her principal." Her reaction was to sell her bond fund and run back to the stock market.

How did Ms. Prather lose money by investing in government bonds? They are rated triple-A and are touted to be super-safe. How did she go wrong? Her major problem was that she did not really invest in government bonds, and her strategy was misguided.

- She did not invest directly in government bonds but rather in a mutual fund that owned government bonds and other kinds of bonds and bond products. She may have assumed that because the word *government* was included in the title of the fund it must be a safe investment. She did not investigate the bond fund's holdings. (See Chap. 12.)

- She did not understand the difference between owning a bond that can be redeemed at face value at maturity and a bond fund where the shares must be sold at the closing price of the day. (See Chap. 11.)

- She did not know that the bond maturities held in the fund would significantly affect her risk.

- She did not understand market risk, the risk that bonds decline in price when interest rates increase. If she had purchased and held individual Treasury bonds to maturity, she would not have had to worry about the fluctuation of interest rates. (See the section entitled "Market Risk" in Chap. 4.)

- She panicked when the price of the fund declined. If she had not sold her shares in 1994, she would have recouped all of her paper losses by March 1995.

The Risks of Stocks versus Bonds

The media usually treat bonds the same as stocks. Bonds are viewed as trading vehicles, a view which is encouraged by the brokerage industry. Each trade generates profits while holding bonds only results in much smaller fees for brokers. A 1 percent decline in long-term bond rates from the level of 7.5 percent would result in a total return of 21 percent, while a 1 percent rise in interest rates would only precipitate a 3 percent loss. Stocks could easily generate that kind of loss and more over a short period of time. That is if you realize the gains and the losses. We believe that unless you are a trader by profession, bonds should be viewed as a buy-and-hold investment and analyzed on that basis.

In our view, the purpose of buying a bond is to receive a stream of income and to protect your principal. A bond represents a debt of the corporation or a government entity. The debtor will make fixed interest payments twice a year and at the end of the term of the bond you will receive back the face value of the bond. If the required interest and principal payments are not made when due, the bond has defaulted and the debtor will be in bankruptcy. This gives the debtor a powerful incentive to meet its obligations on schedule. In a bankruptcy, the law requires that the bondholders are all repaid in full before anything is paid to the shareholders who own stock.

By contrast, stocks may pay a dividend if a dividend is declared each quarter by the board of directors. There is no obligation to pay a current dividend even if a dividend was paid in the past. Since stock represents an equity interest in the corporation, rather than a debt of the corporation, no principal is ever required to be repaid with respect to the stock. Thus, as a shareholder you depend upon another buyer to purchase your shares at a price greater than you paid for them. A bondholder by contrast looks to the legal obligations of the corporation to receive interest payments and a return of principal.

One strategy that a bondholder, but not a stockholder, can use is to monitor the price of the bond. If interest rates have gone down, the price of the bond will go up and the bondholder can take the gain by selling the bond. If interest rates have gone up, the price of the bond will go down. In this case the bondholder can hold the bond to its due date, at which time the bondholder will receive back the face value of the bond. The foregoing strategy is of value only if you will reinvest the gain on the bonds into an investment other than bonds.

Technical Buy-Sell Tip_____

If the value of your bond increases, that is because you are getting a larger cashflow than a bond selling at the prevailing market rate. If you realize the gain, then you pay transaction costs and give up the better cashflow. If prices decline and the value of your bond diminishes, you may be getting less than an average return on your bond. However, if you can hold the bond to maturity, it is not necessary to realize the loss because the bond will eventually come due at its face value. If interest rates were to stay the same for three years, the value of a three-year bond would still increase because it is coming closer to maturity.

Risks of Investing in Bonds

All investments have risks attached to them and bonds are no exception. The continuum of risk on bonds ranges from minimally to very risky. When properly understood, bonds can be a low-risk investment with a competitive return.

There are many different kinds of risks associated with bonds. However, it is possible to control your exposure to the risks. We will discuss how to minimize the impact the following risks could have on your investments:

- *Default risk.* The risk that the issuer is unable to meet the interest and principal payments when due
- *Market risk.* The risk that interest rates will rise, reducing the value of the bonds
- *Liquidity risk.* The risk that the bonds cannot be sold quickly at an attractive price
- *Early call risk and reinvestment risk.* The risk that high-yielding bonds will be called away early, and the money will have to be reinvested at a lower interest rate
- *Event risk.* Uncertainty created by the unfolding of unexpected events
- *Tax risk.* The possibility that changes in the tax code or in your tax position might adversely affect the value of your bonds

- *Political risk.* The likelihood that an issuer will exercise its legal right to terminate appropriations

- *Inflation risk.* The possibility that the value of your investment might be eroded with increased inflation

Default Risk

Default risk sounds very scary. Simply put, bonds default because the issuer doesn't have the money to pay the interest or principal at the designated time. Bonds can default in a number of ways. Issuers can miss an interest payment, or they can pay after the due date for payment. The issuer can pay all interest payments, but fail to redeem the bonds at maturity. It is also considered a default if an issuer does not pay money into a debt-service account at the appropriate times. A debt-service account is the account where money is held for the payment of bond interest and principal.

The risk of default should not be ignored. However, a corporation or a municipal issuer cannot walk away from a loan and expect to be able to access the debt markets again or at the same rate of interest. The large lenders, the rating agencies, and the bond insurance companies would make it difficult for the issuer to borrow again. In this way the marketplace disciplines the issuers. Even if there is a default, all is not lost for the investor. There is usually a reorganization of the corporate or municipal issuer and its debt. The principal and interest are paid out over a different time frame or at a lower interest rate or both.

Bond Ratings. Bond ratings provide investors with some guidelines as to the riskiness of the investment. Though ratings do not provide absolute protection, they generally give a good indication of risk. Bonds rated double-A or triple-A are considered to have excellent economic support.

People care about ratings. Investors care about them because they are a guide to risk. Ratings don't guarantee a risk-reward relationship, but they are the best pathfinder. Issuers care about ratings because a better rating reduces borrowing costs. In December 1994, the Wissahickon School District in Pennsylvania issued $5 million of bonds. It was able to save $60,000 in issuing costs because with its double-A rating it did not need to purchase bond insurance. Most A-rated school districts purchase bond insurance to raise their rating to triple-A. When the insurance premium is smaller than the amount the insurance will save by lowering the borrowing costs, insurance is added to the bond issue.

When the price of a bond issue drops because of a rating downgrade, the yield increases dramatically. Speculation abounds as the news of possible resolutions of the problem percolates through the marketplace. Should you sell your bonds at that time? By the time the bad news has circulated, the traders have already reduced the value of the bonds in the marketplace. Unless you need the money immediately or want to use the loss for tax purposes, it is often prudent to wait and see how the financial difficulties will be resolved.

You will often have a choice between a lower yield and more safety or a higher yield and less safety. The broker calls with a great deal! The yield sounds so attractive compared to what else is being offered. Be disciplined! Consider why one bond is offering to pay more than another. Is the risk increasing more than the return? If a triple-A bond is yielding 6.5 percent, and a triple-B bond is yielding 7 percent, the question to ask yourself is whether you wish to take a greatly increased risk for an extra 0.5 percent return. If the bond had a value of $10,000, the extra return on the lower rated bond would be $50 per year. Over a five-year period that would amount to $250. Another way to deal with the temptation is to tell brokers that you do not wish to hear offerings below a certain grade. Nonrated bonds? No, thank you! They do not fit into my investment profile. All too often, investors are swayed by the yield, and they forget about the risk.

Tip_____

If you wish to invest in high-yield bonds, which are by definition more risky, consider purchasing a high-yield bond fund rather than buying individual bonds. High-yield bonds are called junk bonds by some.

Bonds issued by the federal government are considered to be virtually riskless under our current economic and political systems. Rating agencies evaluate bonds issued by private corporations and federal, state, and local governments and their agencies. The rating agencies provide an indication of the bonds' strengths and weaknesses at the time of the rating. Bond buyers evaluate corporate bonds with the same information used by stock buyers when they assess the strength of a company. The SEC has moved to set up depositories of updated information on municipal bonds in order to make recent financial data accessible to municipal bond investors. That information should be available to investors through their brokers.

The Rating Agencies.   There are four primary rating agencies: Moody's Investors Service, Standard & Poor's (S&P), Fitch, and Duff & Phelps (DCR). These agencies are paid by the issuers to evaluate bond offerings. The rating assigned will affect how much the issuer will have to pay to borrow money. When an issuer brings a new issue to market, all the preceding issues may be rerated if there is a change in the evaluation. Issuers may be placed on *credit watch* if there is a likelihood that their bonds might be downgraded or upgraded.

There are basic similarities in the ratings by the four agencies as shown in Table 4-1.

Standard & Poor's and Moody's also indicate quality within a given rating category. S&P and DCR might give an A-rated bond a plus (+) or minus (−) to indicate a strong or weak A rating. Moody's, on the other hand, would use A1 to indicate a higher credit quality, while A2 indicates a midrange ranking, and A3 indicates a rating at the lower end of the single-A scale. The rating agencies generally agree with each other, but they do sometimes differ in their evaluation, resulting in *split ratings*. One rating agency might give an issuer a triple-B rating and another might grade it single-A.

A fairly new addition to bond ratings is Standard & Poor's "r" rating. S&P attaches an "r" symbol to some securities such as structured notes that could exhibit high volatility or dramatic fluctuations in its expected return. *Structured notes* are bonds that are especially sensitive to fluctuations in interest rates. The "r" indicates interest-rate risk, although the notes have a strong credit rating. Nearly all the notes are rated double-A or triple-A and may be found in mutual funds, pension funds, and other investment vehicles.

Table 4-1. The Rating Agencies

Moody's	S&P	Fitch	DCR	Credit quality
Aaa	AAA	AAA	AAA	Solid as a rock
Aa	AA	AA	AA	Very fine quality
A	A	A	A	Strong capacity to pay
Baa	BBB	BBB	BBB	Adequate ability to pay; lowest investment grade for banks
Ba	BB	BB	BB	Somewhat speculative; risk exposure
B	B	B	B	More speculative; risk exposure
Caa	CCC	CCC	CCC	Major risk exposure
Ca	CC	CC		Crucial risk exposure
C	C	C		Default on interest payments
D	D	D	DD	General default
NR	NR	NR		No rating has been requested

The ratings on bonds change as the rating agencies assess changes in the ability of an issuer to meet its obligations. When the changes are gradual and the issuer comes to market frequently, the ratings are more apt to be accurate than when an issuer only infrequently comes to market.

The accuracy of a rating can change not only as the result of changes in a particular corporation or municipality but also with the fortune of an entire industry or region. For example, the health-care industry is going through massive changes and restructuring. The rating agencies are reevaluating their criteria for measuring the economic health of the industry. They all agree that financial statistics are only reflections of past performance and not indicators of future success as the industry shifts to managed care. Other factors that had not formerly played such a big role assume much greater weight, such as market environment and competitive position. Thus, the ratings on hospital bonds will shift as the pressures on the industry bring about change.

Tip_____

Diversify the issuers of your bonds so that if there is a default the overall impact on your portfolio will be smaller.

You may have read about the financial difficulties in Orange County, California. The county treasurer, Robert Citron, ran an investment pool for the county, municipal entities within the county, and other municipalities that wanted to invest in the pool. This investment pool was able to provide above-market returns by taking above-market risks. Citron invested the pool in highly leveraged derivatives.

One or more underlying instruments determine the value, in whole or in part, of the *derivative*. A derivative is a synthetic concoction derived from more traditional securities such as bonds or stocks or from other economic instruments such as currencies and loans. They are used to defray the risk of changes in interest rates, stock prices, foreign exchange rates, and commodities prices. They have many names, including interest rate swaps, Treasury strips, and collateralized mortgage obligations. *Leverage* means using borrowed money to achieve a greater rate of return. By investing more than the investor actually owns, the effect of a small change in price is multiplied.

Instead of investing only the dollars in the pool, Citron borrowed three times the amount of money invested in the pool. He leveraged the pool more than he was legally allowed. Citron placed a large bet that interest rates would decline. When interest rates began to go up instead of down, the value of the pool dropped so sharply that Citron was unable to meet the margin calls.

A *margin call* is the demand from the broker carrying a customer's position for additional cash to guarantee performance on an investment position. A margin call results from a lack of money in a margin account to meet the broker's borrowing requirements. If you borrowed three dollars for every dollar you invested, and the value of the bond or stock declined, then you would have to put up more money. If you didn't have additional cash, then the broker would sell out your positions to protect the brokerage firm. That is what happened to Citron.

As a result of Citron's failure to meet the margin calls this Aa/AA-rated county, the richest in all of California, filed for bankruptcy. This bankruptcy brought down with it local school districts and smaller municipal entities that were required to invest in the fund. The debt that immediately defaulted was $600 million of one-year taxable notes issued on July 10, 1994. The county officials devised a plan to satisfy most of their creditors.

If a double-A–rated municipality defaults, what hope is there for lesser-rated entities? The rating agencies are the watchdogs and should give advance warning to the investors of any major changes. In the case of Orange County, they failed to do so. As a result, the rating agencies are looking into the possibilities of other problems with derivatives lurking unnoticed in other states' and municipalities' portfolios. Some states, such as Florida, are establishing investment guidelines for all the municipal issuers within the state to prevent similar problems from happening.

The SEC, in conjunction with the Treasury Department, undertook a campaign to educate municipalities about safe investing. The SEC held widespread discussions about establishing guidelines for the sale of derivatives to municipal entities. Tax-exempt money-market funds also applied pressure to Orange County and the state of California by expressing their dismay that Californians failed to honor their debt. The funds threatened to demand higher interest rates, not only for Orange County but for all California borrowers. The state of Maine blamed Orange County and Merrill Lynch for increasing Maine's short-term borrowing costs.

Moody's announced a new rating criteria for tax and revenue anticipation notes. Their objective is to protect investors against a cashflow crunch in the event of a shortfall in the issuer's general fund. The investment community joined forces to prevent this debacle from happening again.

Tip_____

There are times when the spread or difference in the yields between higher-rated bonds and lower-rated bonds is very small, reflecting fairly stable economic conditions. At those times, purchase only the higher-rated bonds!

Summary of How to Protect Yourself from Default Risk

- Purchase bonds with a horizon where you can foresee the issuer repaying the debt.
- Purchase insured (or credit-enhanced) bonds.
- Purchase bonds in thriving areas and growing sectors of the economy.
- Purchase bonds that are simple to describe and understand.
- Take a minute to consider if the extra yield is worth the extra risk. You should spend more time picking out a bond than a shirt.
- Buy bonds with a rating of single-A or better.
- Use a consultant who charges a flat fee to advise you. Don't take pitches from brokers.

Market Risk

All bonds are subject to market risk! It doesn't matter whether they are Treasury bonds or junk bonds. It doesn't matter if they are rated triple-A or triple-B. Understanding market risk will enable you to protect your portfolio.

The principal cause of a price decline is generally a rise in interest rates. As interest rates rise, the values of bonds decline. Even if the value of a bond declines, the *face value*, the value of the bond at maturity, remains the same.

For example, the state of Wisconsin issues a $10,000 bond with an interest coupon of 5 percent. One year later, interest rates rise to 6 percent. The value of the bond declines in order to make the effective rate of interest for a new buyer equal to 6 percent. If the bond had 10 years remaining to maturity, the dollar price would be approximately $9261. These bonds are now selling at a *discount* to their face value. As the bond approaches its due date, it will appreciate until it reaches its face value. No matter how interest rates fluctuate, the state of Wisconsin must repay the face value of the bond at its due date. In our example, if the bond had only a 5-year maturity instead of a 10-year maturity and was being sold at the same 6 percent, the value of the bond would be $9573. The longer the maturity of the bond, the greater is its possible decline in value. However, bonds with short maturities can also experience price volatility. In early 1995, in an effort to stem inflation, the Federal Reserve raised short-term interest rates four times. Bond prices declined as yields increased. If you can hold bonds selling at a discount until redemption, you earn less than the going rate of interest but your principal is returned. If your money was invested in a short-term bond fund, you necessarily lost principal.

There are other factors that may affect the market price of a bond. The price of a bond downgraded by the rating agencies from double-A to single-A will drop because the traders will view it as a more risky credit. Bad publicity may similarly reduce the demand for the bond and result in a price decline. The oversupply of a bond may also result in a lower market price.

Should you be concerned about a price decline? If a stock drops in value, you have lost money. If you own a bond and can hold the bond until it comes due, you will receive the face value of the bond, whether interest rates are up or down or whether you purchased the bond at a discount or a premium. The idea is to purchase bonds that will come due before you anticipate needing the money.

If you own a bond fund, the rise and fall of interest rates will immediately affect your portfolio because bond funds are *marked to market* every day. That means that every day the bonds in the portfolio are repriced, which immediately affects the redemption price. You must expect this roller coaster ride and decide how you are going to react before you put your money in the fund. The fund companies are trying to make the public more aware of the volatility of the funds. The SEC has been gathering information on how to improve open-ended bond fund's disclosure to investors. T. Rowe Price, Fidelity, and Vanguard have been in the forefront of trying to make buyers aware of the risks of investing.

Tip_____

You only experience market risk if you have to sell your bonds. Before you purchase a bond, decide when you will need the money. Purchase a bond that will mature at or before that time.

As interest rates rise, the price of a bond declines. As interest rates decline, the price of a bond rises. This is counterintuitive. A 5 percent bond with a 10-year maturity would sell for $1080 if interest rates declined to 4 percent, a possible gain of $80 per bond. When brokers say that bonds are performing well, that means that the prices of bonds have risen and the

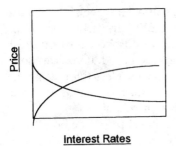

Figure 4-1. Effect of the rise and fall of interest rates on bond value.

yields have declined. If you are looking to purchase bonds, then a price rise is not in your favor. It is in your favor if you own bonds and you are looking to sell.

Tip_____

If your plan is to buy and hold securities to maturity, use the principal amount (face value) of the bonds for your record-keeping.

Unless a bond has traded recently, bonds are priced according to a matrix. A bond matrix shows what a bond of a specified quality should yield in a particular year. A bond of a certain maturity and rating and from a particular market sector is priced like similar bonds that recently sold in the marketplace. This may not be reflective of the price your bonds will fetch. There are many factors to consider:

- Number of bonds being sold
- Availability of the bonds
- Demand for the bonds
- Size of the issue
- Call features

What this means to you is that the prices you see on your brokerage statement every month may not be precise. Unless the bonds are offered for sale, you cannot know their value exactly. Their value is determined by the marketplace. Bonds are worth what buyers are willing to pay for them. All buyers will not necessarily agree on their exact value. That's what makes the market!

Summary of How to Protect Yourself from Market Risk

- Purchase bonds you can hold to maturity.
- Buy individual bonds rather than bond funds.
- Be prepared for a fluctuation in value of your bond fund as interest rates rise and fall.
- Consider tax consequences and transaction costs before selling.

Liquidity Risk

Liquidity risk is the risk that you may not be able to sell your bonds quickly at an attractive price. There is a very active market in the purchase and sale of bonds. Certain kinds of bonds are more vulnerable than others to liquidity risk, but none are immune.

Poorly rated bonds and bonds that are unrated have less liquidity because dealers have more trouble reselling them. Odd lots of less than $25,000 face value are less liquid than lots of $25,000 or more. Some investors may not have the patience you did to listen to the story of bonds with an unusual description. Some investors don't understand premium bonds. Others dislike bonds with lower-than-average coupons because the difference between the purchase price and the face value is subject to capital gains or ordinary income tax. To some, a callable bond might fit the bill; to another investor, it might be poison. Small-issue, infrequently traded bonds have higher yields when purchased but much worse yields when sold.

Bonds may lose their liquidity because the issuer is in the vicinity of another issuer in jeopardy of default. The bankruptcy by Orange County, California, made it more expensive for neighboring Los Angeles County to borrow. The unrelated losses racked up by Cuyahoga County's investment pool led Ohio's State Treasury Asset Reserve to seek a triple-A rating from Standard & Poor's in order to reassure investors of its solid, conservative practices.

If an industry is in trouble, bonds may lose liquidity. Hospitals have been under siege as health management organizations have negotiated to reduce costs. Hospitals have merged in order to form more integrated systems with large networks dominating the delivery of service in order to establish stronger bargaining positions. In the constant flux, some hospitals will be winners and others losers in the merger game. Uncertainty makes buyers more reluctant to purchase hospital bonds.

Some bonds trade actively and will therefore bring a better price when sold. If you want to know how much you would lose if you decided to sell tomorrow, ask the broker to tell you what he would pay for the bond if his firm were a buyer. That information will give you an idea about the *markup,* the amount added to the cost of a security, taking into account overhead and a profit margin.

Tip_____

To find out how liquid an investment is, ask what you could sell the investment for tomorrow if you bought it today.

In a low interest-rate market, brokers will sometimes try to switch an investor into closed-end bond funds instead of bonds. Closed-end funds appear to have a higher yield. They are said to have high liquidity if they are traded on the New York Stock Exchange, like a stock. However, the only buyers of these closed-end funds are other retail buyers. The difference between the purchase and sale price is wider than the spread on bonds that might also appeal to institutional customers.

Summary of How to Protect Yourself from Liquidity Risk

- Purchase bonds that will mature when you need the cash.
- Select bonds from stable market sectors, both regional and industrial.
- Avoid bonds with extreme discounts or premiums.
- Select bonds which have wide market appeal.

Early Call Risk and Reinvestment Risk

A call is never favorable to the investor because issuers only call bonds when interest rates have declined. This is a reinvestment risk because the money returned from a called bond is reinvested at a lower interest rate. If it were not favorable to the issuer to call the bond, then it would remain outstanding. Call risk is a risk that is avoidable. Ask the broker to describe all the calls on a bond, including sinking funds and extraordinary calls (which we'll explain shortly). Make a judgment about the effects of the calls on your investment portfolio.

There are calls with a specified call date. It is quite usual for a new issue to have a call after 10 years. Sometimes the first call is at seven or eight years. With municipal bonds, after the call date the bond may then be callable every year until it matures. Corporate bonds might become callable with 30 days' notice after the first call. In general, corporate bonds have many more calls than municipal bonds. Some bonds, such as bonds issued by housing agencies or hospitals, are callable anytime if there are unexpended funds or a catastrophe occurs. These are *extraordinary call* provisions. Some bonds have *sinking fund* provisions. A lottery decides which bonds are called in a particular year.

If you ask your broker the question, "What are the calls on this bond?" it is likely that you will only be told about the *fixed* calls. Those are the definite dates that the bond may be called by the issuer. You might only be told the par call, when the bond will be redeemed at face value. It is quite likely that you will not be told if there is a special call provision unless you ask. To elicit those calls, you will have to ask, "Are there any extraordinary or catastrophic calls or sinking fund provisions?" On housing bonds and hospital bonds there are always extraordinary calls.

Summary of How to Protect Yourself from Early Call Risk and Reinvestment Risk

- Ask for all calls, not just the fixed calls.
- Buy par bonds or noncallable bonds.
- Ask the broker to send you a copy of the Bloomberg or J.J. Kenny descriptions of the bond if you want more complete disclosure about the calls on a bond. They provide an electronic data bank containing descriptions of bond features.

Event Risk

The term *event risk* was formulated in response to the changes in the corporate world during the 1980s. During that decade, a wave of corporate takeovers and acquisitions occurred. The result was that some companies tried to make themselves unattractive by loading up on debt and using other measures called "poison pill provisions." In the wave of takeovers, a highly rated company could be downgraded to junk status, often overnight. The investment-grade bonds of RJR Nabisco became junk bonds after the company was acquired in the largest leveraged buyout in history. These takeovers are often impossible to predict. Every so often, talk of major changes in a corporate structure make the news. In April 1995, Kirk Kerkorian, a 10 percent shareholder in Chrysler Corporation proposed using Chrysler's cash hoard as well as other money to buy back the stock from the public shareholders. Had Mr. Kerkorian been successful, that would have been good news for the shareholders but bad news for the bondholders, who would have watched the credit quality of their bonds deteriorate to junk status. Though the pace of mergers and acquisitions has slowed, event risk remains a consideration in purchasing corporate bonds.

In 1994, event risk came to municipal bonds. The Mexican government devalued the peso by 38 percent in December 1994. The border cities in Texas rely heavily on sales tax revenues generated by cross-border traffic. Would they be able to cope with the decline in the sales tax revenues? These cities had weathered the peso's devaluation in 1983 and 1987. Their officials knew that they would have to reduce spending if revenues did not meet expectations, and they had diversified their economies in anticipation of a similar event. President Clinton stepped in with $40 billion in emergency loan guarantees to help the country meet its financial obligations. The Mexican president, Ernesto Zedillo, promised to reduce government spending and sell more state-owned industries. The overall effect was moderate and short-lived.

Corporate bondholders can also be caught in a web. Unsuspecting owners of Marriott Corporation bonds found themselves restructured into a debt-laden company. Marriott divided the existing corporation into two separate corporations, putting most of its debt into one unit. The bondholders were not happy because one corporation was strong and the other contained all the debt. The latter had a double-B rating. A decision by a company to spin off a subdivision, loading debt onto the new entity, is not entirely unusual.

Another potential problem facing corporate-bond owners is how management decisions affect the health of the company. Before the takeover mania, junk-bond investors could be assured that if the issuer's business did as well as projected, then the credit rating of the bonds, and therefore the value of the bonds, was likely to improve. However, a company could decide to releverage in order to become a private company, buy out a competitor, or protect itself from a takeover.

Summary of How to Protect Yourself from Event Risk

- Include different geographic regions in your municipal bond portfolio, even if you are in a high-tax state.
- Diversify your corporate holdings by purchasing bonds from different market sectors.
- Diversify your holdings by issuer.

Tax Risk

There is always the risk that the federal or state government will change the tax code, to the detriment of your investment. Capital gains have been taxed as high as 50 percent and as low as 20 percent. Purchasers of limited partnerships found that their tax shelters turned into tax nightmares. For purchasers of bonds there are potential problems that could be under your control.

Investors hate to pay taxes! This general feeling often leads people to choose municipal bonds as an investment. While this is an excellent choice if you are in the 28 percent tax bracket or higher, it is not a good choice if you are in a lower tax bracket. This often affects couples where both partners are working. Upon retirement their tax bracket might fall to 15 percent, but their dislike of paying taxes and their habit of municipal bonds leads them to continue to purchase them. In fact, they are doing themselves a disservice by purchasing such bonds. In the 15 percent tax bracket, they will net more from purchasing taxable bonds and paying taxes on the interest than by purchasing tax-exempt municipal bonds.

A flat tax would negatively affect investors in municipal bonds and help investors in taxable bonds. If a flat tax were to be passed, then investors in municipal bonds would not be adequately compensated for accepting the lower yields compared to yields on currently taxable bonds. However, if the flat tax were passed, it would tend to push all interest rates down, thereby minimizing the market impact on outstanding municipal bonds. The marketplace has already figured in the possibility of a tax change by keeping municipal yields at a higher ratio to Treasuries than they had been traditionally.

The likelihood of a flat tax passing is not considered very great despite its simplicity. The flat tax is viewed by some people as a sharp tax reduction for upper-income individuals and as a tax increase for moderate-income people who depend mostly on their paychecks. Whatever its wisdom, the flat tax looks like a giveaway to the rich, making it a very unpopular proposal.

The *de minimus rule* on discount bonds passed in 1993 adversely affected deep discount bonds by requiring that the investor pay income tax on the amount of the difference between the discounted purchase price and the value of the bond when it comes due. For example, if you were to purchase a bond for $800 and it comes due at $1000 five years later, then $200 would be subject to tax at your ordinary income tax rate. (The top rate was 39.6 percent in 1995.) Before this rule was passed, the $200 gain was subject to the capital gains rate of 28 percent. Since buyers in the higher brackets tend to avoid deeply discounted bonds on which they would have to pay the higher rates, these bonds become more difficult and more costly to sell.

Summary of How to Protect Yourself from Tax Risk

- Know your tax bracket.
- Find out how taxes will affect your return.
- Weigh tax-free bonds against taxable bonds before making your choice.
- Find out if the fund you intend to buy will generate capital gains and taxable dividends.

Political Risk

If the people within a political unit, or the managers of a corporation, are not in favor of a debt that was incurred, they will use every means they have to wiggle out from under an obligation. In the 1970s, there was popular opposition to nuclear power plants. The Washington Public Power Supply System set out to build five nuclear power plants in Washington State. Mismanagement and incompetence led to the default in bonds used to build plants four and five. The mammoth project raised electricity costs throughout the Pacific Northwest. In 1983, the Washington State Supreme Court ruled that the utilities located in the state did not have the authority to enter into the contracts with the Supply System. Since the other participants would not have entered into contracts without the Washington utilities, the judge excused them as well. Units four and five were terminated after much wrangling, and bondholders received a settlement. There was no political will to see the projects through or to pay for the blunders.

A recent concern is about lease-backed debt. The people of the Richmond School District in California, of Brevard County, Florida, and of Orange County, California, tried to walk away from lease-backed debt, believing they had a right to ignore debt that bypassed the voter booth, that is, bonds issued on the say-so of political officials. Traditionally this type of debt has been rated one notch lower than the general obligation bonds of the same issuer. The citizens must vote "yes" on general obligation bonds before they can be issued.

The rating agencies believe that they will be able to apply pressure to the political entity to meet its obligations, whether legal or moral. This is the "economic coercion doctrine" that says if an issuer defaults it will raise the issuer's borrowing costs and limit its access to the bond market. When Orange County defaulted it had to purchase a letter of credit from a foreign bank, and its costs of borrowing increased by 1 percent. The electorate would not incur a small addition to the sales tax in order to keep their credit rating and reduce borrowing costs. Economic reasons are not always sufficient in an era of tax revolt.

Summary of How to Protect Yourself from Political Risk

- Read the newspapers and magazines.
- Think twice about an investment if the sector, market, or region is getting bad press.

Inflation Risk

One risk that none of us can avoid is the inflation risk. This is the risk that the purchasing power of our money diminishes because all the things we buy become more expensive. Bonds are subject to the inflation risk because they provide a fixed rate of return with a return of principal in the future.

There is, however, a hopeful note for bond investors with respect to inflation. After the big inflation that occurred in the late 1970s through the early 1980s, bond investors took note of the erosion of their capital. They demanded an increase in interest rates to keep up with inflation. The interest rates on long-term Treasury bonds went from 6.5 percent in 1975 to over 14 percent in 1981, at least matching the inflation rate. As inflation began to diminish, beginning with the severe recession in 1981 and 1982, interest rates began to decline. It seems to be well established at this time that whenever inflation begins to erupt, creditors immediately demand and get a higher interest rate to keep pace.

It is interesting to note that stocks are said to be a hedge against inflation. However, in the high inflationary period of the early 1980s, stocks went down, not up. Moreover, stocks had their biggest rally beginning in 1983 and continuing as inflation receded. As an inflation hedge, stocks flunked their biggest recent test. Bonds, however, reacted powerfully to inflation by an increase in interest rates.

Summary of Protecting Yourself from Inflation Risk

- Ladder your portfolio with different bonds coming due each year.
- Use your bond income to make new investments as interest rates rise with inflation.
- Consider selling your bonds that come due in two years or less, taking a small loss on their face value so you can lock in higher interest rates with longer-term bonds.

5

The Meaning Behind the Numbers

"Have I got a deal for you." How often have you been offered deals that sound too good to be true? The retort is: "What kind of return is this investment going to give me *and* when will I get my principal back?" The answer to this question is more predictable with bonds than with most other investments, though it is not as straightforward as it might first appear.

Bond professionals do not trade bonds on the basis of cashflow and neither should you. *Cashflow* tells you how many dollars you will get each year, but it leaves out other important considerations. Bond professionals buy and sell bonds on the basis of yield-to-maturity and other yield calculations. This yield tells you what your financial return will be each year in dollars and as a percentage of your investment. Traders use the yield-to-maturity to compare different bond issues in a meaningful way. So should you. The four yield concepts are:

- Current yield
- Yield-to-maturity
- Yield-to-maturity after tax on capital gains (for discount bonds)
- Yield-to-call (if bonds are callable)

Take the time to understand the yield concepts. You will make better decisions on what bonds to buy and whether to buy individual bonds, a bond fund, or a bond trust.

Cashflow from Bonds

Cashflow provides the most basic understanding of investing money in and getting money out of a bond investment. If your purpose for investing in bonds is to receive a steady stream of income, cashflow answers the question "How many dollars will I receive each year?" Compute the cashflow by multiplying the rate or bond coupon by the face value of the bond. Thus, a $10,000 bond issued with a rate (or coupon) of 6 percent has a cashflow of $600 per year.

Cashflow per year = Face value of the bond × Rate or amount of the coupon

$$\$10,000 \times .06 = \$600$$

If the bond has a 5-year life or maturity, it would pay the owner $3000 over the lifetime of the bond ($600 per year × 5 years). If the same bond had a 9 percent coupon, it would pay $900 per year or $4500 over its 5-year life.

Sales tactics for unit investment trusts in particular emphasize the relatively high current cashflow. (See Chap. 11 for an explanation of unit investment trusts.) New issue bonds might have coupons of 4 percent to 5.5 percent, while the trusts are promising returns of 6 percent to 7 percent. Does that mean that the unit investment trusts are more attractive than the individual bonds? There may be more cash coming in from the unit investment trust, but some of that cash is a return of principal. The fee is deducted from your initial investment. If you invested $100, only $96 might actually work for you after the fee is deducted.

You have to ask yourself, How can I get a better return after paying a fee or load to purchase a trust, when a similar investment that has no fee is paying out less cash? Is there a free lunch after all? The answer is that there is more to the story than cashflow. A short answer in this case is that if the current cashflow is at an above-market rate, the principal value of your investment must decline to make up for it. In other words, if the deal is too good to be true, you will probably pay for it later. There is no free lunch. The reverse also holds. If your cashflow is at a below-market rate, then the value of your investment will increase as the bond approaches maturity.

The total cashflow over the life of the bond equals the bond's annual interest income times the number of years you owned the bond plus the face value of the bond when it comes due. Thus, if the bond's interest income was $600 per year and you held the bond for 10 years, the bond paid out $6000. If the bond had a face value of $10,000, your total cashflow would be $16,000. This computation does not take into consideration the price you paid, and the reinvestment of your interest payments. If you want to know a good investment when you see one, you will have to understand more than cashflow.

Current Yield (or How Does the Price You Pay Affect Your Cashflow?)

The current yield is one of the figures most frequently quoted by bond sellers. It is easy to understand but often misleading. The *current yield* is a ratio that compares the interest that you receive for the year to the amount that you paid for the bond. Compute the current yield by dividing the amount of annual interest earned by the amount you paid for the bond.

$$\text{Current yield} = \frac{\text{Coupon interest received for the year}}{\text{Amount paid for the bond}}$$

For example, a bond with a 6 percent coupon and a price of $1000 per bond has a current yield of 6 percent.

$$6 \text{ percent} \times 1000 = 60; \quad \frac{60}{1000} = 6 \text{ percent}$$

However, the same bond priced at $900 has a current yield of 6.67 percent.

$$6 \text{ percent} \times 1000 = 60; \quad \frac{60}{900} = 6.67 \text{ percent}$$

If the bond were priced at $1100, the current yield would be 5.45 percent.

$$6 \text{ percent} \times 1000 = 60; \quad \frac{60}{1100} = 5.45 \text{ percent}$$

The current examples illustrate how to make the current yield computation but not the market reality. In reality a discount bond will have a lower coupon than a premium bond. The purpose of the price adjustment is to give the buyer an acceptable yield-to-maturity. The result is that a premium bond will have a higher current yield than a discount bond.

The current yield combines cashflow and the amount paid for the bond into one number. If the bond is a long-term bond with a maturity of 20 years or more, or is purchased near par, the current yield is a relatively good measure of true return. In other situations it is not a good measure of return. For deeply discounted bonds selling way below their face value, the current yield does not fully reflect the increase in the face value received at maturity over what you paid for the bond. For example, a 5-year $1000 bond selling at $900 will return the $100 discount all at once when the bond comes due in year 5.

Zero-coupon bonds are the ultimate example of a discount bond. Certificates of deposit and U.S. government EE bonds are examples of zero-coupon securities. In the case of zero-coupon bonds, the current yield would be zero because the bonds pay no interest until maturity. A 10-year $1000 face-value zero-coupon bond might be purchased at $600. It would provide no current yield or cash return until maturity. At the end of 10 years, the investor receives $1000. Of the $1000 received at maturity, $400 is interest.

Bonds sold at a premium, a price above face value, have a high current yield. However, an early bond redemption dramatically diminishes the expected current return. For example, a 10-year bond purchased for $1100 has a $100 premium. The $100 premium is theoretically returned $10 per year for 10 years as higher semiannual interest payments. A bond redeemed after two years at $1000 loses $80 of the $100 that you expected to receive.

Many people who invested in unit investment trusts fell into this trap. They bought the trusts because of the higher current yield. As interest rates declined, early redemption of high-coupon bonds followed. The cashflow from the trust diminished with each large bond call. For example, assume a unit trust is purchased for $1200 and pays $84 per year. It has a *current yield* of 7 percent, while the return in the market for similar bonds is 6 percent. The current yield was accurate, yet also misleading to some investors. Was this a good investment? The trust contains long-term high-coupon bonds subject to early redemption. If the investors received back only $1000 of face value for their investment of $1200, they did not receive a 7 percent overall return on their investment after five years. They lost $200 of their principal. Current yield, therefore, is not an accurate measure for investment comparisons.

Bond funds also may increase their holdings of premium bonds to increase their monthly payouts. The bond funds often quote a current return when you call them on the phone to ask about the yield. The SEC does not require the funds to give investors a yield-to-maturity number. This is one reason why it may appear that you are earning more from a bond fund than from the actual bonds. Even the SEC 30-day yield is not a true yield-to-maturity computation.

Yield-to-Maturity

Bonds come in all varieties of maturities. Some bonds will pay interest for one year, and other bonds will pay interest for 5 years or 30 years. The year that a bond issuer is obligated to repay the loan is the bond's *maturity.*

The yield-to-maturity is the basis professionals use to determine the market price of bonds. It is the common denominator used for comparing the worth of the "apples and oranges" of bonds. It enables you to compare bonds with a longer maturity to short-term bonds, high-coupon bonds to low-coupon bonds, and premium bonds to discount bonds. Along with yield-to-call and yield-to-maturity after tax, it is the key calculation used by professionals in the purchase of bonds. Unlike current yield, the yield-to-maturity considers both the *reinvestment of interest* and the *discount or premium* paid for the bond.

Tip_____

Yield-to-maturity determines the price! Focus on the yield-to-maturity number. Do not lose sight of it.

The reinvestment of interest results in interest compounding over time. Time adds value to money. The compounding of interest is intrinsic to the yield-to-maturity calculation. It is the application of the Rule of 72 to bonds. The Rule of 72 tells you approximately how many years it takes money to double. If you take a rate of return and divide it into the number 72, the result is approximately how many years it takes money to double. For example, if the rate of return is 10 percent, the number of years it takes money to double is approximately 7 (72 divided by 10 = 7 years). Similarly, if the rate of return is 5 percent, it would take money 14 years to double (72 divided by 5 = 14).

Money has time value because it can earn interest at a compounded rate over time and grow into a larger amount in the future. A dollar received in the future is less valuable than a dollar received today because of the "magic" of compound interest.

The general concept of compound interest is simple. Principal earns interest. Interest earned on the interest creates compound interest. Thus, the first dollar of interest is more valuable than the last dollar because the first dollar of interest earns interest for the life of the bond.

Table 5-1 shows that if you invested $8870 each year for five years at 6 percent interest compounded annually, you would have $50,000 at the end of the five-year period. Similarly if you invested $2718 a year for 20 years at 6 percent interest, you would have $100,000. The magic of compound interest is the alchemy of geometric compounding over time.

Tip_____

The number of years of compounding is more important than how much you invest.

The reinvestment of coupon interest is what gives the yield-to-maturity computation its compound interest magic. In the following example (compared in Table 5-2), each bond has the same cashflow—$800.

The yield-to-maturity on a $10,000 bond with an 8 percent coupon bought at par is 8 percent. If you owned these bonds, you would receive $800 interest each year for ten years. The yield-to-maturity on the discount bonds purchased for $9000 is 9.57 percent rather than 8 percent. You would receive the same $800 interest payment each year. In addition, in the 10th year you would receive a $1000 gain on which you would have to pay taxes. The amount of tax paid on the $1000 will lower the yield. The premium price of $11,000 knocks the yield-to-maturity

Table 5-1. The Power of Compound Interest

If $8,870 is contributed each year to a fund for 5 years and compounded annually at 6%, the fund will be worth $50,000.

If $3,793 is contributed each year to a fund for 10 years and compounded annually at 6%, the fund will be worth $50,000.

If $1,359 is contributed each year to a fund for 20 years and compounded annually at 6%, the fund will be worth $50,000.

Table 5-2. Par, Discount, and Premium Bonds Compared

	Face value	Coupon	Unit price	Price	Maturity	Yield-to-maturity
Par bond	$10,000	8%	100	$10,000	10 years	8%
Discount bond	$10,000	8%	90	$9,000	10 years	9.57%
Premium bond	$10,000	8%	110	$11,000	10 years	6.6%

down to 6.6 percent because you would receive only $10,000 back at maturity. There may be reasons guiding the decision to buy a discount bond or a high premium bond. The yield-to-maturity figure provides a valuable benchmark that all professionals understand and use in their evaluation of bonds. You should use it too for your bond comparisons. Always ask the broker for it.

Basic Assumptions Underlying the Yield-to-Maturity Calculation

- Bond ownership does not change for the life of the bond.
- The bond is held until its due date.
- All interest payments are reinvested. Spent interest payments cannot compound.
- All interest payments are reinvested at the same rate as the yield-to-maturity.

What happens if the *actual* rate of reinvestment of the interest payments is higher than the stated yield-to-maturity rate? Good news! The investor receives a higher return than the yield-to-maturity he expected to receive. Bad news comes if the actual rate of reinvestment is lower than the stated yield-to-maturity. The investor then receives an overall lower rate.

Yield-to-Call

A bond call might result in a shortening of the bond's life if the issuer decides to exercise its right to redeem or repurchase the bonds from an investor before the bond's due date or maturity. Traders, therefore, price bonds to the earliest call date. When the bonds are first sold, the issuer might have agreed to pay a premium of $10 or $20 a bond if it decides to call the bonds. Often bonds initially will have a premium call. If the bonds are not called, the call price usually declines to par after two or three years. Bonds priced to a premium call are frequently attractive buys in a yield-hungry market.

If the call price of the bond is the same as the purchase price, the yield may not be much different. However, if the call price is more than 100 ($1000 per bond), then the yield-to-call may be higher than the yield-to-maturity. Call prices might be 100.5 ($1005), 101 ($1010), 102 ($1020), or even as high as 103 ($1030). Newspapers like the *Wall Street Journal* quote the lowest possible yield of either the yield-to-maturity or the yield-to-call on Treasury or U.S. government agency bonds. Some bond advisers call this the *yield-to-worst*—how much you would get at the earlier of the call date or the final maturity date. This assumes the most unfavorable result occurs.

Bonds offered on the basis of price instead of yield are usually callable anytime. Corporate bonds may have calls anytime with 30 days' notice. A yield-to-maturity may not be useful in this situation. There are many unpredictable factors that enter into the decision to call a bond.

Yield-to-Maturity after Tax

The interest income from corporate bonds is subject to federal income tax and, generally, to state and local income tax as well. Unless the bonds are being purchased in a tax-deferred entity such as a 401(k) plan, Individual Retirement Account, or a Keogh plan, the taxes due on the interest income will lower the bonds' yield.

U.S. Treasury bonds are subject to federal but not state or local income tax. In high-tax states, Treasury bonds may be a better selection on an after-tax basis than corporate bonds even if the Treasury bonds appear to yield less. Treasury bonds are a better credit risk than corporate bonds. The Treasury yield may be higher after calculating the taxes on the corporate bonds or at least not so low as to justify the added risk of corporate bonds.

Tax-free municipal bonds are not subject to federal income tax. Some states subject income from certain municipal bonds to tax even if the bonds are issued within the state. Some states and counties subject income from out-of-state bonds to an intangibles or personal property tax. The territorial bonds of Puerto Rico, Guam, and the U.S. Virgin Islands enjoy full tax exemption in all 50 states.

A municipal bond purchased for less than its face value is generally subject to tax on the difference between its purchase price and redemption price. However, a zero-coupon bond may not be subject to this tax unless it too sells at a discount to its accreted value. A $1000 bond purchased for $900 has a discount of $100. On the $100 discount, the investor pays ordinary income tax or capital gains tax at maturity or when the bond is sold.

Calculate the yield-to-maturity after tax in the same way as the yield-to-maturity, with one difference. The redemption price used is not face value but face value minus the amount of tax on the discount. You can also ask the broker for the yield-to-maturity after tax at your particular tax bracket. "If I am in the 28 percent tax bracket," you say, "what is my yield after I pay the tax on the discount?"

The Yield Curve

The *yield curve* is the name given to a line on a graph that plots the interest rate paid by bonds of similar types but different maturities. The Treasury yield curve is the most publicized chart. It tracks bonds with maturities of three months to 30 years. Buyers of other types of fixed income securities compare those offerings to the interest rates paid by Treasuries of similar maturities.

Daily newspapers, and magazines like *Forbes* and the *Economist*, publish current yield curve information. The municipal yield curve may not look quite the same as the Treasury yield curve. There are factors unique to the municipal market that affect its yield curve.

A regular-shaped yield curve shows that the bonds with the shortest maturity pay the lowest yield and the bonds with the longest maturity pay the highest yield. From the left corner of the graph, the line slopes upward, gradually flattening out between 10 and 15 years. The longer maturities generally yield more because there is more volatility in longer yields and more risk of the value of the investment being eroded by inflation. In bond investments other than Treasuries, there is also the question of the borrower's ability to pay. In February 1993, there was roughly 350 basis points (3.5 percent) separating the long and short ends of the curve. A flat yield curve indicates that there is little to no yield benefit from purchasing long-term bonds. In 1995, the yield spread was less than 200 basis points from 5.11 percent on a 1-year Treasury note to 6.8 percent on a 30-year Treasury bond. Sometimes the yield curve inverts, so that a 1-year bond yields more than a 30-year bond. A recession often follows a yield inversion. As with any other economic indicator, the result is unpredictable. The only reason to buy longer-term bonds that yield less than shorter-term bonds is to lock in the yield in anticipation of declining long-term rates. In the early 1980s, investors could have purchased 30-year Treasury bonds paying 12 percent. If an investor had bought short-term Treasuries because they yielded more, she would have missed a big opportunity to lock in a high yield for many years.

How to Calculate Yields

Yield-to-maturity calculations are too complex to describe. The best way to check the yield-to-maturity given to you by the broker is to purchase a calculator that performs financial functions. Such calculators cost $50 to $100. You can either use the regular function keys or the more accurate computer programs built into some calculators. The information you need to calculate yield-to-maturity includes:

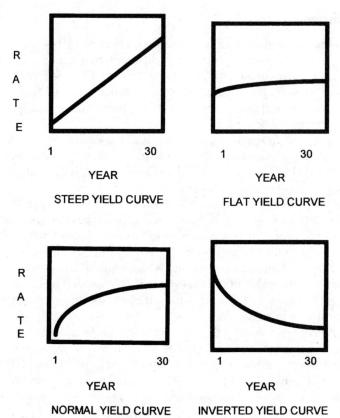

Figure 5-1. The shapes of the yield curve.

- The coupon or rate at which the bond was issued
- The settlement date of the trade
- The maturity date of the bond
- The price at which the bond will mature or be called
- The unit price or cost of the bond

Alternatively, you can buy a *basis book,* which contains mathematical tables of yields, equivalent rates, and maturity dates.[1]

In addition, there are computer programs that calculate yield-to-matu-

---

[1]*The Bond Values Tables* can be purchased from the Financial Publishing Company, Boston, MA 02215.

rity. Some of these are stand-alone programs that act primarily as calculators. Other programs have the ability to store a portfolio or to print out different analyses. Some work in conjunction with the larger spreadsheet programs. These programs sell for as little as $15 or more than $300.[2]

Yields on Bond Funds

You will not be able to calculate the yield on bond funds with a financial calculator. Bond fund yields are not directly comparable to yields on individual bonds. The SEC mandates bond fund yield calculations, but this calculation will not predict what return you will get. Instead, the calculations represent the average annualized yields of a bond fund, based on the recent past. Money-market funds must use a 7-day SEC average, and other bond funds must use a 30-day SEC average. Modifications to the yield calculation reflect the eventual loss of principal in premium bonds when they mature and the end gain on any discount bonds. The purpose of the SEC averages is to enable you to compare the yield of one bond fund with another.

The *distribution yield* of a bond fund tells you how much cash the fund has distributed over the last 12 months. It is not a fixed amount, like the interest payments on an individual bond. The distribution yield reflects the coupon income and the gains and losses produced by the fund in the past 12 months divided by the fund's share price. It tells a story of what has already happened, with no guarantee that it will happen again.

For a bond fund, the concept of total return is more important than the current yield. The concept of yield alone may be misleading. If the touted current yield is well above the return you could get on individual bonds of similar maturity, there is a reason. Don't ignore the danger signal. The result of an extraordinarily high current yield is a decline in the underlying value of the fund. There is no free lunch.

Total Return

The concept of *total return* combines the current yield with all capital gains or losses realized by the investment. Total return is none of the above. Total return combines the amount of interest earned each year

---

[2]A summary of information about bond calculation programs for the computer can be found in the annual *Individual Investor's Guide to Computerized Investing,* American Association for Individual Investors, Chicago, IL.

Table 5-3. The Concept of Total Return

Interest rate	Maturity	Purchase price	Change	% Increase or decrease	Total return
6%	5 years	$1,000	+$50	+5%	11% (6% + 5%)
6%	5 years	$1,000	−$70	−7%	−1% (6% − 7%)

and the change in value of the bond or bond fund. Two examples given here and shown in Table 5-3 may help explain this concept.

Assume you purchased a 6 percent, five-year bond for $1000 and wanted to calculate its current return at the end of the first year. Further assume that the value of the bond at the end of the first year appreciated to $1050 because interest rates declined during the year. The total return for this bond would be 11 percent, calculated as follows: 6 percent from the cash interest payments received during the year plus 5 percent from bond appreciation ($1000 to $1050). The formula is as follows:

$$\frac{\text{Value of the bond at the computation date} + \text{interest payments} - \text{amount paid for the bond}}{\text{Amount paid for the bond}}$$

Assume you purchased the same bond, however, and it declined in value during the year from $1000 to $930 because interest rates increased during the year. The total return would be −1 percent. The cash interest payment received during the year gave a return of 6 percent, but the bond declined in value from $1000 to $930 for a 7 percent *loss*. The total return of −1 percent, while accurate, need not be the final return for this bond. If the investor held the bond for the full five-year term, he would receive back the $1000 face value of the bond, rather than the current value of $930.

The fact that bonds come due at a fixed date is one of the key differences between stocks and bonds. When a stock goes down in value, it might stay there forever. If a short- or intermediate-term bond declines in value and you hold it until its maturity date, you will get back the face value. Thus, the holder of a short- or intermediate-term bond may decide that total return is not an appropriate measure of his return.

Total return is, however, a valid concept with respect to bond mutual funds. Mutual funds have no due date. Bond mutual funds constantly trade their large portfolio of bonds. They trade the bonds for profit and to meet purchase and redemption requests of shareholders. Total return is the best measure of the return on stock and bond mutual funds since stocks also do not come due.

Some funds focus on providing an attractive current yield in order to keep the cashflow steady for those investors who are seeking a reliable income from their investment. Perhaps you are like the investor who said, "I want a high current yield. I need to maximize the dollars I get each month because I live off the income from my bond funds. I don't care if the price of the fund fluctuates, because I have no intention of selling it!" With this in mind, many investors seek out high-yield taxable and tax-free bond funds. They provide the highest current yield. In order to generate high yields, these funds must hold long-term bonds maturing in 20 to 30 years or find other ways to boost their return. The very long maturities make the price of these funds very sensitive to interest-rate shifts. When interest rates decline even moderately, the value of these funds will rise significantly. Funds provide customers with a high current yield by purchasing high-coupon premium bonds. To achieve a high total return, the fund managers sell the bonds for a profit and purchase new bonds with lower coupons. This strategy eventually reduces the current cashflow to the investor. To keep investors happy, many bond funds buy derivatives and engage in aggressive trading in order to increase the total return. They may not be successful. These practices make the price of the bond fund more volatile than it would be otherwise.

The major newspapers and magazines list the total return for bond funds. The bond fund literature contains historical summaries of total return. Holders of individual bonds have to compute total return themselves. If you plan to hold your individual bonds to maturity, total return may not seem relevant. The formula for calculating total return for bond funds is as follows:

$$\frac{(\text{Present value} + \text{dividends} + \text{distributions}) - \text{purchase price of the fund}}{\text{Purchase price of the fund}}$$

Assume you bought 100 shares of the fund on January 1 for $10 a share for a total price of $1000. Further assume that the value of your 100 shares of the fund at December 31 is $1050. During the year there were dividends of $20 and distributions of $10. The total return for the year on your 100 shares of the fund is 8 percent, computed as follows:

$$\frac{\underset{\text{(Present value of the fund)}}{1050} + \underset{\text{(dividends)}}{20} + \underset{\text{(distributions)}}{10} - \underset{\text{(purchase price of the fund)}}{1000}}{\underset{\text{(Purchase price of the fund)}}{1000}}$$

The $1050 value at December 31 is computed by taking into account all the costs, including loads and other charges. There has to be a reason to invest in a bond fund rather than in an individual bond that you could hold until maturity. Individual bonds provide a predictable flow of income each year. However, certain types of bonds are better bought in bond funds because the funds provide needed protection. If you want to invest in junk bonds or GNMAs, for example, we recommend that you do so using funds because of the particular risks involved in these securities.

Bond Volatility, Maturity, and Use of a Bond Ladder

Bond price volatility, how much the price of the bond varies, increases with the lengthening of maturities. Let's say you purchased 30-year bonds because they had the highest interest rates. You knew you needed the money in 5 years because of an upcoming college tuition payment. To get your money back in 5 years, you must sell your bonds. If market interest rates went from 7 percent to 8 percent, a 7 percent bond with a 5-year maturity would drop in price from $1000 to $959, a $41 decline. If, however, the bond had a 30-year maturity instead, its price would drop to $887, a $113 decline. So, under the same conditions, the shorter-term bond lost 4.1 percent of its value, and the long-term bond lost 11.3 percent.

To protect yourself from price fluctuations, plan ahead. Purchase bonds so that they will come due when you anticipate needing the money. Parents of college students can purchase bonds that mature at the beginning of each semester, when the bills come due. Nearing retirement? Buy bonds maturing when your paychecks end, softening the transition into a new lifestyle. Owning a number of bonds with different maturities, known as *laddering*, lowers your overall risk to price changes.

Laddering is a powerful technique. Step by step, build your ladder by purchasing equal dollar amounts of bonds of different maturities. A simple example is a ladder containing bonds maturing after one year, three years, and five years. When the first bond matures after one year, purchase another bond with a five-year maturity. When the three-year bond matures, purchase another with a five-year maturity. The average maturity of this portfolio will always stay at about three years if the investor keeps replacing the maturing bonds with others having the longest maturity in the ladder.

If you are saving for a particular goal, such as payment for college expenses, the ladder can be targeted to mature after high-school graduation. It can be modified so that bonds mature in each of the college years. Replace maturing bonds with other bonds, filling in the rungs on your portfolio ladder.

A laddered portfolio has several advantages. A ladder averages the rates of interest over a period of years. A ladder provides more overall return in a rising interest-rate market than a single bond. It provides less risk than investing only in longer-term bonds. It provides flexibility by giving you access to your funds without having to entail the costs of selling a longer-term bond. It is a strategy for individual investors who don't know where interest rates are going. It produces a steady, predictable stream of interest income that pays more than a strategy based on short-term investments only. Enjoy the cash cows, and don't fret about the stingy payers. They too will come due.

Bond funds can also be laddered. However, the ladder does not work as well as with individual bonds. Fund companies have short-, intermediate-, and long-term bond funds. The fund managers also shift the average maturity of the bonds within the fund, buying and selling as they see fit. They extend or shorten maturities depending upon where they feel they can maximize the return and how they view the direction of interest rates. Instead of a one-time cost of purchase, funds charge annual, never-ending fees. The value of the fund—any fund—fluctuates daily. The main difference between a bond-fund ladder and a ladder containing individually purchased bonds is that a bond fund never comes due. When you decide to withdraw the money from the bond fund, there may be more or less money than you expected.

How to Decide if the Yield Is Good Enough

There are a number of strategies buyers use to decide at what yield to buy. One popular technique is to call three brokers. If they tell you that the yield to the year 2000 is 5 percent, immediately tell them that you will buy at a 5.20 percent yield. Let them know that you know that they are holding out on you, and you won't buy unless you get an above-market yield. Will you be successful with this strategy? Brokers want to sell you bonds, but they need to make a living too. They won't work for nothing, even if you are a nice guy.

Bonds of similar quality and maturity will trade in the same range as each other. If you don't like the return on the triple-A insured bonds, then maybe you'll like lower-quality bonds with higher yields. Is the added risk worth the return? For example, how do you decide between two $10,000 bonds, one an AA-rated credit yielding 5.6 percent and the other a lower-rated triple-B credit yielding 5.85 percent. Translate the extra yield into dollars. Calculate how much interest each bond will pay you each year.

$$5.6 \text{ percent} \times \$10,000 = \$560 \text{ interest per year}$$

$$5.85 \text{ percent} \times \$10,000 = \$585 \text{ interest per year}$$

Subtract the return of one bond from the other and find out how much more the higher-yielding bond will return annually. In this case:

$$\$585 - \$560 = \$25 \text{ per year}$$

Big deal—$25. Over 10 years the total difference is $250. Do you have to lose sleep for that?

PART 2
Categories of Bonds

6
U.S. Treasury Bonds

Treasury securities are backed by the full faith and credit of the U.S. government. They are virtually free of default risk, though no investment is ever guaranteed to be foolproof. Treasury securities are sold in three varieties—bills, notes, and bonds—which have many features in common.

- Treasuries are backed by the full faith and credit of the U.S. government. However, if the Treasury securities are held by a fund, you are not protected against the risks of mismanagement by the fund.

- There are no limits on how many Treasuries you may own.

- Interest income from Treasuries is subject to federal income tax, but not to state and local taxes. The interest income from Treasury bond funds is subject to federal income tax and may also be subject to state and local taxes.

- Bills are taxed at maturity. The interest on notes and bonds is subject to tax in the year the interest is credited to your account.

- Treasuries are all issued in book-entry only format. This means that you cannot receive a certificate of ownership. They must be held at a brokerage house or at the Treasury. Banks will also hold your Treasury bonds in custody. When held by a bank, they are not considered deposits of the bank.

- Treasuries can be purchased through a bank or brokerage house or through Treasury Direct from the Federal Reserve Bank.

- Treasuries can be sold immediately for settlement the following day. This means that you can convert them into cash in one day. They are considered to be the most liquid investment available. If interest rates rose since you purchased the bonds, you may lose money if you sell the securities. Traders call this *interest rate risk* or *market risk.*

- Treasuries can be sold as one lot or sold and transferred in part only. For example, if you own a $10,000 bond, you can sell only $5000 if you chose.

- Treasuries can be used as collateral for a loan. You can borrow up to 90 percent of their value at the broker loan rate. For example, assume you have a $10,000 Treasury bond in your brokerage account and need cash either for another investment or for a personal expense. Your brokerage firm would lend you up to $9000 and use the Treasury bond as collateral (security) for the loan. The interest rate charged on the loan would be a floating rate that would be much lower than a credit card loan because the Treasury bond is considered such good security.

Treasury Bills

When newly issued, Treasury bills (T-bills) have original maturities of 13 weeks (91 days or 3 months), 26 weeks (182 days or 6 months), or 52 weeks (365 days or 1 year). T-bills are a very attractive investment if you have the minimum amount of $10,000 to invest, with incremental amounts of $1000. T-bills are considered a cash equivalent. They are bought as a safe short-term investment by managers of pension funds, money-market funds, and corporations, and by individual investors and governments.

Like EE savings bonds, T-bills are sold at a discount to their face value. Interest is paid at maturity only. For example, a $10,000 13-week bill might be sold for $9790. At maturity, the T-bill will pay $10,000. The T-bill will provide $210 of interest income, taxable in the year it comes due.

T-bill Funds

If the minimum purchase price of $10,000 for T-bills is more than you want to spend, an alternative way of buying Treasury securities is to purchase shares in a mutual fund. There are money-market funds which hold only T-bills. Two good no-load funds are Benham Capital Preservation ($1000 minimum, 1-800-4-SAFETY) and Dreyfus 100 Percent U.S. Treasury Money Market ($2500 minimum, 1-800-Dreyfus).

Tip_____

Treasury bills can be used for tax planning. All interest income from Treasury bills is reportable on your federal income tax return in the year in which the bond comes due. To move interest income from one year to the next, buy a Treasury bill this year which has a maturity date next year.

Information Sources on Treasury Bills

Treasury bills, notes, and bonds are listed in the daily newspaper. If you want to purchase Treasuries on the secondary market, you would pick out which issue you wanted to buy and tell your banker or your broker to purchase them for you. In this way you can tailor the maturity precisely to your needs. This is a very active market, so Treasury securities can generally be found for sale in all maturities.

As you will see from the offerings listed in Table 6-1, bills maturing in some weeks are cheaper than others. This is the result of more demand by buyers for one issue than another. Terms used in the listing and terms relevant to it have the following meaning:

- *Date.* The date the bills are maturing.

- *Bid.* The interest rate at which the buyer offers to buy. The price is computed from the rate.

Table 6-1. Trading Treasury Bills

Date (1995)	% Bid	% Asked	Chg	Yield
JUL6	5.20	5.18	+0.16	5.28%
JUL13	5.08	5.06	−0.11	5.16
JUL20	4.9	4.88	−0.09	4.98
JUL27	5.24	5.22	+0.10	5.33
AUG3	5.31	5.29	+0.09	5.41
AUG10	5.34	5.32	+0.07	5.45
AUG17	5.37	5.35	+0.04	5.48
AUG24	5.31	5.29	−0.02	5.43

SOURCE: *The New York Times*, June 29, 1995, p. D8. Copyright © 1995 by the New York Times Company. Reprinted by permission.

- *Asked.* The interest rate at which the broker is willing to sell. The price is computed from the rate.

- *Chg (Change).* Difference between the bid price at close yesterday and the bid price today on trades of at least $1 million.

- *Yield.* The annualized rate of return if held until the bill comes due based on the asked rate. This yield is calculated on the amount invested, not on the face value of the T-bill.

- *Rate.* The interest rate at which notes and bonds were issued. For bills, the rate is always zero, so it is never included as a column.

- *WI (When Issued).* Indicates that the bill has not been issued yet and is trading in anticipation of its issuance.

Since the date refers to the date the bills are maturing, the July 6 bills were maturing in one week. (The listing appeared June 29.) They had a bid that was + 0.16, or 16 basis points higher than the yield for the previous day. The difference in the yield reflects the differences in supply and demand.

The spreads are very narrow. That is, the difference between the bid or offer to buy and the asked price, the price at which the broker is willing to sell, is very small. The spreads you see in the newspaper are on million-dollar lots. If you were purchasing an odd lot, the spread would be greater. The prices would be higher and the yields lower. The spread on the bill due on August 24 was only two basis points—a 5.31 percent bid and 5.29 percent asked.

Treasury Notes and Bonds

Treasury notes and bonds have longer maturities than T-bills. Treasury notes have maturities longer than 1 year but less than 10 years. The bonds have maturities longer than 10 years. Aside from their maturities, Treasury notes and bonds are essentially the same as T-bills and function in the same way as municipal and corporate bonds. Treasury notes and bonds function quite differently than EE savings bonds, which are also issued by the federal government.

Like Treasury bills, Treasury notes and bonds can be purchased in the over-the-counter market or at the Treasury auction. Just to make matters more complicated, Treasury notes and bonds are quoted in 32ds, while bills and other bonds are quoted in 100ths. As we said, a basis point is 1/100 of a percent. There are 100 basis points in 1 percent. A 32d is 1/32. If the price of a Treasury bond is listed as 104.8, it means 104 and 8/32.

If an investor bought one bond with a face value of $1000 at a price of 104.8, it would cost $1042.50, calculated as follows: Convert the 8/32 into a decimal, which is .25. The price of the bond would then be 104.25. To get the dollar price of one bond, multiply 104.25 by $10. Thus, the dollar price of the bond would be $1042.50.

If the note or bond is callable, the call date rather than the maturity date is used to calculate the yield. When a Treasury bond is callable, it is indicated in the newspaper by two maturity dates. The date might read "Feb. 02–07" indicating that the bonds are callable on any interest-payment date, from February 2002 until the final maturity in February 2007.

Zero-Coupon Treasury Securities

Zero-coupon Treasury bonds are constructed by taking a Treasury bond, stripping off the interest coupons, and selling the interest coupons separately. For example, assume that a brokerage house buys a $1 million Treasury bond coming due in 30 years which has a 6 percent coupon rate. There will be 60 coupons, one coming due every six months, worth $30,000 each. Remember that 6 percent of $1 million equals $60,000 in interest per year and thus the semiannual interest payment would be $30,000. Each $30,000 coupon would be a separate $30,000 zero-coupon bond. For example, if the coupon in year 12 were sold, it would pay $30,000 in year 12 and would be purchased by the investor for about $15,000. Each of the other coupons can be sold separately for a different price, depending on its maturity. The $1 million face value becomes a zero-coupon bond coming due after 30 years.

Interest on the zero-coupon bonds must be reported annually to the Internal Revenue Service and is taxed as ordinary income, even though it has not been received by you. As a result, these bonds are most often used in retirement accounts because no tax is paid on the income until the money is withdrawn. The interest from Treasury zero-coupon bonds is exempt from state and local taxes.

There are two basic categories of zero-coupon Treasury securities. The first type are proprietary products sold by brokerage houses. These are brand-name zeros. They are a very simple form of derivative security, a product derived from another security. The dealer unbundles the security and sells each interest payment and the principal payment separately. The original issuer, in this case the Treasury, has nothing to do with the whole process.

Proprietary zero-coupon bonds are book-entry only bonds which are deposited with a custodian who issues certificates against the coupon and principal cashflows. The function of the custodian is to insure that the purchasers of the bond components will receive the appropriate rights to cashflows, without endangering the tax advantages of the bond: namely, freedom from state and local taxes.

Each brokerage house issues its own brand of zero-coupon bonds and gives its product a different name. Some of the acronyms are: LIONs, TIGRs, CATS, ETR, TBR, and TRs. They are not interchangeable, and each represents a separate market product.

After the development of the proprietary zero-coupon bonds, the Treasury began issuing its own version of zero-coupon bond called STRIPS, (Separate Trading of Registered Interest and Principal of Securities). This second category of zero-coupon Treasury securities is a generic product that is now generally accepted in the marketplace. It is a better trading vehicle than the proprietary products produced by the brokerage houses. STRIPS tends to cost a little more than the proprietary zero products for the same maturity because they are a direct obligation of the federal government. The minimum purchase size is $1000.

Federal agencies and corporations also issue zero-coupon bonds. The advantage of a zero-coupon bond is that you can lock in a particular yield-to-maturity. For a low initial investment, you can plan to have the bond mature when your major financial obligations are expected. The downside is that if interest rates rise, you will have no income from the bonds to reinvest at the higher rate. For this reason, all zero-coupon bonds, whether they are derived from other securities or originally issued as zeros, have above-average price volatility, both on the upside and the downside. It is important to remember that if the zero-coupon bonds are not purchased in a retirement account, you will have to pay a current yearly tax liability on the interest income that you will receive in the future.

Selected Treasury zeros are listed in the *Wall Street Journal, The New York Times,* and other papers with financial news. The prices represent transactions of $1 million. If you compare the yields on Treasuries which pay interest currently to zeros which are sold at a discount, you will find that as the maturities lengthen, the spreads widen between the two types of securities. This represents the perceived increase in market volatility of the zeros. Thus, the ten-year February 2005 zero-coupon strip yields 4 basis points more than its interest-paying counterpart, while the thirty-year 2025 strip yields 29 basis points more than the interest-paying bond. A 29 basis-point spread is not fixed. As interest rates become more volatile, the spread will increase. If the interest rate environment is quiet, the spread will narrow. Zero-coupon bonds are more sensitive to interest rate changes because they do not pay any rein-vestible interest that can cushion the impact of changing rates.

Buying Treasuries through Securities Dealers

All Treasury securities can be purchased from a bank or a brokerage house, either in the open market or at the Treasury auction. If you buy them in the open market, you can purchase any of the outstanding issues. Like purchasing any other bonds, there is a bid and an asked price. The bid and asked prices quoted in the daily newspapers are for $1 million transactions. The price spreads on smaller trades would be wider, and your purchase price higher. You can purchase bonds at the Treasury auction through your broker. The fee for the service generally ranges from $50 to $75 per transaction. The broker does not earn a spread on the transaction.

The American Stock Exchange (AMEX) is expanding its system to trade odd-lot Treasury notes, bonds, and zero-coupons. A Treasury odd-lot is any size less than $1 million worth of bonds. The service will provide more pricing information than has ever been available to the public before. The AMEX will provide bid and asked prices and the price of last sale information on a continuous basis throughout the day. The market specialist will guarantee that the bid-asked spread on Treasury trades never widens beyond 0.25 percent of a bond's value, which is attractive for odd lots. Currently, individuals may pay a transaction fee in addition to the spread of 0.25 percent or more. Institutions usually pay a spread of 0.03 percent to 0.06 percent of a bond's value. When the service is up and running, you will be able to follow the bond prices in the financial newspapers. If nothing else, this will provide the individual investor with a basis for cost comparisons and increase the liquidity of her Treasury holdings.

Buying Treasuries through Treasury Direct

You can also purchase Treasury bonds at auction for no charge through Treasury Direct from the Federal Reserve Bank. To do this you must fill out a form, a sample of which is shown in Fig. 6-1. A check must accompany the form. If you are planning on purchasing Treasury *bills*, the check must be certified at your local bank. When a check is certified, it

PD F 5174-3
Department of the Treasury
Bureau of the Public Debt
(Revised April 1994)

OMB NO. 1535-0069

TREASURY DIRECT®

5-10 YEAR TREASURY NOTE TENDER

TENDER INFORMATION		FOR DEPARTMENT USE

AMOUNT OF TENDER: $ _____

TERM _____

BID TYPE (Check One) ☐ NONCOMPETITIVE ☐ COMPETITIVE AT . ____ %

TREASURY DIRECT ACCOUNT NUMBER = ____ — ____ — ____

TENDER NUMBER
912827

CUSIP

ISSUE DATE

INVESTOR INFORMATION

ACCOUNT NAME

RECEIVED BY

DATE RECEIVED

ADDRESS (FOR NEW ACCOUNT ONLY)

EXT REG ☐
FOREIGN ☐
BACKUP ☐
REVIEW ☐

CITY   STATE   ZIP CODE

TAXPAYER IDENTIFICATION NUMBER

1ST NAMED
OWNER   ____ — ____ — ____   **OR**   ____ — ____
SOCIAL SECURITY NUMBER   EMPLOYER IDENTIFICATION NUMBER

CLASS ☐

TELEPHONE NUMBERS   (FOR NEW ACCOUNT ONLY)

WORK (____) ____ - ____   HOME (____) ____ - ____

PAYMENT ATTACHED   **TOTAL PAYMENT: $** _____

NUMBERS

CASH (01): $ _____   CHECKS (02/03): $ _____

SECURITIES (05/06): $ _____ $ _____

OTHER (07): $ _____ $ _____

DIRECT DEPOSIT INFORMATION   (FOR NEW ACCOUNT ONLY)

ROUTING NUMBER
FINANCIAL INSTITUTION NAME
ACCOUNT NUMBER
ACCOUNT NAME

ACCOUNT TYPE   ☐ CHECKING
(Check One)   ☐ SAVINGS

AUTHORIZATION

I submit this tender pursuant to the provisions of Department of the Treasury Circulars, Public Debt Series Nos. 2-86 (31 CFR Part 357) and 1-93 (31 CFR Part 356), and the applicable offering announcement.

Under penalties of perjury, I certify that the number shown on this form is my correct taxpayer identification number and that I am not subject to backup withholding because (1) I have not been notified that I am subject to backup withholding as a result of a failure to report all interest or dividends, or (2) the Internal Revenue Service has notified me that I am no longer subject to backup withholding. I further certify that all other information provided on this form is true, correct and complete.

_____   _____
SIGNATURE   DATE

SEE INSTRUCTIONS FOR PRIVACY ACT AND PAPERWORK REDUCTION ACT NOTICE

*U.S. GPO: 1994-387-620/01226

Figure 6-1. Treasury Direct tender offer form.

means that the money is in your checking account and a lock has been put on the funds so they can only be used to pay for the certified check. The purchase of Treasury notes and bonds *does not* require checks to be certified. This is logical, though at first it may not seem so.

When you send in a $10,000 check for a Treasury bill, the Treasury refunds to you the difference between the discount price and the face value of the bill. When the Treasury bill matures, you then receive the face value, but no additional interest. You must pay for the bills with a certified check. The Treasury would not want to find itself in the position of having sent you a refund, only to find that your check bounced. By contrast, Treasury notes and bonds are not sold at a discount to face value. Therefore, you can pay for them with a personal check.

When you make your first purchase at Treasury Direct, you receive an account number. All future purchases that you make in the same name will be entered into that master account. The account number is unique. If you accumulate more than $100,000 of securities in your account, the Federal Reserve will charge you a $25 fee per year for maintaining your book-entry account. Otherwise, the account is free.

If your securities are held at Treasury Direct, you will get a statement *only* when there is a change in your account. If you buy Treasuries or they are redeemed, then you would get a statement. You will get notification of an impending redemption. You do not get a statement every month, not even on an interest payment date. If you wish to request a statement because you have not received one for some time, you can call Treasury Direct and one will be sent.

Each bond that you purchase has a CUSIP number. That number is unique to a particular bond issue and is used to distinguish the bond from all others. If you want to transfer a bond from Treasury Direct, you would identify it by providing that number.

Treasury bills only pay interest at maturity. Treasury notes and bonds pay interest semiannually. Treasury Direct wires the interest directly into the account you specify. Upon redemption, the principal is wired the same way. Your Treasury Direct account never holds cash. Using the electronic routing of money eliminates the possibilities of lost or stolen checks. The routing number is found at the bottom of your bank check (see Fig. 6-2). You can call your financial institution to verify the deposit.

Do you want the proceeds from your Treasury bills reinvested through Treasury Direct? At the time of your first investment in Treasury bills you can elect to have the proceeds from a maturing Treasury bill reinvested automatically in new Treasury bills. For maturing notes and bonds, you will be mailed a form giving you reinvestment choices before the next Treasury auction.

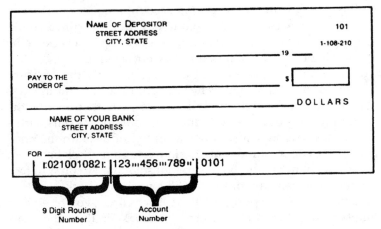

Figure 6-2. Check routing numbers.

Bonds can be purchased at Treasury Direct by submitting a competitive tender or a noncompetitive tender. A competitive *tender,* or application, is a bid by an investor or a dealer which specifies a price at which the bidder will buy. The bid is on the basis of 100 with two decimal places, e.g., 99.95. Competitive bids are filled starting from the highest bid price and then on down. All noncompetitive tenders are accepted first. Individual investors generally submit noncompetitive tenders. They are priced based upon a weighted average yield of accepted competitive tenders. Noncompetitive tenders must be postmarked the day prior to the auction date and received by the issue date. At the bottom of the envelope in which the purchase request is submitted, you should print "Tender for Treasury (bill, note, or bond)."

The application for the purchase of Treasury securities should be submitted on a form provided by Treasury Direct. If you do not have a form, but have already opened an account at Treasury Direct, you can write a letter. The letter should include: your account number, what securities you wish to purchase, the amount of the purchase, your mailing address, the name and social security number of the prospective owner, and a telephone number where you can be reached if there is a problem. It should contain all the information that is required by the form, including your signature.

Advantages of Using Treasury Direct

- You pay no fee and no spread to purchase or redeem Treasury securities.

- The interest income and proceeds from the redemption of Treasury securities are wired automatically to your designated bank account. There is no charge for this service.

- The cost of the Treasury Direct account is free to those with less than $100,000 of securities in the account and only $25 to those with more.

- The custodian of your Treasury securities is the federal government. Thus, the possible risks associated with a failed brokerage firm holding your securities do not exist.

Disadvantages of Using Treasury Direct

- You can only purchase Treasury securities at the time of an auction.

- You can't sell a Treasury bond that is in your Treasury Direct account before its maturity date. It must first be transferred to a brokerage house or a bank, often with considerable delays.

- Treasury Direct will not make a margin loan. To use the bonds as collateral for up to 90 percent of the bond's value, the bonds must be transferred to a brokerage house or a bank.

- There is a $1 million limit on each noncompetitive bid.

The sale of bonds through the Treasury follows a usual but not unchangeable pattern. There is an auction schedule (see Table 6-2), which includes an announcement in the week before the auction stating that the auction will actually happen. If you are interested in a particular auction, you can call the week before to verify that it will take place. Notice of an impending sale can be found in the major financial newspapers as well.

The broker dealers as well as individuals buy securities at the auction. If you need the flexibility that a bank or brokerage house can give you, then it is worth the fee to purchase them through a broker. If you are going to hold your bonds to maturity and do not plan to borrow, then you might as well save yourself some money and buy through Treasury Direct.

Tip_____

To purchase Treasury bills through Treasury Direct, you must send in a

Table 6-2. Treasury Direct Auction Schedule

Maturity date	Minimum investment	Additional $	Announcement time	Auction time	Issue time
13-week bill	$10,000	$1,000	Tuesday	Monday	Thursday
26-week bill	$10,000	$1,000	Tuesday	Monday	Thursday
52-week bill	$10,000	$1,000	Every four weeks on Friday	Thursday	Thursday
2-year note	$5,000	$1,000	Near the middle of every month	One week later	Last business day of each month*
3-year note	$5,000	$1,000	First Wednesday of the quarter	One week later	2/15, 5/15, 8/15, 11/15, or next business day*
5-year note	$1,000	$1,000	Near the middle of every month	One week later	Last business day of each month*
10-year note and 30-year note	$1,000	$1,000	First Wednesday of the quarter	One week later	2/15, 5/15, 8/15, 11/15, or next business day*

*These are the usual dates of issuance. The announcements are generally made two weeks before, and the bonds are sold one week before delivery.

certified check. For the purchase of Treasury notes and bonds, a regular bank check is acceptable.

Forms of Ownership

One area of confusion in purchasing bonds is frequently that a clear statement of form of ownership is not declared. If two people are planning on purchasing some bonds together, they often write their names separated by a comma. For example, Mary Doe, John Doe. This is very ambiguous, and more information is needed.

- *And.* Mary Doe and John Doe. The *and* means that both parties have a right to the account, and each party owns half. To withdraw the securities, both signatures are required. If one person dies, the other person must show proof of death to obtain the other half of the account if the account has Right of Survivorship. Both social security numbers are required.

- *R.O.S.* Mary Doe and John Doe, Right of Survivorship. If an account is R.O.S, the two owners are each other's beneficiary. If one person dies, the other person has a right to the entire account. If the account is titled as an *and* account and is Without Rights of Survivorship, then half the value of the bonds goes to the decedent's estate upon death of one of the signers. The cosigner does not have any rights in the other half of the account.

- *Or.* Mary Doe or John Doe. This type of account only requires one signature to effect any transaction. If one of the signers dies, half the account automatically belongs to the surviving cosigner on the account. Only one social security number is required. There should be a further designation of R.O.S. or not.

- *P.O.D.* Mary Doe P.O.D. John Doe. In this case, the account belongs to Mary Doe. When she dies, the account is Payable on Death to John Doe.

- *Natural Guardian.* John Doe as natural guardian for Jack B. Jones, a minor. Minors cannot own bonds in their own name. The minor's social security number is provided. John Doe supervises the account as long as he is the guardian of Jack B. Jones and Jack is considered a minor under state law.

- *Custodian.* John Doe as custodian for Mary Jones, a minor under the Uniform Gifts to Minors Act. The child's social security number is provided. In this case you have given the child a gift, and you are supervising it until she is not considered a minor under state law.

Though these forms of ownership are listed here with Treasury securities, the same format refers to the titling of bank accounts as well as other bond purchases.

Why Buy Treasuries?

There are several good reasons for the individual investor to buy U.S. Treasury bonds.

- They are free of state and local taxes.
- Treasuries are backed by the federal government's full faith and credit, providing maximum safety.
- They are easily salable.
- They come in many maturities, but they are all "plain vanilla." There are no hidden surprises.
- Five-, ten-, and thirty-year bonds can be bought in the minimum size of $1000.

7

Certificates of Deposit and U.S. Savings Bonds

Certificates of Deposit

You may not realize how reliant on bonds and bondlike investments most people are. For example, a certificate of deposit is a bondlike investment that is not a bond. When you deposit $100 in a bank CD, you are really lending the bank $100. The bank promises to pay you $105 when the CD matures in one year. The CD is an IOU, a promise to return your $100 and pay interest at a fixed rate on the $100 at the end of the year.

The FDIC insures up to $100,000 per ownership category deposited in an account at an insured savings institution. The FDIC is an independent agency of the U.S. government. Banks that display the FDIC or eagle sign at each teller window are FDIC-insured.

Certificates of deposit are like zero-coupon bonds. They pay no interest until the certificate matures. The interest represents the bank's payment for its right to use your money for the specified period of time. The bank in turn lends the money to other borrowers at a higher interest rate. CD interest is subject to federal, state, and local income taxes. You can redeem or cash in your CDs prior to maturity. However, if you do, you will be subject to penalties.

A bank may use the money collected from the sale of CDs to make mortgage, business, or personal loans. Alternatively, a bank may use the cash to purchase Treasury bills and notes issued by the federal government.

On October 24, 1994, the *Philadelphia Inquirer* reported that the yield on six-month bank CDs ranged from 3.04 percent to 5.45 percent, while the yield on six-month Treasury bills was 5.75 percent.

What is the story here? Why didn't everyone invest their money in the higher-yielding Treasuries rather than CDs? The Treasury bill has the full faith and credit of the U.S. government behind it and is the better credit of the two, yet it yielded more. In addition, the income from the Treasury bill is free of all state and local taxes, while the CDs are subject to state and local taxes.

There are a number of reasons why people invest in CDs rather than Treasuries.

- CDs can be bought in very small amounts. Treasury bills require a minimum investment of $10,000.

- With CDs there is a penalty for early redemption but no market risk.

- Investors are familiar with CDs and know they are a safe investment.

- The local bank advertises CDs but not Treasury bills.

- CDs rollover automatically if you do not personally redeem them. There is only a 10-day window between the maturity of the last CD and the start of a new one.

Some banks offer more attractive CDs than others. It is easy to buy a CD by mail. The newspapers often carry CD rates from a variety of banks. If you are a serious CD shopper you might want to subscribe to *100 Highest Yields,* a weekly newsletter (1-800-327-7717).

U.S. Savings Bonds: Are They an Investment for You?

One of the Treasury issues most popular with investors are EE savings bonds. (The last E bonds were issued in June 1980.) You can invest as little as $25 or a maximum of $15,000 a year in EE bonds. U.S. savings bonds sell at a discount to face value. The U.S. government calls these *accrual bonds* because the government pays interest by increasing the redemption, or cash-in value, of the bonds every six months. For example, a $100 bond costs $50. Bonds are available in $50, $75, $200, $500, $1000, $5000, and $10,000 denominations or face value. The minimum investment amount is $25.

Tip

In other market sectors, accrual bonds are called zero-coupon bonds. With zero-coupon bonds, the investment may be more or less than half of face value.

One of the aspects of EE bonds that made them so attractive was that there was an interest-rate floor, i.e., a minimum rate of interest. In 1995, Congress did away with the interest-rate floor. Now, all EE bonds issued after May 1995 and held for five years or more will receive interest at 85 percent of the average return on five-year marketable Treasury securities. The market-based rate is determined by the Treasury every six months, as of May 1 and November 1. Bonds held for less than five years are pegged to the market rates of the average six-month Treasury security yield. Since the six-month Treasury bill generally yields quite a bit less than the five-year Treasury bond, there is a big penalty for cashing in the EE bonds before the five-year holding period. Thus, if you don't think that you can hold the EE bond for five years, you would be better off to consider another investment.

If EE bonds pay only 85 percent of the average of a five-year Treasury bond, why not buy five-year Treasury bonds instead? If you can afford the minimum purchase price of $1000 for the five-year Treasury bond, the Treasury bond makes sense. Investors find EE bonds attractive for the following reasons:

- The initial investment can be low.

- Payroll deductions provide a forced savings discipline.

- The incremental value of the bonds is not taxed until you redeem them.

- There is no interest-rate risk. If interest rates rise, the value of the EE bond will gradually increase rather than decrease.

- In certain cases, all interest may be excluded from taxable income if the proceeds from the bonds are used for college tuition.

The redemption value of EE bonds rises every six months as interest accrues. Bondholders who cash in EE bonds a few months or weeks before the semiannual adjustment of interest rates would lose several months of interest. On bonds issued before May 1995, the interest payment month was not the month of purchase. Nothing on the bond would tell you when this increase occurs. On the bonds issued after May 1995, the six-month period begins with the month of purchase. Now the EE bonds will pay interest the same way that all other bonds pay interest, every six months beginning six months after the date of issue. (See Table 7-1.)

Table 7-1. Earning Schedule for EE Bonds

Rate announcement date	Month the interest earning period begins	Month the interest is added to bond value
May 1	May	November
	June	December
	July	January
	August	February
	September	March
	October	April
November 1	November	May
	December	June
	January	July
	February	August
	March	September
	April	October

If you need to redeem your EE bonds, do so carefully. It matters which bonds you choose to cash in. Bonds issued before 1995 have different interest-rate floors, depending upon your date of purchase. One EE bond can be earning a high interest rate of 8.5 percent while another may be earning a low of 4 percent. The EE bonds issued after May 1995 have no guaranteed rate at all. However, if the market-based rates are not sufficient for a bond to reach face value in 17 years, the Treasury will make a one-time adjustment to increase it to face value.

When you purchase savings bonds can affect your interest. If you purchase savings bonds at the end of the month, you receive interest for the entire month. If you plan to purchase the bonds on the last day of the month, and it is near the end of the day, the agent might not post the transaction until the next day, which would be the first day of the new month. You would lose a month's interest if this happened. Since these are not bank products, if you purchase EE bonds at a bank, you can expect delays in posting.

Tip_____

Ask the teller how long the bank will take to register your EE bonds with the federal government. Make sure you leave enough time to get the bond recorded in the month of purchase.

Tax Rules on E, EE, and HH Bonds

EE and E bonds are issued at a discount, which means that you pay less than the face value for the bonds. The face value of the bond is payable to you at maturity. The difference between the price that you paid for the bond and the amount that you receive when you cash in the bond is reportable by you as taxable interest income on your federal income tax return. This is the usual way of reporting your interest income. However, there is an alternative way to report your interest income. You can choose to report the increase in redemption value as interest income each year on your federal income tax return.

Tip_____

A great advantage of EE and E bonds is that the interest income is exempt from state and local taxes.

Series HH bonds are issued at face value rather than at a discount. The Federal Reserve pays interest twice a year by check or by direct deposit to your bank account. You must report interest on HH bonds as interest income in the year that you receive it.

The extended maturity period of E bonds issued between May 1941 and November 1965 ends 40 years from their issue dates. The importance of the multiple maturity extensions is that as long as the E bonds' maturities are extended you don't have to report any of the interest that you have earned. The Department of the Treasury has announced that there will be no further maturity extensions for these E bonds. Therefore, if you have postponed reporting interest on E bonds purchased in 1956, you have to report the interest on your 1996 return because the 40-year period has expired; the same holds true for succeeding years.

Tip_____

EE bonds that formerly paid a higher interest rate will earn 4 percent if the possible life of the bond was extended beyond its original maturity after March 1993.

There is a great tax advantage if you trade your E or EE bonds for HH bonds. You can continue to postpone paying the interest that has accrued on the E or EE bonds. However, you must begin to pay tax currently on the interest that you earn from your HH bonds. Even if your EE bonds were accruing interest at a higher rate, the rate you will receive on the HH bonds is the current rate.

An example might be helpful. Assume that you bought an EE bond for $500 and it is now worth $1000. If you trade your EE bond for an HH bond worth $1000, you would continue to postpone reporting the $500 of interest income that you earned on your EE bond until you finally cash in your HH bond. However, the interest income that you earn on your $1000 HH bond will be subject to tax each year.

Series HH bonds are only sold in denominations of $500. If the cash received from the EE bonds is not in even $500 units, then the owner of the EE bonds must either take the difference and pay taxes on the money received or add more money to purchase another $500 unit. (See Table 7-2.)

If you inherit E or EE bonds from a decedent, the tax rules are a bit complex. If the decedent had postponed reporting the interest income while he was alive, there are two choices for reporting the deferred interest income.

1. All the postponed interest income can be reported on the decedent's final income tax return. In this case, you (the heir) will not have to include any of this income in your tax return. You would include only interest earned after the date of death.

2. All of the interest income earned before and after the decedent's death can be reported on your tax return. However, you would have the right to continue to postpone reporting any of the interest income until you cash in the bonds or they finally mature.

If you are making a gift of EE bonds, you should supply the social security number of the recipient. If you do not know that person's social security number, you must supply yours. Make sure you say that the bond is a gift so you will not be accountable for tax on the interest. The word *gift* will be inscribed on the bond. For Treasury record-keeping purposes, such bonds are not commingled with bonds owned by the purchaser.

Table 7-2. Rollover of EE Bonds to HH Bonds

Redeemed EE bonds = $2328

Option 1. Purchase 4 HH bonds for $2000 and pay taxes on the remainder or $328.

Option 2. Purchase 5 HH bonds for $2500 and pay the difference of $172.

Questions to Ask about Your EE Bonds

1. What is the date of the crediting of interest on my EE bonds? Will I lose interest if I cash them in before that date?

2. What is the final maturity of my bond? Is there an extension to the final maturity on my bonds? Will my EE bonds still accrue interest if I hold them after their final maturity?

3. How should I handle the tax consequences of the EE bonds I inherited?

4. Which bonds should I redeem first?

5. How much are my old EE bonds worth now?

U.S. Savings Bonds: Tax-Free for Education

You may be able to exclude all or part of the interest you receive on the redemption of qualified U.S. savings bonds from your income. This exclusion applies to qualified higher educational expenses that you pay for yourself, your spouse, or your dependents. This exclusion is known as the Education Savings Bonds Program. You must meet the following requirements for the exclusion to apply:

- EE bonds must be purchased after 1990.
- EE bonds must be held in the name of the parent or parents.
- The parent must be 24 years of age or older.
- EE bonds must be redeemed in the year the tuition is paid.
- The bond proceeds can be used for tuition and fees but not for room and board.
- The amount of income you earn may affect whether the interest from the bonds is free of federal income tax. Income limits apply to the year of redemption of the bonds.

Assume that you are married and buy U.S. savings bonds in your name. When your child is ready for college you cash in the bonds and use all the proceeds for college tuition. If you meet the income test at the date that you cash in the U.S. savings bonds and use the proceeds for your child's college tuition, all of the interest earned on the savings bonds will be tax-free. Thus, U.S. savings bonds become as tax-efficient as investing in tax-free municipal bonds. To get this benefit you must meet the income test. You can satisfy the test requirements if you are married and your gross income is below $63,450 (this is the 1995 number that will be adjusted for inflation in later years). Above $63,450, the exclusion is phased out so that you would have no exclusion if your gross income exceeded $93,450. Single parents get a complete exclusion of all interest income on their U.S. savings bonds if their gross income is less than $42,300. A single parent has a phase-out as his or her gross income increases so that there is no exclusion above $57,300. (These are also 1995 amounts that will be adjusted for inflation in future years.)

These bonds are in direct competition with college savings bonds issued by states. Before purchasing bonds, compare college savings bonds issued by your state that are free of state and local taxes to the U.S. savings bonds that are free of federal taxes. Depending upon interest rates and your tax bracket, one may be a better buy than the other.

You can purchase savings bonds for your child's education through the payroll savings plan, but segregate them from your other EE bonds. You should keep a record of each bond's serial number, issue date, and face value.

Until your child is 14, you should keep most of the money you have earmarked for your child in your own name. There are many reasons for this. When your child applies for financial aid, the college expects the child to contribute a larger percent of his or her own money than you are expected to contribute of your total assets. Thus, your child might be penalized for having money in his or her name rather than in yours. Also, keeping money in your name provides more flexibility for the family if an emergency should arise.

The IRS views a child's 14th birthday as a key date. Up until your child is 14, any *passive income*—dividend or interest income your child earns above $1300 (in 1995) is subject to federal income tax at *your* highest tax bracket. The first $650 of your child's passive income is not subject to federal income tax and the next $650 is subject to a 15 percent tax. To take advantage of the tax rules you might consider putting enough money in your child's name to get the benefit of the low federal income tax rates on the first $1300 of taxable income. If your child is under 14 and has more than $1300 of passive income, there is no tax break for putting money in your child's name. On the taxable income above $1300 you must pay taxes at your own tax rate. However, there may be a tax advantage in putting those EE bonds that mature after your child is 14 in the child's name. Once your child is over 14, he or she will pay tax on the postponed interest income at his or her own lower tax bracket when the EE bonds are cashed.

Why Buy EE and HH Bonds?

There are many reasons an investor may choose to buy EE and HH savings bonds.

- On the whole, EE and HH bonds are free of many of the risks of other investments. There is no default risk. The federal government is not going to walk away from these debts.

- There is little liquidity risk. After the first six months, EE bonds can be cashed in for the amount paid plus accrued interest.

- There is no interest-rate risk. If you do not like the interest rate you can cash them in. Unlike fixed-rate marketable bonds, the value of which will fluctuate, the EE bonds never decline in value. They cannot be sold for a profit, however, even if interest rates decline. You can always redeem them for the going rate.

- Call risk is not an issue. These bonds cannot be called. You will not have to face the problem of reinvesting the income at lower rates.

- Purchasing power risk occurs during periods of unprecedented inflation. EE and HH bonds are somewhat shielded from this risk because they will increase in value as the interest rate on the five-year Treasury bond increases. In other market sectors they would call EE bonds variable-rate bonds.

- They can be purchased monthly though a payroll deduction plan.

- Federal taxes on the interest can be deferred on EE bonds until they are cashed. By rolling over your E and EE bonds into HH bonds, the tax on the accrued interest can be postponed even further.

Considerations When Purchasing EE Bonds

- EE bonds pay less interest than you could earn if you purchased corporate or Treasury bonds.

- Cashing in EE bonds will result in a large tax liability in the year they are redeemed.

Where to Purchase Savings Bonds

EE and HH bonds can be purchased through your neighborhood bank or directly from the Federal Reserve Bank. These bonds are not bank products. The bank acts as agent for the Federal Reserve Bank. If you decide to purchase them directly from the Federal Reserve, you can visit your local office or you can mail in the forms. You can obtain the forms and information from your local Federal Reserve by calling 1-800-245-2840. For recorded information on the current rate call 1-800-487-2663.

Included here is a list of selected Federal Reserve Banks. If you cannot find a listing in a city near you, you can call or write to one of these for the address and phone number of the Federal Reserve Bank nearest you.

FRB Atlanta
104 Marietta Street, N.W.
Atlanta, GA 30303
404-521-8653

FRB New York
Federal Reserve PO Station
New York, NY 10045
212-720-6619

FRB Chicago
PO Box 834
Chicago, IL 60690
312-322-5369

FRB Pittsburgh
PO Box 867
Pittsburgh, PA 15230-0867
412-261-7802

FRB Houston
PO Box 2578
Houston, TX 77001
713-659-4433

FRB San Francisco
PO Box 7702
San Francisco, CA 94120
415-974-2330

Additional Help on Your Savings Bond Decisions

What is supposed to be a simple investment for the general population, is actually very complex. If you do not get the proper information, you could cash in the wrong bonds first or pay more taxes than you need to. A new book, *U.S. Savings Bonds: A Comprehensive Guide for Bond Owners and Financial Professionals,* written by Dan Pederson, provides comprehensive information about savings bonds. He also provides a service for people who want their portfolios personally reviewed. For either the book or the service, call Mr. Pederson at 1-800-927-1901.

8

U.S. Federal Agency Bonds Including Mortgage Pass-through Securities

Federal Agency Bonds

Agencies of the federal government have issued bonds for over 30 years to fund their activities. The number of agency bonds has ballooned as the federal debt has grown. The major agencies that issue bonds or mortgage pass-through securities are the following:

Federal Farm Credit System (FFCS)

Federal Home Loan Banks (FHLB)

Federal Home Loan Mortgage Corporation (FHLMC—Freddie Mac)

Federal National Mortgage Association (FNMA—Fannie Mae)

Financial Corporation (FICO)

Government National Mortgage Association (GNMA—Ginnie Mae)

Resolution Funding Corporation (Refcorp)

Student Loan Marketing Association (SLMA—Sallie Mae)

Tennessee Valley Authority (TVA)

Agency Bonds Compared to Treasury Bonds

Treasuries have many advantages compared to agency bonds. Treasury bonds are considered a better credit than agency bonds, although all agency bonds have an implied triple-A rating. It is easier to sell Treasury bonds than agency bonds because the Treasury bond market is a trading market. Treasuries are bought and sold for speculation as well as for their long-term value. Because of the market activity, the spread between the bid and the ask prices is smaller on Treasury bonds than on agency bonds. As a result, agency bonds yield somewhat more than Treasury bonds.

GNMAs, FNMAs, and FHLMCs are mortgage pass-through securities issued by agencies. The mortgage pass-through securities are a different kind of security than a bond. They are discussed in detail later in this chapter.

In August 1995, agency bonds generally yielded between 20 and 50 basis points more than Treasury bonds of similar maturities. Remember that there are 100 basis points in 1 percent. Thus, 50 basis points is equal to one half of one percent (0.5 percent). If all you can earn is 20 basis points more on an agency bond, consider buying the Treasury bond because of the advantages noted above. In the past agency bonds have yielded 100 basis points or more over Treasury bonds and may do so again in the future.

Advantages of Agency Bonds

Although most agency bonds are not well known to most of the investing public, they are attractive investments in certain circumstances. Some of the agency bonds are directly backed by the federal government and thus have no credit risk. The rest of the agency bonds are considered extremely safe and the credit risk is considered negligible because the federal government is unlikely to let one of its agencies default. Thus, agency bonds are a better credit than all corporate bonds and most municipal bonds.

Bonds issued by the following agencies are exempt from state and local taxes, but all are subject to federal income tax:

Federal Farm Credit System

Federal Home Loan Banks

Financial Corporation

Resolution Funding Corporation

Student Loan Marketing Association

Tennessee Valley Authority

The following popular agency bonds are *not* exempt from state and local income taxes:

Federal Home Loan Mortgage Corporation

Federal National Mortgage Association

Government National Mortgage Association

The agencies mentioned above are all very large and thus the bonds issued by these agencies are generally more liquid than corporate and municipal bonds. Those agency bonds that are exempt from state and local taxes have a significant tax advantage as well as credit advantage over corporate bonds. Agency bonds are suitable investments for tax-sheltered accounts such as IRAs and pension accounts. Minimum purchase requirements for agency bonds generally range from $1000 to $50,000.

Descriptions of the Agencies

Federal Farm Credit System

This is a nationwide system of banks that lend to ranchers, farmers, and certain farm-related businesses. The country is divided into 12 districts, and there is a Federal Farm Credit System bank in each district. Banks in the system issue three kinds of securities: short-term discount notes that range in maturity from 5 to 270 days and sell in minimum denominations of $50,000; short-term bonds with maturities of three to nine months that sell in minimum denominations of $50,000; and longer-term bonds with maturities of 1 to 10 years that sell in minimum denominations of $1000.

Federal Home Loan Banks

The Federal Home Loan Banks support the savings and loan banks in the United States. There are 12 regional banks. The Federal Home Loan Banks borrow money in the open market from investors, then they lend it to the savings and loan banks, which in turn lend it to home buyers. The Federal Home Loan Banks issue short-term discount securities in minimum amounts of $50,000. They also issue noncallable longer-term bonds in denominations of $10,000, $25,000, and higher.

Financial Corporation

The Financial Corporation was begun in 1987 to help create liquidity for the Federal Savings and Loan Insurance Corporation (FSLIC) after the stability of the savings and loan banks was threatened.

Resolution Funding Corporation

The purpose of the Resolution Funding Corporation is to provide financing to bail out the large number of thrifts that failed in the 1980s. Although the bonds issued by this corporation are not direct obligations of the U.S. government, the U.S. Treasury guarantees the interest and Treasury bonds secure the principal. Thus, there is little if any default risk on these bonds.

Student Loan Marketing Association

Sallie Mae was created in 1965 to guarantee student loans and provide liquidity for banks, educational institutions, and others who lend to students. Sallie Mae purchases student loans from these lending institutions.

Tennessee Valley Authority

The TVA is a wholly owned corporate agency of the U.S. government that was set up to develop the resources of the Tennessee Valley and adjacent areas and to strengthen the regional economy. The TVA bonds are not guaranteed by the U.S. government. The principal and interest of the bonds are payable only by the TVA. The bonds sold by the TVA are in denominations of $1000.

Mortgage Pass-through Securities

Mortgage pass-through securities are not bonds. They are much more complex than bonds and are a different kind of animal altogether. The way to understand mortgage pass-though securities is to first understand the purpose of a mortgage.

When you buy a house you can pay for it all in cash from your own funds. If this were the only way to buy a house, few of us would own one. We need help in buying the house. So you go to the bank and the bank lends you money for the house purchase. The piece of paper that the bank makes you sign in order to get your money is called a mortgage. The purpose of the mortgage is to secure the bank's interest in the property and make sure the bank gets repaid.

Years ago the bank held the mortgage itself until you paid it off. As you may recall, in the 1970s many of the savings and loan banks got in trouble because they lent money on 30-year fixed-rate mortgages at say 6 percent or 7 percent. A few years later their cost of funds went up and the banks had to pay interest at 9 percent or 12 percent. For these and other reasons, banks and other institutions wanted to be able to sell the mortgages that they wrote so that they would not have to take the risk of holding them. Mortgage pass-through securities were invented to enable the easy trading of mortgages, such as the mortgage that you have on your house.

Let's take a look at how this works. You go to the bank and borrow $100,000 for 30 years to finance the purchase of your house. You also pay the bank three points or $3000 for making this loan. You give the bank a $100,000 mortgage representing your debt. The bank without your knowledge or consent turns around and sells your mortgage together with many other mortgages written at the same time.

GNMA

The most standard mortgages are sold to the Government National Mortgage Association (GNMA). The bank now has all of its $100,000 back and can lend it to another borrower. The $3000 in points you paid is profit for the bank. The bank may still collect your monthly mortgage payment for GNMA and send you your statements. For these services, the bank earns a yearly fee from GNMA.

GNMA does not want to hold your mortgage either, so it combines your mortgage with many other mortgages in a mortgage pool and sells shares in the pool to investors. When the pool is sold, GNMA has all of its money back and it can buy more mortgages. GNMA earns a fee for two services. First, it guarantees all mortgage payments that the home owners like you have to make. Second, GNMA sells the interests in the pool to institutional investors. Once the investors buy the securities, called GNMAs or Ginnie Maes, they can trade them in the market.

GNMAs are a good deal for the bank. The bank gets its money back quickly, takes no risks, and earns fees for its services. GNMAs are good for home owners because the GNMA loan guarantee enables them to borrow mortgage money at the lowest rate available. When mortgage money is cheap, it enables more people to buy homes. GNMAs provide an excellent investment for investors.

All the home owners' mortgages are bundled in mortgage pools. Each pool is unique, although mortgages in the pool may share certain characteristics. There are pools which just own 15-year fixed-rate mortgages and some that just own 30-year fixed-rate mortgages. All mortgages in the pool may have the same interest rate.

The monthly payment made by the home owner and received by the owner of the GNMA security consists of interest and principal payments, including prepayments. Payments of principal are not taxable since it is a return of the investor's capital. The interest is subject to tax as interest income. Each month the payment will be of a different size, and the proportion that is principal and interest will be different as well. The originator/servicer of the mortgage pool collects all of the interest, principal, and prepayments and pays each investor his pro rata share of the cash collected. The originator/servicer charges a 0.5 percent fee for this work.

A home owner might decide to reduce her mortgage by paying an extra amount. This is a *prepayment*. Prepayments will also occur if a home owner sells his house and pays off the entire mortgage. Mortgage refinancing because of a drop in interest rates also triggers prepayments. The owner borrows from another institution and pays down the original mortgage loan. Prepayments are such a big part of the process, that pools of 30-year mortgages are generally paid off in 12 to 14 years. This is called the *average life* of the pool.

GNMAs are very safe because they are backed not only by the mortgages in the pool but also by a U.S. government guarantee. What if a home owner defaults and can't or won't make his mortgage payment? In this case, the pass-through agency will make the required payment since the agencies guarantee all payments in the pool. A guarantee by the federal government is one of the major advantages of a GNMA.

Freddie Mac and Fannie Mae

Federal Home Loan Mortgage Corporation, known as Freddie Mac, and the Federal National Mortgage Association, known as Fannie Mae, are two other major entities that guarantee and sell mortgage pass-through securities. The securities represent pools containing 15- and 30-year mortgages. The guarantees are of both principal and interest.

Like GNMA, Freddie Mac is a federal agency. Fannie Mae is not a federal agency. Fannie Mae is a public corporation whose stock is owned by private shareholders and traded on the New York Stock Exchange. However, Fannie Mae is a U.S. government–sponsored corporation that is subject to regulation by the Secretary of Housing and Urban Development. Although Fannie Mae has an implied triple-A credit rating, its securities yield more than GNMAs and Freddie Macs because the latter two are federal agencies. The mortgages included in the GNMA pools are more uniform and less unconventional than those in either the Fannie Mae or Freddie Mac pools. The differences in the nature of the pools result in a yield difference of about 0.25 percent or less. There has been little real difference in safety between a Fannie Mae and a GNMA security as far as credit quality. Neither entity has ever defaulted or missed a payment to an investor.

Freddie Mac guarantees mortgages in the same way as GNMA. However, the guarantee of GNMA is more highly regarded than the guarantee of Freddie Mac because GNMA's guarantee is a direct obligation of the U.S. government. By comparison, Freddie Mac's loans are guaranteed by the Federal Home Loan Bank, a federal agency. Freddie Mac guarantees mortgage pools of 15- and 30-year mortgages.

Advantages of Mortgage Pass-through Securities

Mortgage pass-through securities provide a high current cashflow. In fact, the current cashflow is greater than would be received on a Treasury security. You get back not only interest but also some mortgage principal. As an investor, you are in the position of a lender. When you are repaid, you receive back mostly interest in the early years and mostly principal in the later years. This is just what happens when you make your fixed monthly payment to the bank on your mortgage. You pay mostly interest in the early years and mostly principal in the later years. A pass-through security pays its cash out each month, while bonds pay interest only every six months.

Since there are billions of dollars invested in outstanding mortgage pass-through securities, they trade frequently. They are traded in large lots. Pass-through securities pay a higher yield than Treasuries because of their disadvantages.

Disadvantages of Mortgage Pass-through Securities

At first blush, you might conclude that a mortgage pass-through security is as good an investment as a Treasury. The GNMA has the same safety as a Treasury and a larger cashflow. However, all mortgage pass-through securities are subject to state and local income tax as well as federal income tax. By contrast, Treasury bonds and many other agency bonds are not subject to state and local income taxes.

The cashflow from mortgage pass-through securities is uneven and unpredictable. The cashflow includes the homeowners' regular monthly payments and their additional prepayments. Prepayments are a real wild card. They make it impossible to predict the overall cashflow from the pass-through securities. If you can't predict cashflow, you can't predict current return and you certainly can't compute a yield-to-maturity.

The prepayment assumptions used for pass-through securities are based on complicated statistical models. Usually, the payment history of the securities is compared to prepayment patterns prepared by the Federal Housing Administration. If interest rates change markedly, the FHA may issue new prepayment guidelines. Unless you purchase GNMAs and other pass-through securities through a fund, the relatively small blocks that an individual can purchase might actually be statistical aberrations from the norm.

Unpredictable prepayments cause other problems. If the estimated yield on the GNMA is based upon the pool remaining in existence for say 12 years, prepayments may result in a pool coming to an end in only 9 years. This might result in a lower yield on the pass-through security. In this scenario, if you purchased GNMAs, Fannie Maes, or Freddie Macs at a premium, you would lose money.

Prepayment risk also means that you are likely to get back a large amount of your investment at the very time that interest rates are low. For example, if interest rates drop sharply, home owners will have a big incentive to refinance their mortgages at a lower rate.

Capital depletion is another potential problem. For the inexperienced investor, the large cashflows look like manna from heaven. If you spend all of the interest payments from the pass-through securities as it comes in, you will deplete your capital. You will have nothing to reinvest. Thus, a pass-through security is similar to an investment in oil and gas; large payments in the early years, but declining payments in the future.

Pass-through securities also have interest-rate risk. If interest rates rise, home owners will generally not refinance, thus keeping the pool alive for a longer period of time. This might result in a yield lower than estimated. You will not get your capital back to reinvest at a higher rate. What is best for pass-through securities investors is for interest rates to remain within a narrow range.

The yield on GNMAs and other pass-through securities is not directly comparable to corporate bonds or Treasury bonds. Since the GNMA payments are uneven and unpredictable, the yield is only an estimate and probably not a good estimate at that.

With all of these disadvantages why would anyone buy a pass-through security? Because of these known risks, pass-through securities are generally priced to have a higher expected yield than a Treasury. If you purchase GNMAs, the estimated yield may be 1.5 percent more than Treasury bonds with the same estimated maturity. Fannie Maes and Freddie Macs would yield slightly more.

It is difficult for the individual investor to evaluate information about pass-through securities and to commit enough cash to properly diversify a pass-through security portfolio. For these reasons, mortgage pass-through securities are generally not suitable securities for individuals to purchase on their own. Most fund families that have pass-through security pools fill them with GNMAs. If you wish to purchase GNMAs, the simplest way to do it is to buy a GNMA fund. Vanguard and Benham both have well-regarded GNMA funds with excellent prior performance records.

Despite the disadvantages noted above, certain investors may find the GNMAs attractive. An investor who desires a large cashflow and doesn't care if his principal is returned unpredictably may enjoy owning mortgage pass-through securities.

Collateralized Mortgage Obligations

Collateralized Mortgage Obligations are known as CMOs. They are relatively new financial products, first developed in 1983. CMOs are pass-through investments based on underlying mortgages as are GNMAs. The so-called "rocket scientists" of the investment-banking revolution developed CMOs in part to solve the problem of how to deal with the prepayment of the mortgages in GNMAs. It is difficult to predict a yield on GNMAs because mortgage prepayments can't be predicted. The CMO allows greater certainty of returns for at least some of the CMO investors. CMOs created a whole new range of profitable financial products for Wall Street.

CMOs are much more complicated than GNMAs. The creators of the CMOs have come up with endless variations on how to dice and chop the cashflows coming from a large pool of mortgages. The key concept is that the mortgage pool is broken up into anywhere between 3 and 17 different slices or tranches. The mortgage pool documents provide the order in which mortgage prepayments are paid to the different tranches.

Let's take the simplest case of a CMO with three tranches. We will call them A-tranche, B-tranche, and Z-tranche. The last tranche is always called the Z-tranche. The A-tranche might pay a fixed rate of interest of 6 percent and the B-tranche a 7 percent fixed rate of interest until the tranches are retired. Interest is accrued but not paid on the Z-tranche. The Z-tranche receives no principal payments from mortgage prepayments until all the other tranches are fully paid off. The Z-tranche bears some similarity to a zero-coupon bond in that interest is accrued but not paid.

The CMO provides that all *prepayments* go first to the A-tranche; and when the A-tranche is retired, the prepayments then go to the B-tranche until it is retired. Finally, the rest of the payments go to the Z-tranche. The Z-tranche may have a very long life and no definite maturity. It may also be difficult to determine the tax consequences of the Z-tranche.

The return on the A-tranche is more predictable than the return on a GNMA. In the CMO, *all* prepayments first go to the A-tranche. The A-tranche is similar to a short-term bond. It might be possible to predict with a high degree of reliability that the A-tranche will be retired in about three years. The return on the B-tranche is more difficult to predict than the A-tranche.

The last tranche, the Z-tranche, will receive no interest or principal payments until all of the others are repaid. While the first tranche may have an expected life of three years, the Z-tranche may not be retired for 20 or 30 years. The return on the Z-tranche obviously is the most difficult to predict. It has the highest yield, and it loses value quickly when interest rates rise because prepayments decline. The Z-tranche was the cause of many government bond fund holders' woes. Thus, in the pricing of these securities, the A-tranche would probably yield less and cost more than a GNMA and the Z-tranche would yield more and cost less than a GNMA.

Not all CMOs have the same credit quality. Some CMO mortgage pools are backed by GNMA and some by Fannie Mae, both of which have minimum risk. Private insurance backs some CMO pools. These pools may have greater risk because the insurer may not be as creditworthy as GNMA or Fannie Mae.

Yield predictions may be very far from the actual outcome. What may appear to be a short-term investment because of rising interest rates may lengthen by many years if interest rates later drop precipitously. Even the shortest tranches are not immune to maturity extensions.

The Z-tranche may be particularly hard to analyze and sell. The Z-tranche will also be more volatile than other mortgage-backed securities, particularly when interest rates are moving rapidly. In addition, the Z-tranche may have difficult accounting and tax aspects for the investor to deal with.

The marketability of your CMO may be limited. CMOs are *proprietary products,* products that are created by the rocket scientists at a particular brokerage house. They are not easily sold, and the bidders could be limited to the broker that originally sold you the deal. In this case you can expect a relatively low price if you need to sell your investment.

Advantages of CMOs

There are only some slight advantages to CMOs over other investments.

- Cashflow is more predictable than in GNMAs for the A- and B-tranches, which resemble short-term bonds with less predictable maturities.
- Later tranches have less prepayment risk because they are paid after the earlier tranches.
- CMOs generally provide larger pools and thus the prepayments are more spread out.
- There is no credit risk if the CMO is guaranteed by GNMA or Fannie Mae.
- Smaller minimum investments are required for some CMOs ($10,000) than for GNMAs ($25,000).

Recommendations

Because of the disadvantages inherent in CMOs, unless you are a very aggressive investor, CMOs will not be for you. CMO investments are generally considered proper for institutional investors that have the staff and time available to gain a deep understanding of the terms of the CMO offering. Unless you have a great deal of time, information, and knowledge about the CMO, you will not be able to understand its terms well enough to project a meaningful yield. While all GNMAs have the same structure, most of the CMOs have different structures. Many are unique. Thus, understanding each one is a new exercise. CMOs were originally sold only in large pieces to large institutional investors. However, they are now being sold to investors like you.

If you are thinking about investing in mortgage-backed securities, an entertaining and informative book to read is *Liar's Poker* by Michael Lewis. Lewis details the development of the mortgage-backed securities department at Salomon Brothers through the trading and management skills of Lewis Ranieri. He describes the growth of the market in witty and scathing detail.

If you want to invest in CMOs, the best way to do it is through a well-regarded mutual fund that has experienced management in this area. Some mutual funds that invest in mortgage pass-through securities are restricted to investing only in GNMAs. One example of this is the Vanguard GNMA fund. Other mutual funds are allowed to invest in any mortgage pass-through securities available. These funds use CMOs as a vehicle to attempt to earn higher returns. These funds are obviously more risky. Their returns may be significantly higher or lower than a plain GNMA fund.

If You Are Looking for Income, Should You Buy Pass-through Securities?

- Pass-through securities provide high monthly cashflow. Some of it will be returned principal. Don't spend it!

- Quotations of yield are unreliable.

- The fluctuation of interest rates affects when you will get your principal back.

- They are less liquid than Treasuries.

- The minimum individual purchase is $25,000, except for CMOs that sell in smaller units.

- This is one investment better bought through a fund.

Do you want to invest in pass-through securities? You decide!

9
Municipal Bonds

*Since the Depression, no general obligation
bond of a major issuer has ever defaulted.*
ARTHUR LEVITT, SECURITIES AND EXCHANGE
COMMISSION CHAIRMAN

*It is not best that we should all think alike; it
is difference of opinion which makes horse
races.* MARK TWAIN

Why Invest in Municipal Bonds?

Bracket creep, the hidden tax increase caused by inflation that silently
pushes the investor into higher tax brackets, has attracted millions of
people to municipal bonds. The 1986 Tax Reform Act effectively shut
down all tax shelters other than municipal bonds. Municipal bonds
(munis) benefit not only wealthier investors, but also the states, cities,
and their agencies that issue them. Munis enable these governments to
sell their debt at lower costs. Municipalities use debt to finance new
schools, adequate roads, clean water, sewers, hospitals, and a host of
other services that benefit the people on a day-to-day basis. The federal
government exempts municipal bond income from federal income tax
as a way of helping the states and municipalities borrow at lower costs.

Not only are municipal bonds an investment that directly benefits
local communities, but they have also proved to be an excellent investment. "When investment risk is introduced, municipals actually outperformed equities on an after-tax risk-adjusted basis over the last 10 years,"

says John Nuveen analyst Richard B. Harper, Jr. Though stocks actually performed better than municipal bonds, after factoring in both the risks taken to achieve those gains and municipal bond's tax advantages, municipals came out ahead. These findings were supported by James McGinley, associate vice president of the municipal strategy group at Prudential Securities Inc., and Richard Ciccarone, executive vice president of strategic advisors at Kemper Securities Inc.[1] "Municipal bonds trailed stocks by only 25 basis points between 1990 and 1994," Harper said. Municipal bonds have a low default rate and pay interest quite predictably. With their tax advantages and low risk, munis provide an excellent alternative to stock investments. As with any investment, however, the past is no predictor of the future.

The Birth of a Municipal Bond

Before a bond issue is conceived, the municipal officials must perceive a need. A school district, town, county, state, or supplier of service to the community identifies a need for a construction or improvement project. The municipal officials consider how to finance the project. A school district, for example, could face a burgeoning student body housed in temporary classrooms. Where are the funds going to come from to buy land and build another school? The school district's supervisors and school board develop a budget and research the different ways the needs can be satisfied. They hold town meetings to gain support for a bond referendum. The backing for the loans are real estate taxes paid by the residents of the school district.

If the city of Miami decides to float a bond issue, it would ask brokerage houses and bank *underwriters* to submit bids to purchase the bonds. The bond issue is usually bought by a *syndicate* or group of brokers in order to spread the remarketing risk. They then sell the bonds to funds, insurance companies, banks, and individuals. The underwriters make a profit by marking up the price of the bonds and keeping the difference as their profit. If it judges the market correctly, the syndicate makes money. If it misjudges the market and is unable to sell the bonds at the expected yields, the syndicate will lose money. In the same way that the city asks contractors to submit bids on construction jobs, the city asks the under-

---

[1]Peter List, "Munis Have Beaten Equities Since 1985, Says Analyst's Study," *The Bond Buyer*, September 7, 1995, p.7

writers to submit bids for the bond issue. In a competitive bid, the city might receive three bids with overall yields of 5.5 percent, 5.4 percent, or 5.68 percent. The city would take the lowest overall bid of 5.4 percent.

From an issuer's point of view, the lowest rate is the best rate. A lender always prefers the higher rate. The broker and the brokerage house earn money on all bond transactions in the same way. They sell to you for a higher price than they bought the bond. The energy derived from the differences in the lender's and the borrower's need is what fuels the bond market.

In some instances, the issuer opts for a negotiated bond issue instead of a competitive bond issue. In a negotiated issue, the issuer would contract with only one syndicate to manage the deal and sell the bonds. Large, complex issues often result in negotiated deals. However, many more deals were negotiated than necessary because the politicians wanted to repay favors for political contributions. These contributions have been substantially restricted by the actions of the SEC and the Municipal Securities Rulemaking Board.

Whether a deal is negotiated or competitive, the yields and prices are fixed for all members of the syndicate during the selling period. The selling period may last one day if all the bonds trade immediately, or it may last longer. When the syndicate disbands, any unsold bonds are free to trade in the open or secondary market. In the secondary market bonds trade according to supply and demand. The yields may be higher or lower than the new issue yields.

General Obligation Bonds

The issuance of some bonds requires voter approval. When the Wissahickon School District in Pennsylvania decided to borrow money to build a new school, it had to put the issue to a vote by the community. On the ballot at the next election was a description of the proposed construction project. The voters approved the referendum, empowering the school board to issue *general obligation* bonds (GOs). These bonds are backed by the issuer's full faith and credit. Thus, a GO bond is supported by all the resources of the state, municipality, or school district that issued it. The Wissahickon school bonds are principally backed by real estate taxes, but they may also be backed by the receipts from income tax, sales tax, and other taxes.

Not all GOs are equal. The strength of a general obligation bond is based upon the financial health and economic potential of the taxing power of the state or municipality that issued it. Analysts evaluating a

GO bond determine the financial strength of the issuer by exploring its economic and financial base. They determine trends in employment, the growth of population, the riches of the region, and the nature of local industry, among many other factors. Most municipalities receive federal and state aid in addition to more local sources of income.

States have the most diversified revenue sources, including personal income taxes, corporate and business taxes, property taxes, sales taxes, user fees, death and gift taxes, severance taxes, and federal grant-in-aid. State legislators have the ability to broaden the tax base by raising new taxes. Many anti-tax groups have emerged to resist tax increases. Local governments, including counties, municipalities, and school districts rely mainly on property taxes, unless the state government allows the local government to levy additional taxes. A broadened tax base might include sales and income taxes.

Issuers use various techniques to improve the credit ratings of their GO bonds. A higher bond rating results in a lower interest rate. For example, Wisconsin has waived its right to immunity from suits from bondholders to show good faith. Other GO bonds have double protection because they are secured by both the credit of the issuer and also by the credit of a particular state agency. Illinois issued general obligation transportation bonds that were secured and paid for from the gasoline taxes of the state's transportation fund and also secured by the resources of the state. These are called *double-barreled bonds* because they have two sources of security. These and other credit enhancements by a state are reflected in the credit ratings given to the bonds by the rating agencies.

There are also factors that tend to decrease the credit rating of municipal bonds. In many states the response of the voters to increasing demands for more taxes is to pass limitations on the tax rate. California voters passed Proposition 13, limiting real estate property taxes. Massachusetts followed with Proposition 2½, reducing the amount of real estate taxes collected. Other states did likewise. The voters followed up those votes by saying "no" to proposed bond issues, momentarily tying the hands of their elected representatives. Some general obligation bonds are *limited tax general obligation* bonds (LT GOs) because they can only be paid off with a specified stream of income, rather than from all of the municipality's revenues.

Limitations on taxation resulted in a proportional decrease in the amount of general obligation bonds issued. In 1970, GO bonds accounted for 75 percent of all municipal bond issues compared to only 40 percent in 1982. Since 1982, GO issues have fluctuated between 35 percent and 40 percent of the bonds issued. In response to the declining source of funds that can be raised by GOs, other alternatives were expanded. Municipalities issued more bonds backed by a specified stream of revenue. New authorities and agencies were created that had new borrowing capabilities. Bonds backed by lease revenue became more common as did certificates of participation (COPs). The funding source for COPs is the annual appropriation of funds by the issuing municipality.

Case Study: Orange County, California

General obligation bonds of states have always been considered the most desirable credit because of the variety of taxes that support the bonds. However, the ability to raise revenue is not the only important factor. The willingness of the voters to support indebtedness is even more important.

Voting to limit the ability of the state or local government to tax is one way to slow the issuance of municipal bonds. A less savory method is the repudiation of the debt. In Orange County, California, the majority voted against new taxes to pay for the fiscal management mistakes of an elected official. The politicians claimed that Orange County was like New York City. In New York City there was widespread talk of possible defaults because of the city's difficult economic straits. However, Orange County was in very good financial shape. The county supervisors and treasurer took risks called unreasonable when the strategy failed. Having declared bankruptcy, the Orange County politicians and residents would have liked to walk away from the situation, sticking the note holders with nonpayment. The default could have been cured if a majority of the residents had voted to raise the sales tax by one-half of one percent. The officials of the state of California said the default was not their problem. Governor Pete Wilson vetoed a bill that would have given him the tools to take over most of Orange County's operations. Initially he did not want to be involved in helping to bail out one of the richest counties in the United States with other taxpayers' money. It was a political hot potato.

On June 27, 1995, Orange County voters defeated the one-half of one percent sales tax increase by an overwhelming margin. County officials had hoped to defer payment of new short-term notes by one year and then use the $130 million revenue from the sales tax as the basis of a new borrowing to repay the $975 million in bond debt. The voters' repudiation of the additional tax showed that they did not feel any responsibility for the actions of their elected officials. This attempted repudiation of debt by a rich county with the ability to pay set a very bad precedent.

On the same day that the voters were defeating the sale tax increase, the county tried to sell $155 million of short-term notes paying 1 percent more than the market rate. Despite the high yield, the notes did not sell well. "It was a clear-cut boycott of Orange County paper. Price was not an issue," said Paul Nussbaum, a county financial advisor.[2]

The need for additional revenue sources grew directly out of Proposition 13, which severely limited tax revenues available to local governments. Rather than come to grips with how to pay for the services they receive, county residents preferred borrowing now and paying later to paying their debts currently by raising the sales tax. The county had come to rely on funds garnered from investments in lieu of higher taxes.

The county supervisors who opposed passage of the sales tax proposed to sell county assets in order to meet county obligations. However, the supervisors were really hoping to sue Merrill Lynch successfully for the monies because the officials alleged that Merrill Lynch sold unsuitable securities to the county. Merrill Lynch, the county's broker, maintained its innocence.

Pete Wilson, the governor of California, approved a legislative recovery plan on October 9, 1995, that was expected to take Orange County out of bankruptcy by mid-1996. Part of the plan called for the county to raise money by selling county assets, such as unused land and buildings. The county would also raise money by importing the trash of neighboring communities to its underused landfills. In addition, over 200 local governments that participated in the Orange County Investment Pool would forgive about $800 million owed to them. These local governments would only recoup this $800 million to the extent that Orange County was successful in its suit against Merrill Lynch and other brokers.

The immediate cause of the Orange County default was the use of excessive *leverage*. Leverage is the use of borrowed money to achieve a greater rate of return on capital. Robert Citron, Orange County's treasurer took risks which turned sour. Citron had been making the same kind of investments for 10 years. He had generated above-average returns for the county for all that time. Citron had to keep increasing the level of risk with the county's investment portfolio in the hopes of maintaining his excellent performance. The income generated by the pool rose to a third of the county's budget while the income generated by property tax fell more than half to 25 percent. In 1994 his luck ran out as market conditions changed.

[2]Seth Mydans, "Uncertainty in California as County Goes to the Polls," *The New York Times*, June 26, 1995, p. A10.

What is of particular interest in the Orange County case is that Citron's hazardous investments were not a secret. During Citron's 1994 reelection campaign, his opponent John Moorlach, a Costa Mesa CPA, told the voters how precarious the investments were in the face of rising interest rates and that there could be massive losses. The voters, however, approved of Citron's actions and reelected him by an overwhelming vote. The voters, it seems, were more interested in paying less taxes while getting more services. Calvin Grigsby of the municipal bond firm of Grigsby Bradford & Co., described the Orange County vote as follows:

> The Orange County vote almost said, we don't like debt and so we don't care if we can't issue anymore. We don't want any services, we don't want any government, and if you have debt, you have government. We don't want any more government.[3]

Municipal treasurers in Ohio, Hawaii, Florida, Maine, and Michigan also made risky investments and incurred substantial losses. However, Orange County, California, suffered the largest losses. In the other municipalities, steps were taken to cut services and raise taxes to pay for the losses. Only Orange County felt it was entitled to seek a more comfortable path.

Revenue Bonds: Who Pays the Bills?

Do you realize if it weren't for Edison we'd be watching TV by candlelight?
AL BOLISKA

I know of no more encouraging fact than the unquestionable ability of man to elevate his life by a conscious endeavor.
HENRY DAVID THOREAU

If it weren't for revenue bonds, electricity might not have been developed on the current scale, and our governments would have no way of funding the big infrastructure projects to get the electricity into our

---

[3]Kieran Beer, "Grigsby Seeks to Transcend Minority Firm Status," *The Bond Buyer*, August 1, 1995, p. 29.

homes. Revenue bonds pay for the big projects that can't come out of the current operating budget. Revenue bonds fund our roads, stadiums, sewers, and a host of other projects that we now take for granted. The stream of revenue to support the bonds can come from traditional revenue sources or innovative and creative ones. Florida backs some bonds with revenue from jai alai. Many states are considering backing bonds with proceeds from the state lotteries. More traditional sources of revenue are produced by the services they support.

Revenue bonds generally fall within one of the following categories:

- Electric utility bonds
- Water and sewer bonds
- Toll road, bridge, and port authority bonds
- Airport bonds
- Hospital bonds
- Housing bonds
- Industrial development bonds
- Pollution-control bonds
- University and student loan bonds

Unlike GO bonds, a public referendum is not required for the issuance of revenue bonds. Revenue bonds are backed and supported only by a designated stream of income for a particular bond issuer rather than by a municipality's general taxing power. The stream of income is usually from user fees. For example, a Philadelphia sewer authority's bonds are backed by the fees paid by the residents of Philadelphia for sewer service. If the sewer fees are not great enough to support the bonds, the sewer authority can request a rate increase. Neither the city of Philadelphia nor the state of Pennsylvania has any *legal* responsibility for supporting the sewer authority's bonds.

Highways and bridges raise funds through tolls and concessions. A toll is a fee for usage and a concession is a fee for access. For example, a restaurant might pay an access fee for permission to open along a highway. Docks and airports charge fees to shipping companies and airlines for the use of space. Housing bonds are supported by mortgage payments (a fee for the use of money), by rents, and by payments for the use of living space. Student loan bonds are paid by interest on the loan, again a fee for the use of money. College and university bonds are funded by fees paid by students, rents from university housing, entertainment charges to the general public, and contract fees for special research. Utility bonds are secured by user fees. Nursing home bonds are secured by payments from the residents. Hospital bond revenue is based upon hospital utilization. Patients and doctors decide which hospital to use. The government has increased its control of hospitals. Health maintenance organizations, medicare, medicaid, and other third-party payers limit hospital stays, forcing mergers of hospitals, shorter stays for the same treatments, and a general squeezing of hospital revenue sources.

Tip

Diversify the types of bonds you purchase. Electric companies used to have a lock on the area they served. Now purchasers of electric power can buy from the cheapest provider because the electricity can be transported over lines owned by another company. This is called "free-wheeling," and it will dramatically alter the strength and bond-paying ability of many electric utilities.

Lease-Backed Bonds: When a Bond Is Not Quite a Bond

Lease-backed bonds are bonds backed by municipal leases on buildings and equipment. Payments on the leases are often dependent upon an *annual* vote by the legislature to appropriate funds to pay rent or fees under a lease. If the annual appropriation is not made, the bonds will be in default. Some states allow greater latitude for nonpayment than others. Some lease agreements allow a municipality to terminate the lease at its sole discretion for any reason. Lease payments may not be made, for example, if the financed facility is not available for use. The security of lease-backed bonds ranges from excellent to fair.

Certificates of Participation (COPs) are a special kind of lease-backed security. This type of debt is generally more expensive for an issuer to sell because it offers the lender less protection against default. COPs pay a higher interest rate than revenue bonds supported by a dedicated stream of earnings, or GO bonds backed by the full faith and credit of a municipal entity. COPs may be issued without voter approval. COPs are frequently issued in California because local general obligation debt requires approval of two-thirds of the voters. That is a goal not often met by even the most essential projects.

Case Study: Brevard
County, Florida

Brevard County, Florida, issued COPs in 1989. The proceeds funded the construction of a government office building in the city of Viera. The Brevard County government had always been decentralized, with government offices located throughout the 72-mile-long county. This building was located far from the most populated areas of the county, and was being used to anchor new development. Many voters were dissatisfied with the location of the building. In the 1992 election, the voters elected two new commissioners who were opposed to this office building.

Unlike most bonds, the interest payments flowing from the lease-backed debt was funded by annual appropriations. The county commissioners decided not to automatically appropriate the money for this unpopular project.

The commissioners resolved to hold a referendum to ask the voters whether they thought that the county should continue to pay for the office building. Wall Street financiers were upset because the referendum signified that the voters had the right to repudiate debt legally contracted by their elected officials. A default in Brevard County would have flashed a danger signal to other buyers of lease-backed debt.

The referendum had a two-part question. First, the commissioners asked the voters if the county officials should stay in the Viera office building. If the answer was no, then the county would default on the Certificates of Participation. The second question asked if the county should issue general obligation bonds to pay off the COPs. In a narrow vote, the residents supported the use of the Viera office building, but they rejected the issuance of general obligation bonds to redeem the COPs. Ultimately, revenue bonds were issued to redeem the lease-backed issue.

The favorable vote was the result of heavy lobbying by MBIA, the insurance company that was responsible for covering the costs of the COPs in the event of default. The insurance company spent almost $375,000 to support local political-action groups that backed the Viera site. The rating agencies put the county on their credit watch list and downgraded another competitive issue the county was about to sell before the referendum. Wall Street predicted higher borrowing costs for the county if the voters rejected the lease-backed debt. There was a general fear that if Brevard County walked away from the COPs, then lenders of similar issues around the country would also suffer. In the end, the COPs were refunded with a revenue bond issue, and the furor died down. It won't be forgotten.

As some municipalities face budget crunches, leases subject to annual appropriations may become an early casualty of an economic downturn.[4] When the politicians in Orange County, California, backed away from their obligations to repay county debt, and the state of California failed to step in, saying it was a county problem, lenders began taking a hard look at California lease-backed bonds. If any securities were going to be repudiated, lease-backed bonds top the list. In good economic times everyone gets paid. In states such as California where limitations on the rights to taxation have been passed, creative financing has been required to raise funds for projects felt to be essential. Keep in mind that a lease-backed bond is not very secure. If it is backed by annual appropriations, the issuer has a right to terminate payments, and the voters do not feel a strong obligation to pay back the debt.

Local taxpayer revolts have resulted in challenges to the moral and legal obligation of lease-backed bonds. In 1991, the Richmond Unified School District in California tried to walk away from $9.8 million in lease-backed bonds. The school district argued that it did not have voter approval of long-term debt and that the funds were used largely for operating deficits rather than capital projects. The judge hearing the case rejected the school district's arguments, saying that there were funds available to pay the debt on an annual basis, that the school district had the legal right to negotiate the lease, and that the district was legally obligated to pay it. After losing the battle, this school district changed its name.

Voters do not like being bypassed. When politicians support lease-backed bonds, they do an end-run around the voters in order to float the projects they want. Investors believe that, even though the bond indenture says "subject to annual appropriation," the community has a moral obligation to continue to support the lease-backed bonds.

Moral Obligation Bonds

Some revenue bonds are called moral obligation bonds. A bond is called a moral obligation bond if there is an *implied* obligation that the state will support the bonds in the event of a default. Note that the state does not have a *legal* obligation to support the bonds in case of a default. Moral obligation bonds are designed to circumvent debt limits that would apply to GO bonds. Moral obligation bonds do not require voter approval because they are not a legal obligation of the state.

---

[4]Brad Altman, "Lease Deals: A Tool Might Need a Crutch," *The Bond Buyer*, May 19, 1995, p. 8.

In 1968 the New York State Urban Development Corporation (UDC) issued moral obligation bonds. The UDC was established by the New York State legislature primarily to construct subsidized housing and other projects in urban renewal areas. Six years later in 1974, the UDC defaulted on $100 million of moral obligation bonds. New York State made good on the defaulted bonds. Other states have also exhibited a similar willingness to support moral obligation bonds.

The cases show the need for approval by officials, of municipalities, and voters to pay for what they did not approve. The issue gets more complicated when there are projects which must be built under mandated federal or state law. Officials have a choice of asking for voter approval or sidestepping the issue altogether and issuing lease-backed debt. Expect a higher yield if the voters have not been consulted by their elected officials. There is more risk to your bond holdings in this situation.

Potential Problem Areas for Revenue Debt

How do you know what the danger signs are when you purchase revenue debt? Some issues are potentially more unstable than others. Look for these warning signs:

- Start-up situations, where the users never materialize; for example, a new housing development to which no one moves.

- Cost overruns on projects without public support; for example, nuclear power plants.

- Second lien bonds; first lien bonds are paid first in full before the second lien bonds.

- Voter dissatisfaction; for example, residents may not vote rate increases if they do not see the value provided by public utilities.

- One source of payment, instead of a pool of payers. The theory is that a weak link in a chain can be mended.

- Any limitations on profit or income of the issuer.

- Debt service coverage less than $1\frac{1}{2}$ times the interest cost to the issuer. If the amount to be paid in interest to the bondholders is $100,000 per year, the issuer must have at least $150,000 in revenue per year to allow a margin for error.

Things to Note

- Most housing bonds and hospital bonds have extraordinary calls and can be called at any time, even if the call is not mentioned by the broker.
- Most calls occur when interest rates have declined significantly. Calls are not your friend. They are always in the issuer's interest, not yours.
- Housing bonds issued under the Department of Housing and Urban Development (HUD) only provide a rent subsidy, which can be terminated.
- Uninsured housing bonds are rated single-A or triple-B. Insured bonds are rated triple-A or double-A.
- Uninsured student loans may be risky because students often default on their loans.
- Nursing home bonds, including those issued by religious institutions, have the highest default rate.
- Tax allocation bonds, which are supported by the development in the area to be assisted, will not be repaid if the expected property taxes do not materialize.
- Nonrated bonds may be very risky. Read the prospectus carefully before investing.

Taxes and Municipal Bonds

The Tax Reform Act of 1986 took away most tax shelters but left the municipal bond exemption intact. While people with high incomes benefit most from an investment in municipal bonds, anyone in the 28 percent tax bracket or higher can reap an advantage by investing in them.

Tip_____

In 1995, a single person reached the 28 percent tax bracket when taxable income exceeded $24,000. A married couple reached the 28 percent tax bracket when their taxable income in 1995 exceeded $40,100. These numbers change yearly.

Sometimes people with tax brackets below 28 percent invest in tax-exempt municipal bonds, even though they would make more money from other investments. They buy munis to avoid paying income taxes.

Since 1986, individuals have become the dominant force driving the municipal bond market via direct purchases and purchases of mutual funds which hold municipal bonds.

Are Municipals Right for You? Taxable Equivalent Yields

Before buying municipal bonds rather than taxable bonds, ask yourself how you can make the most money *after tax* on your invested dollar. To figure this out, you must know what is your highest federal income tax bracket. Then you compare the return you would get on a bond which is taxable to the return on a bond which is not subject to tax. The result is called the *taxable equivalent yield*. This comparison is done by using the following simple formula:

Taxable bond rate $\times$ (1 − your top tax bracket) = Tax-free bond rate

For example, assume that the taxable bond rate is 7 percent and your top tax bracket is 28 percent. The computation would be made as follows:

$$7 \times (1 - .28) =$$

$$7 \times 0.72 = 5.04 \text{ percent}$$

In this example, a taxable yield of 7 percent is equivalent to a tax-free yield of 5.04 percent, if you are in the 28 percent tax bracket. Thus, if you can get more than 5.04 percent on a tax-free bond, the tax-free bond would give you a higher after-tax return than a 7 percent taxable bond.

Brokerage houses or bond funds can provide you with a table that will show tax equivalent yields. Table 9-1 lists tax brackets and inter-

Table 9-1. Taxable Equivalent Yield Table

Federal Marginal Income Tax Bracket	Taxable equivalent yields based on tax-exempt yield of:						
	4%	5%	6%	7%	8%	9%	10%
15%	4.7%	5.9%	7.1%	8.2%	9.4%	10.6%	11.8%
28%	5.6%	6.9%	8.3%	9.7%	11.1%	12.5%	13.9%
31%	5.8%	7.2%	8.7%	10.1%	11.6%	13.0%	14.5%
39%	6.6%	8.2%	9.8%	11.5%	13.1%	14.8%	16.4%

est rates. If, for example, you are in the 39 percent marginal (top) bracket, a 9.8 percent taxable return is equivalent to a 6 percent tax-free return.

The most sophisticated buyers look at the spreads between Treasury bonds and munis to see whether munis are reasonably priced. If they are not, these buyers will purchase Treasuries or other taxable bonds. Treasuries are compared to municipal bonds through ratios. For example, a statement in the paper might read: Yields on long-term high-grade GOs are now almost 90 percent of the yields on long-term Treasury bonds. This is translated into standard English as: If you invested $1000 in a 10 percent, 30-year Treasury bond, you would receive a 10 percent pretax yield. By comparison, a 30-year secure tax-free bond would yield 9 percent. The 90 percent ratio of municipal yield to yield on taxable Treasury bonds is computed as follows: 9/10 = 90 percent. Analysts often consider municipals a good buy when the ratio of municipal bond yield to Treasury bond yield is above 80 percent.

All Your Eggs in One Basket? Out-of-State Yield Comparisons

If you live in a high-tax state like New York or California, it is necessary to compare the yield on an out-of-state bond issue after taxes to the benefit of purchasing a bond issued by a municipality within your state. "Hey," you might say, "I thought municipals were tax-exempt!" Tax laws are never so simple. Most states tax municipal bonds issued by other states, referred to as out-of-state bonds.

All munis are free of federal income tax except for taxable municipal bonds. Most municipal bonds are tax-free within their state of origin, though a few states tax their own bonds. For example, in New York State all bonds issued by the state and any municipality within the state are free of New York tax. When the advertisement says "triple tax-exempt," it means a resident of New York City can buy bonds issued anywhere within New York State and still enjoy the exemption from federal, state, and city taxes.

Bonds issued by the territories of the United States are tax-exempt in all the states. That provision makes the bonds of Puerto Rico particularly desirable despite the risk that Puerto Rico might become independent. Guam and the Virgin Islands bonds are also tax-free in all states.

The Alternative
Minimum Tax

Certain municipal bonds, called AMT bonds, are subject to the federal
alternative minimum tax (AMT), but only for individual investors
whose tax bracket makes them subject to the tax. Bonds that primarily
benefit individuals or private companies, as defined by Congress, are
subject to the AMT. These include certain state agency housing bonds,
industrial development bonds, and resource recovery bonds.

Tip_____

*For investors not subject to the AMT, this may be an opportunity rather
than a burden. AMT bonds yield about 20 to 25 basis points more
than non-AMT bonds, often without any sacrifice of credit quality. AMT
bonds may also prove valuable because their higher yields can
cushion investors from the blow that potential tax reform may deal to the
municipal bond market.*

   Put your accountant to work and see if you can take advantage of
AMT bonds and earn higher returns. Be aware though that these bonds
are less liquid than non-AMT bonds. They are cheaper to buy, but they
will be more expensive and difficult to sell. Consider also whether you
may become subject to the AMT in the future before you buy.

Market Discount—Sounds
Like a Bargain!—Or Is It?

If you were to buy a municipal bond for $900 which has a face value of
$1000 in 10 years, have you found a bargain? The answer is maybe. What
we have here is called a "discount bond" because the bond is sold at a
discount to its face value. The amount of the discount in this case is $100.
   If you bought a zero-coupon muni when it was originally issued at
$600, you would pay no federal income tax on the discount of $400
when the bond came due. This is called the *original issue discount* (OID).
However, if you bought a bond for $900 which was originally issued at
$1000, the $100 discount would be subject to tax when the bond came
due or if you sold it for more than $900 before it came due. This is true
even though we are dealing with a tax-free municipal bond. There are
further complicated rules to determine whether the discount is taxable
as ordinary income or as a capital gain. Remember to ask your broker to

advise you on this point before you buy a discount bond. The discount bond may not be a bargain after you compute the taxes on the discount.

Speaking of Changes: Flat Tax Discussions

There is always talk of changes to the tax code. The latest flap is about doing away with the old complex Internal Revenue code and replacing it with a simplified "flat tax" system. The purpose of the current proposal is to increase incentives for saving and to make the system simple and "fair." The basic idea behind the flat tax is to do away with all deductions, credits, and exemptions and tax everyone's income at the same rate.

Supporters of the flat tax foresee a general overall lowering of taxes by cutting the top tax rates and a freeing up of markets currently fettered by high taxes. For example, investors sitting with large stock market gains would pay less tax under the flat tax system than under the current tax on capital gains. Opponents of the flat tax system say it would be unfair to the middle-income taxpayer and perhaps overly generous to the high-income taxpayer. It would be very complex to institute.

There are many proposed ways of instituting a flat tax. One proposal would impose a single tax rate of 17 percent and eliminate all deductions. Another proposal would tax consumption and exempt from tax all income that is saved. A proposed alternative to that is to do away with the income tax altogether and replace it with a national sales tax.

A flat tax is not a favorable development for municipal bondholders. The market response to these proposals has been to narrow the spread or difference in yield between taxable and tax-free bonds in the 10- to 30-year maturities. Some individual investors took their money out of tax-free mutual funds in the spring of 1995. Municipal bonds did not fully participate in the huge Treasury bond rally in June 1995, as investors considered the implications of possible tax changes.

One possible consequence of these tax changes for the municipalities is to increase their borrowing costs by as much as 2 percent because municipal bonds would become less desirable for tax purposes. In effect, this is another attempt by our federal legislators to pass the buck to the state and local governments. Under the flat tax, municipalities would continue to borrow, but they would issue taxable bonds. The taxable municipal bonds would be eligible for inclusion in pension funds and tax-deferred accounts.

If the flat tax became a reality, the current value of municipal bonds would decline. However in this case, the investor in individual municipal bonds would hold existing short- and intermediate-term bonds until they matured. Ten- to thirty-year bonds purchased in 1995 or later have already taken the flat tax into account in their pricing by providing a higher return than usual as compared to Treasury bonds. Municipal bond fund values will fluctuate more widely as the fortunes of the flat tax wax and wane until a decision is finalized. Full implementation of the flat tax, if enacted, would take years.

Credit Enhancement: Does an Ugly Duckling Become a Beautiful Swan?

Issuers purchase credit enhancements for their bonds because it makes the bonds more attractive to investors. Credit enhancements also reduce the issuers' borrowing costs and make the bonds easier to sell to unsophisticated retail investors. Sophisticated buyers always ask what the rating on an insured bond would be without the insurance. You should ask this question as well. Issuers who come to market frequently often have both insured and uninsured issues outstanding. If the underlying rating is strong, then the investor can rely on the underlying strength of the bond as well as on the insurance for protection. Some bond issuers have only issued insured bonds and have no underlying rating.

Tip_____

A strong A-rated issuer will often forgo insurance, and those bonds may yield more than triple-A insured bonds.

Bond Insurance

Bond insurance is sold by insurance companies, and insurance companies are in business to make money. This may seem like a redundant statement, but it is a fact that few people focus on when they decide to purchase an insured bond with the magic triple-A rating. As *Grant's Municipal Bond Observer* points out, four out of the top five bond insurers are now public companies. Stockholders demand growth. Growth demands expanding markets or new business ventures. The number of new investment-grade municipal issues is not expanding, and the market share for insured bonds is not growing. To satisfy the stock analysts and feed the hungry stockholders with higher stock prices, bond insurers are exploring new ventures in order to increase their business.

The problem with buying only insured bonds is that if an insurance company gets into trouble and its credit rating is downgraded then all the bonds carrying its credit designation will be downgraded as well. As the insurance business gets more competitive, with new entries into the marketplace such as Capital Guaranty Insurance Company (CGIC) and Financial Security Assurance Inc. (FSA), it gets harder for all of them to make a profit. As some of the insurers look elsewhere to increase their profit, they may find that the new areas are not as secure as the municipal bond market. Maintaining that triple-A rating is vital to the ongoing vitality of the insurance company.[5]

AMBAC Indemnity Corporation (formerly, American Municipal Bond Assurance Corporation) began insuring bonds in 1971. Municipal Bond Insurance Association (MBIA) was formed in 1974, and Financial Guaranty Insurance Company (FGIC) was formed soon after. These three companies account for 90 percent of the muni bond insurance market.[6] These insurance companies are composed of consortiums of other insurance companies, which spread the risk.

Bond insurance companies have become very successful. Forty-three percent of all new issues were rated triple-A by Moody's in 1994, and only 11 percent were rated single-A. In 1988 only 29 percent of all new issues were rated triple-A and 20 percent were rated single-A. The great increase in triple-A ratings resulted from more bonds being insured. Bonds rated single-A are no longer plentiful. Insurance converts the lower investment grade bonds to triple-A status.

The single-A-rated bonds yield more than the higher rated bonds. The traders view single-A-rated credits as having little risk. However, it is easier to sell a triple-A rated credit to the retail investors, and it therefore lowers the issuer's costs to insure the bonds.

Tip_____

If you purchase only insured bonds, vary your holdings so that many municipal insurance companies are represented, in order to provide diversity.

[5]Jon Birger, "More Bond Insurance, More Worries for Buyers," *The Bond Buyer*, May 18, 1995, p. 8.
[6]Amy Feldman, "Muni Anxiety," *Forbes*, August 15, 1994, p. 74.

The individual investor is fortunate that his concern about the strength of the bond insurance companies is matched by the concerns of the municipal bond funds. Funds that hold triple-A-rated single-state funds, such as Pennsylvania or California Tax-Free Funds, would see the value of their portfolios decline dramatically if an insurer were to lose its triple-A rating. Other corporate entities, such as banks and insurance companies, are also large holders of municipal bonds. To prevent a downgrade of one of the major bond insurers, corporate entities might step up to help the insurer if there were a threat of a downgrade in order to protect the value of their own investments. It is a comfort to know that the big guys are looking over each other's shoulders.

The effects of a downgrade on an insurer is illustrated by the downgrade of Fuji Bank. Fuji Bank was the biggest provider of letters of credit (LOC) to the municipal market. The LOC is a commitment by a bank to pay principal and interest if an issuer is unable to meet its bond obligations. It is frequently used as a means of increasing the credit-worthiness of short-term borrowing, such as commercial paper, industrial development bonds, and housing bond issues. Fuji Bank's assets deteriorated in quality and value due to the substantial decline of property values in Japan in the early 1990s. Standard & Poor's lowered the bank's rating, resulting in a downgrade of $9.5 billion municipal debt. The bond traders' reaction was to devalue the bonds that Fuji insured. This decline in the insured bonds' value hurt bond traders, bond fund shareholders, and individuals who planned to sell their insured bonds.

Most bonds, if insured, are insured when they are first issued. There are some bonds which are insured after they have been sold. Here is how it works. A brokerage house buys uninsured bonds, stores them for the life of the bond in a depository trust company, and buys insurance. This procedure increases the value of the bonds. The bonds are then sold to new buyers. Since the certificates cannot be removed from the vault, the buyer can only receive a *depository receipt.* This receipt looks like a bond and acts like a bond. It is a receipt which says you own the bond. You can use the receipt to sell your security to any brokerage house or individual, and the buyer will receive interest payments in the mail as if she were holding a registered bond.

Insured bonds, though rated triple-A, do not trade at the same price as bonds which are rated triple-A based upon the financial strength of the issuer in its own right. Instead, insured bonds trade between a single-A and a double-A credit.

As you can see from Table 9-2, the yield on triple-A insured bonds is higher than the return on double-A bonds and lower than the return on single-A bonds. This trading relationship is the same on the shorter and

Table 9-2. Municipal Market Data: General Obligation Yields

Year	AAA	AAA (Insured)	AA	A
1996	3.65%	3.8%	3.75%	3.85%
2001	4.5%	4.65%	4.6%	4.75%
2006	5%	5.15%	5.1%	5.25%
2011	5.45%	5.6%	5.55%	5.7%
2016	5.65%	5.8%	5.75%	5.9%

SOURCE: *The Bond Buyer*, June 15, 1995, p. 29.

longer maturities. This table mirrors the traders' view that the abundance of insured bonds in the marketplace makes them less desirable than the relatively scarce triple-A bonds that reflect the superior strength of the issuer.

Alternative Forms of Private Insurance: Deep Pockets

Private insurance often reaches into the deepest pockets, those of Mother Earth. The Texas Permanent School Fund taps the production of the oil and gas reserves, on land set aside for schools back in 1854, to insure local school district bonds. Rated triple-A by all the rating agencies, the fund enables smaller and weaker districts to tap the bond market at low cost. Due to the depth and breadth of its reserves, it is a well-respected insurer. It is not as widely known, since it only backs the bonds of Texas school districts. Due to its success, Oklahoma and Wyoming have plans to imitate the structure of the Texas Permanent School Fund.

Other states have chosen different models to enhance their debt. Minnesota has a School District Credit Program begun in 1993. It uses a standing appropriation from the state's general fund to enhance local school bonds to the double-A level. This is not GO debt. Michigan, New Jersey, and Virginia have similarly structured debt.

Pension funds have begun to use their ability to leverage to enhance bonds. Oregon Public Employees' Retirement System issued a guarantee on a $50 million taxable Port of Portland issue. California State Teachers' Retirement Fund is also considering backing bonds with a credit enhancement and liquidity program.

Lessons about Bond Insurance

- Bond insurance adds a level of comfort.

- Bond insurers are only as good as their asset base.

- Bond insurers can overextend.

- Owners of insured bonds can see the value of their bonds reduced if the insurer is downgraded. Diversify by insurer.

- To ensure portfolio safety, diversify your portfolio by issuer and maturity as well as by insurer.

- Diversify by issuer.

- All investments have risk! Not investing is also a risk!

Safe! Safe! Safe!—
Pre-refunded Bonds

Perhaps the most desirable form of security enhancement is when a bond is escrowed or pre-refunded. This occurs when U.S. government bonds, U.S. agency bonds, or other obligations are purchased by a municipal issuer and placed in an escrow account at a bank for the sole purpose of meeting the interest and principal requirements of its outstanding municipal bonds. A municipal obligation so backed by Treasury bonds is the safest municipal bond investment available. In the trade, they are called pre-refunded bonds or pre-rees. These bonds are priced to the first call date and will be redeemed on that date. Escrowed bonds are priced to their maturity date.

Pre-refunded bonds are redeemed on the first call date, sometimes at par and sometimes at a premium. The redemption price is based upon the original call price set in the bond indenture. Bonds which are purchased after they have been pre-refunded are priced to the pre-refund date, which is the first call date. These bonds may be listed on your brokerage statement by their original maturity even though they have been pre-refunded. That is because the identity of the bond is still based upon that date.

If you purchase a bond which is pre-refunded after you purchased it, the bond's value increases and its maturity is shortened. If you decided to sell it, it would be worth more because the maturity is shorter and it now has triple-A quality. The bad news is that you will not be able to hold that high stream of income to maturity.

In contrast, an escrowed bond increases in value and can be held until maturity. There have been instances of escrowed bonds being called early. This is an unusual but disturbing occurrence. Usually escrowed bonds have all calls voided. That is, the right to call the bonds has been terminated when the bonds were escrowed.

The downside of pre-refunded bonds is that they usually sell at hefty premiums to the face value of the bond. Bonds are pre-refunded when interest rates have declined from the high cost of original issuance. That means that pre-rees can sell for prices as high as $1400 per $1000 bond, depending upon the original issue rate and the prevailing yield-to-maturity rate.

Some bonds are pre-refunded but not rerated by the rating agencies. Those bonds do not have the stamp of approval of an outside agency, verifying that everything has been done the way it was supposed to have been done. Should you buy those bonds? The escrow agreement may not meet the specifications of the rating agencies because it has been funded with securities which do not match their specifications. Everything may work out just fine, and then again.... Does the extra yield justify the risk?

Guarantees Are Not Always What They Seem

State guarantees do not represent the full faith and credit of the state in support of the bonds in the same way that bond insurance does. State guarantees may be a partial guarantee to help regain solvency, or they may be activated after a time if the issuer fails to resolve a default situation.

Federal Housing Administration (FHA) insurance provides default insurance that covers most, but not all, of the costs of a default of hospital bonds. It is important, therefore, to consider the strength of the hospital as if it were not insured. The incomplete coverage is reflected in a double-A rating on FHA insured bonds.

Insurance Is Not Always Forever

Banks can issue letters of credit (LOCs) on municipal bonds. They provide protection to municipal bondholders similar to the protection provided by insurance companies. The LOC is only as good as the bank's credit rating, which is carefully guarded by the banks. If a bond issuer defaults, the bank will usually retire an issue immediately. LOCs usually run for 10 years or less. They may not run for the life of the bond.

What happens, you may ask, if the LOC runs for 7 years, and the bond matures in 10 years? At the termination of the LOC, the issuer would have to find a new form of credit enhancement. If the issuer were unsuccessful, then the bond would be rerated to reflect the strength of the issuer at that time. The value of the bond would be based on the issuer's own credit strength and the number of years left before redemption.

Tip_____

Find out the specific terms when you rely on insurance and LOCs.

Joined Together: Municipal Bond Banks and Bond Pools

To reduce costs of information and borrowing, small municipal issuers borrow through bond banks and bond pools. School districts, states, school building authorities, and counties sometimes pool their borrowing needs and float one large issue. A bond pool can offer larger issues that attract more institutional bidders and reduce the risk of holding debt of small and often unrated issues.

The bond bank sells bonds, using the proceeds to purchase the debt issued by the local government units. The bond bank debt is secured by payments made by local government units in addition to one or more of the following reserve funds: full faith and credit of the municipality, lien on state grants-in-aid, and the state's moral obligation. States that have adopted bond banks include Vermont, Maine, Alaska, North Dakota, and New Hampshire.

State and sometimes county school building authorities raise money for school construction. The new schools are leased to the communities until the bonds are repaid, at which time the local district acquires them. Pennsylvania, Georgia, and Maine use this method extensively. The Virginia Public School Authority operates similarly, but funds come from the state school construction fund as well as bond revenues.

Investment pools gained notoriety after Orange County, California, declared bankruptcy in 1994 as a result of its investment pool's failed gamble in risky derivative securities. Municipal issuers in Ohio, Wisconsin, and Florida also suffered substantial losses. Investment pools do not have the same credit backing as the bond bank. Orange County bet that interest rates would move down when they moved up. Other investment pools immediately became suspect, but they did not suffer losses as great as Orange County, and they have not sought protection under the bankruptcy code.

One notable loss was suffered by the Wisconsin State Investment Fund. It pools money from the state and over 1000 local issuers. In March 1995, officials announced that there had been a loss of $95 million as a result of swaps based on European and Mexican interest rates. An audit found that swaps were used to increase yields, not to limit risk. The strategy failed when the Mexican government devalued the peso and increased interest rates. Attempts to cover the loss led to further losses. Many other investment pools immediately moved to reduce their risky investments, and many local governments reduced the size of their accounts in response to the disaster.

Questions and Questions: Where Are the Answers?

The J. J. Kenny Wire and the Bloomberg Wire are both sources of information about bonds. The brokers rely on the wires, or electronically transmitted information, to give timely information about the nature of each offering. The wire services give all the pertinent information about a bond—when it was issued, if it is insured, what the call features and extraordinary calls are, how many bonds were issued, and so on. If you have a concern about a bond you are purchasing, you can ask the broker for a printout on your bond.

In the past, it has been difficult to find out information about municipal bonds. The primary sources of information were the rating agencies, which rated new issues of bonds. However, information was not generally available to the public about ongoing events in a municipality. In 1995, the SEC established secondary market disclosure rules. That means that issuers will have to update the key financial and operating information in their official statements for new bond offerings. They will also have to provide information about "material events," events which might affect the ability of the issuer to meet its obligations. This information will be housed in national repositories, and in state repositories where they exist, and will be available to any investor who requests it.[7]

Information about new offerings is usually posted in the newspapers. Descriptions of the main features of a new issue, known as *tombstones*, are published in the financial press. Innovators from the Illinois Development Finance Authority decided to be the first to announce their offering on the Internet in 1995. The Internet source provided a table of contents of the information available and how to get a statement, which is the official

---

[7]Jon Birger, "Market Braces Itself for New Disclosure Rules," *The Bond Buyer*, May 4, 1995, p. 8.

TABLE OF CONTENTS

Figure 9-1. Offering statement table of contents.

offering document. Whether this will increase buyer interest remains to be seen.[8]

Every new issue must have an offering statement. It lays out all the issues which might affect the payment of the bonds. It includes the legal opinion and the financial statement of the issuer. If you have not purchased bonds before, or if you are planning on purchasing bonds from a frequent issuer or in a new region, it would be helpful for you to read

[8]Chris Carmody, "Munis Go Internet: Chicago Bank Posts Details on Offering," *The Bond Buyer,* May 19, 1995, p. 23.

Published every weekday except Saturdays and Holidays by
Standard & Poor's, 65 Broadway, New York, N.Y. 10006
Telephone 212 770-4300   FAX 212 425-6864

The Blue List is a registered trademark of Standard & Poor's.   Printed in U.S.A.

+ Items so marked did not appear in the previous issue of The Blue List.
# Prices so marked are changed from the previous issue.
o Items so marked are reported to have call or option features.

ALABAMA

AMT. M	SECURITY	PURPOSE	RATE	MATURITY	YIELD OR PRICE	OFFERED BY
10	ALABAMA HSG FIN AUTH	MULTI FAM	6.000	05/01/97	4.00	STERNEAG
950	ALABAMA MENTAL HEALTH FIN AUTH	MBIA	5.000	05/01/05	4.90	RAYJAMNY
5	ALABAMA MENTAL HEALTH FIN AUTH	P/R @ 102	7.375	05/01/08 C99	4.75	SEELAUS
225	ALABAMA ST IND. ACCESS RD &		8.000	08/01/13	100	SEIDOWA
145	BIRMINGHAM ALA ARPT AUTH ARPT	PKG WTS AMT	5.750	06/01/18	6.00	BKSOUTH
		AMBAC	5.250	07/01/14	5.85	HOUGHMAG
10	BIRMINGHAM ALA ARPT AUTH ARPT (CA @ 102)	AMBAC	5.250	07/01/14 C03	5.50	STOEVERG
30	BIRMINGHAM ALA MED CLINIC BRD	S/F 00	8.300	07/01/08 ETM	6.20	EMMET
15	BIRMINGHAM ALA SPL CARE FACS	P/R @ 102	7.000	08/01/09 C99	4.25	STERNEAG
1000	BOAZ ALA ELDERLY HSG CORP MTG	MBIA	6.000	07/01/23 C04	6.25	MORKGEAL
20	CITRONELLE ALA UTLS BRD NAT	S/F 01	8.000	08/01/09 ETM	6.00	FANU
40	CITRONELLE ALA UTLS BRD WTR	S/F 95	8.300	12/01/13 ETM	6.70	EMMET
45	EAST ALA HEALTH CARE AUTH	MBIA	5.250	09/01/23	6.10	RICKELGA
30	FAIRFIELD ALA INDL DEV BRD	US STEEL TAXABLE	10.300	12/01/08	100 3/8	WENERAB
65	GUIN ALA	BK.QD	9.500	08/01/08	9.00	STERLING
75	HOOVER ALA		8.500	02/01/08	4.75	STERNEAG
15	HOOVER ALA BRD ED SPL TAX SCH	P/R @ 102	8.700	02/01/13 C01	4.60	STERNEAG

ALABAMA - CONTINUED

AMT. M	SECURITY	PURPOSE	RATE	MATURITY	YIELD OR PRICE	OFFERED BY
1950	HOUSTON CNTY ALA HOSP BRD	CA 02 @ 100	7.625	04/01/07 ETM	5.75	EMMET
50	HUNTSVILLE ALA SOLID WASTE		7.000	10/01/14	5.45	MONARCH
40	JACKSONVILLE ALA HEALTH CARE	Y/M 6.67	7.625	04/01/08	6.40	CREWASSC
25	JEFFERSON CNTY ALA	P/R @ 102	6.875	01/01/10 C00	6.40	STERNEAG
10	JEFFERSON CNTY ALA BRD ED CAP (CA @ 102)	AMBAC	5.00	02/15/12 C03	5.80	STOEVERG
290			4.300	09/01/99	100	
380			4.400	09/01/00	100	
545	MADISON CNTY ALA BRD ED	BK.QD	4.500	09/01/01	100	SYN. .424
525			4.550	09/01/02	4.80	
315			4.600	09/01/03	4.70	
420			4.700	09/01/04	4.80	
	SUNTRUST DWARTL.					
20	MARENGO CNTY ALA PORT AUTH	INSD	0.000	07/01/05	7.20	RICKELFL
190	MARENGO CNTY ALA PORT AUTH		0.000	03/01/19	7.60	CARTYCOM

VOLUME 240. NUMBER 45

TUESDAY SEPTEMBER 5, 1995

Figure 9-2. The Blue List. *(Reproduced by permission of the Blue List, Standard & Poor's)*

about the problems confronting the issuer. The offering statement must list all the potential horribles, even if the likelihood of any of them occurring is very small. You will probably not be able to get an offering statement for the issue you would like to buy because by the time it could be sent to you the bonds would have been sold. However, you can get a good feel for the issuer by reading a prior offering statement.

New issues are sold in the primary market. Bonds which are offered for resale are sold in the secondary market. The Blue List (see Fig. 9-2) is a daily list of municipal bond offerings. It is available to brokers through their computers and in hard copy. If your broker does not have what you are looking for in the house inventory, the broker will search the Blue List for an offering to show you. The trader will buy the offering and then resell it to you. At times of high demand and low inventory, a flip through the Blue List shows just how scarce municipal offerings can be.

A new service geared to help individuals obtain price information about their bonds is sponsored by Standard & Poor's and the Public Securities Association. In cooperation with J. J. Kenny, they will provide the buyer with a "price evaluation" similar to the evaluations on some brokerage statements. It is not a market quote, since that is only available from brokers who are interested in purchasing your bonds. The degree to which the prices reflect market prices will vary based upon the frequency with which an issue trades and the size of the bond lot. Pricing is based on the assumption that the block of bonds is $1 million. Odd-lot trading prices may vary widely. For more information call 1-800-BOND-INFO.

10
Corporate Bonds Including Junk Bonds

What Are Corporate Bonds?

Corporate bonds are simply those bonds that are issued by corporations. The corporate issuers are generally divided into four categories. The categories often help to define the risk that you take when you buy corporate bonds.

The first and largest category of corporate issuers is public utilities. This category includes electric power companies, gas companies, and telephone companies. Examples of utilities include AT&T, Duke Power, and Consolidated Edison Company of New York. Historically, the utilities have been considered very stable and generally safe investments. However, the world is swiftly changing. Electric utilities have become much riskier because their monopoly power has been broken by new laws fostering competition. As a consequence many utilities will become stronger, many will become weaker, and some will be bought by new owners.

The second category of corporate issuers is transportation companies such as airlines and railroads. Many years ago railroads were among the strongest issuers. Over the years they have all become weaker and many have gone bankrupt. The airlines had been strong credits until the government deregulated the airline industry. This led to many credit downgrades, takeovers, and bankruptcies.

The third category of corporate issuers is industrial companies which includes the major retailers such as Sears and the major manufacturing companies such as General Motors, Ford, and Chrysler Corporation. Their fortunes rise and fall as consumer purchasing varies with the economic times.

The fourth category of corporate issuers is financial institutions— banks, finance companies, and brokerage houses. Both foreign and domestic banks issue corporate bonds. American banks such as Citibank, BankAmerica, and NationsBank are frequent issuers. The German-based Deutsche Bank is an example of a foreign issuer that issues bonds denominated in U.S. dollars. General Motors Acceptance Corporation (GMAC) and Ford Motor Credit are both strong finance companies that finance the sale of cars and other items. GMAC is wholly owned by General Motors, and Ford Motor Credit is wholly owned by Ford. Brokerage house bonds—such as those issued by Merrill Lynch; Smith Barney; Bear, Stearns; and Salomon Brothers—also fall into this category.

No matter what corporate sector a bond is in, the bonds are either secured by collateral or unsecured. A secured bond means that the issuer has granted to bondholders a first claim on specific assets if the corporation is unable to pay its debt. Examples of secured bonds are mortgage bonds, collateral trust bonds, and equipment trust certificates. If you see one of these names in the title of a bond, you know that you have a secured bond. A title might be Duke Power, First Mortgage Bonds. This means that the issuer, Duke Power, a utility company, is issuing a bond that is secured by a first mortgage on certain of its property.

All corporate bonds that are not secured are unsecured. Unsecured bonds are called *debentures.* Don't be impressed by this name. It means unsecured. Does it make sense to buy an unsecured debenture rather than a secured bond? Yes, it does. Unsecured bonds issued by General Motors or AT&T are safer than a secured bond of a weaker company. Thus, the security backing a bond is just one factor to consider. The overall rating of the bond and its other features are also considerations.

Notes are a kind of debenture. They are not as liquid as other debentures because they are part of smaller, less widely held issues. Notes should therefore yield more than other bond debentures to compensate for their decreased liquidity.

Tip_____

Prices of corporate bonds in the same sector are whacked by any bad news affecting the sector. Diversify your bond holdings by sector.

The Importance of Bond Sectors

Bond sectors are of more than theoretical interest to bond buyers. Bad news affecting one issuer in a sector can affect the pricing of all the bonds in the market sector. For example, a class-action suit brought against one cigarette company may send the bond prices of other cigarette manufacturers reeling. President Clinton's announcement of further restrictions on cigarette advertising dropped bond prices significantly.

At any one time, bonds with the highest yields tend to cluster in one sector—the one with the most problems at the time. Those bonds are the ones being dumped by the institutional traders. In 1995, for example, big losses in derivatives trading hit the financial sector. Suits ensued against Merrill Lynch and Bankers Trust among others. Piper Jaffray suffered financial losses as it tried to protect the owners of its mutual funds who suffered sizable losses. Others, like Askin Capital, went bankrupt. On another front, Prudential suffered huge financial losses from suits for illegally selling limited partnerships. All those suits threaten the financial bottom line and the corresponding security of the bondholders.

Events that are positive for the stockholder may be neutral or negative for the bondholder. The takeover of one company by another also tends to go in waves. Takeovers may be unfavorable for bondholders but increase the price of the stock. If the purchasing company had a good credit rating but assumed a lot of debt to acquire the target company, the rating agencies might downgrade its bonds. It may also be favorable if the purchasing company has a higher credit rating than the target company. Likewise stock buybacks may be either neutral or negative for the bondholder. If the stock buyback weakens the financial strength of the company, then it is negative for the bondholder.

Tip_____

Most bondholders look for solidity and steadiness. Bonds provide the soft padding in the fluctuating economic cycles.

When Are Corporate Bonds Right for You?

When should you buy corporate bonds? The answer is only in certain situations. While corporate bonds always yield more than Treasury and agency bonds, they are never as secure because corporations are businesses and do not have the unlimited power to raise money as does the U.S. Treasury.

Corporate bonds owned by individuals generally are subject to more taxes than any other type of bond. Except in very limited situations, the interest from all corporate bonds is subject to federal, state, and local tax. Treasury and agency bonds are both subject to federal income tax. However, all Treasury and some agency bonds are not subject to state and local tax, which would make them better buys for someone in a high-tax state. The interest from municipal bonds is free of federal income tax and sometimes free of state and local tax as well. Individuals buy corporate bonds in tax-deferred accounts such as IRAs or 401(k) plans, where the interest on the accounts accrues free of all taxes until distributed.

There are only three situations in which buying corporate bonds makes sense:

- If you are in the 15 percent federal income tax bracket and your state tax bracket is low.

- If the yield on corporate bonds is high enough to offset the tax benefits of municipal bonds and Treasury bonds *and* you have taken the time to evaluate the risks of the corporate bond.

- If you are investing in an IRA or other tax-sheltered account such as a pension plan or a 401(k) plan.

Since corporate bonds provide no tax advantages or credit advantages, the only reason to buy corporate bonds rather than other bonds is to get a higher yield. Traders price corporate bonds in relation to Treasury bonds. Every trading day the price and yield of Treasury bonds fluctuates up and down. Price and yield, you remember, always move in tandem but in opposite directions. As the price goes up, the yield goes down, and vice versa. For example, a newly issued American Express note issued in August 1995 was priced at 40 basis points over the corresponding Treasury of a similar maturity. If you know that the spread is 40 basis points over the corresponding Treasury, you can look at the Treasury yield in the same maturity, add 40 basis points and have an idea about the value of the bond. Thus, if the Treasury bond is yielding 6 percent, the American Express note would yield 6.40 percent.

This knowledge can help you negotiate the price. The price and yield you will actually get depends on how many bonds you are buying, what the trader paid for them, and whether the trader has market indigestion, that is, holds too many of these bonds. Since the corporate market is mainly an institutional market, where a round lot is $5 million, you will not be able to get the same price as the institutional trader unless you are buying a new issue. In a new issue, the issuer pays the broker's fee.

The spread on corporate bonds over Treasuries is not fixed in stone. It is based on *price discovery*. The trader must figure out what a bond is worth based on any new information about the industry and the specific corporation that issued the bond. The trader takes all changes into account when repricing a bond issue. This takes time to discover, especially on less liquid issues.

The less frequently a bond is traded, the longer the time it takes to complete the price discovery. Therefore, the less frequently a bond is traded, the greater the price spread. The average institutional holding is $2 million to $3 million. If the size of the bond issue is $200 million, there could be 30 to 60 holders of a bond. The bond doesn't trade very often. Many bonds trade once a week or even once a month. Each week there is new information about the economy and the industry as well as possible changes in the corporation. A trader can follow only a very narrow range of securities. The more time it takes him to price a bond, the higher the spreads are going to be.

Buying bonds on the New York Exchanges might appear to provide the solution, but it is only a partial one at best. Bond values are based on what someone is willing to pay. Since bonds are infrequently offered for sale, traders sometimes post bonds on the exchange in order to get a fix on their value. They may not actually be for sale at all. Prices that show up in the *Wall Street Journal* and other financial presses may not accurately reflect the value of the bonds in the market. If less than $1 million is traded, the price is suspect. The usual reported trade is less than $100,000. The number of issues traded is usually below 400. If there is a lot of volume, then the price is probably more accurate. The volume numbers on the New York Stock Exchange transactions are very important. If there is no volume, then the price doesn't mean anything. Assume there were 10 odd lots for sale and each one was priced slightly higher than the next. If you bought 3 of the 10 odd lots, you might be the engine driving the price rise. Even in institutional trades there are big spreads.

Reading the Bond Tables

Any broker can sell you corporate bonds. As with most bonds, there are two markets. There is a primary market for new issues and a secondary market for previously issued outstanding bonds. There are two ways to buy and sell corporate bonds. The first is on the exchange for secondary market trading. Daily trades are listed in the *Wall Street Journal* and *New York Times* and many other daily newspapers under the caption "New York Exchange Bonds." Trading reported in the New York Exchange Bonds column is mostly for small trades.

The larger trades are done dealer to dealer in the "over-the-counter" market. Individual trades are the smallest part of the $1.8 trillion corporate bond market, of which individuals own about $200 billion directly. Institutional investors do the bulk of the trades, such as mutual funds and pension plans. Dealers in the over-the-counter market do most of the trading in corporate bonds because these dealers have the large capital required to assume the risk of buying and selling large blocks of bonds for their own accounts. The average trade for the individual investor is about 20 bonds or $20,000.

The New York Exchange Bonds table shows the number of bonds traded, the closing price, the net change from the prior day, and the current yield. There are a number of abbreviations explained in the box called "Explanatory Notes." In September 1995 an AT&T bond is listed as follows:

ATT 7 3/4 07 Cur Yld 7.3 Vol 56 Close 105½ Net Chg. − ½

Decoding the description, here is what we find out:

- The full description of the bond: The AT&T bond has a coupon of $7\frac{3}{4}$ percent and comes due in 2007. Notice that there are a lot of pieces of information not presented, such as whether the bond has any calls or a sinking fund, the credit rating, and whether the bond has any collateral securing it. This information is available from the bond guides published by Moody's or Standard & Poor's, or from your broker.

- The current yield (Cur Yld) is 7.3 percent. The more significant yield-to-maturity is not presented because bond calls complicate the picture. The current yield can be misleading. The novice bond investor tends to view this yield as "the yield" that is quoted among brokers. When the 30-year Treasury is selling around 6 percent, this bond looks great. The only way to know is to do further investigation.

- The volume (Vol) shows that 56 bonds or $56,000 of this bond issue were traded.

- The paper lists closing price for the day at 105½, or $1,055 per bond.

- The change from the closing price on the previous day is off ½. This means that the closing price the prior day had been 106. If you owned $10,000 of this bond, the value of your bonds declined by $50.

The New York Exchange Bond table reports the bonds traded that day on the New York Stock Exchange and American Stock exchanges. There are no price listings for untraded bonds. Thus, if you own a particular bond, you will not find it listed for a day that it did not trade.

You can ask your broker for the last bid and asked prices for corporate bonds listed on the New York Bond Exchange. The *bid* is the price that a broker or other buyer will pay for the bond. The *asked* or *offer* is the price that a broker or other seller wants for the bond. For example, a bond might be 99.5 bid and 99.785 asked. If you *sell* the bond, you'll receive the *lower* bid price, and if you *buy* the bond, you'll purchase it for the *higher* asked price.

Brokerage firms that own bonds adjust the spreads. Factors entering into the pricing include the size of the bond lot, the demand and availability of the bond, and the amount the broker needs to cover the trade.

If you can't get enough extra yield to compensate for the risks of owning corporate bonds, you should not buy them. When corporations are prosperous, as they are now, the spread between Treasuries and corporates is historically narrow. For example in mid-1995, a highly rated corporate bond yielded only about 0.5 percent more than a Treasury bond of the same maturity. Many traders feel this is insufficient compensation for the risks. Years ago the yield spread between Treasuries and corporates was 1 percent or even 1.5 percent. When a recession or other traumatic events occur and market participants become worried, there is a flight to quality. At this time, the spreads between corporates and Treasuries will widen. Treasury and agency bonds become more desirable because of the perceived risks to corporations.

Event Risk and the Making of Junk (High-Yield) Bonds

Large corporations in America have historically been financially strong and stable over the last 50 years. There were always companies that got into financial difficulties and had their bond rating downgraded. Companies near or in bankruptcy reorganized and restructured to rise again. If the reorganization efforts failed, the company's assets were sold to pay off the creditors.

The term *junk bonds* originated in the mid-1970s to describe the bonds of well-established corporations that had fallen on hard times. These so-called "fallen angels" were corporations whose earnings had fallen far enough that there was a sufficient possibility of default on their bonds. However, the more recent junk bonds come from newly issued debt that represents a source of capital for emerging or continuing growth companies. Corporate raiders in the 1980s used junk bonds as a way to finance hostile takeovers.

Traders used the terms *junk* and *high-yield* interchangeably. If you are selling below-investment-grade paper, it is much more attractive if it is called *high-yield.* If you lost money through a bankruptcy, you would call it *junk.*

A bond can be a high-yield bond when it is purchased, or it can be downgraded to junk status as a result of event risks. A letter of credit backing a bond might expire and be replaced with one less favorable for the bondholders. A solid company might be acquired and then burdened with debt in order to finance the acquisition of other financial enterprises. These events cannot be predicted in advance. The result is a decline in the rating of a bond with the attendant increase in the bondholder's risk of not getting paid interest or principal when due.

It is not just takeovers that create event risk and junk bonds. Often in the 1980s, companies turned their own highly rated bonds into junk bonds by paying a large one-time dividend to their shareholders. There were often two reasons for this: to enhance shareholder value and to prevent a takeover. Corporate management chose to ignore the concerns of its bondholders in the process. Standard & Poor's devised "event risk covenant rankings" to create awareness of takeover possibilities. E1 represents the highest risk and E5 the lowest risk.

Up until 1990 junk bonds were good investments because the default rate had been low and they really were high-yield bonds. As a result of this favorable experience, the difference in the yield between Treasury bonds and high-yield bonds narrowed. However, partly as a result of the recession in 1990–1991 the junk-bond market became unglued, resulting in $53 billion in defaults, or nearly 18 percent of the junk bond market. The massive defaults in 1990–1991 caused the spread between Treasury and junk bonds to widen considerably. BB-rated junk bonds yielded about 2.7 percent more than Treasury bonds and CCC-rated bonds yielded almost 9 percent more than Treasury bonds. By the end of 1990, spreads between the lowest-rated junk bonds and Treasuries reached 12 percent. Many low-rated junk bonds declined in price by 60 percent to 70 percent.

The causes of the crash of the junk-bond market in 1990 are easy to identify. The oversight of the SEC forced Drexel Burnham Lambert, Inc., the primary market maker in junk bonds out of the market. It later went bankrupt. Government regulators who were cleaning up the savings and loan bank mess required the banks to dump their junk bonds. The recession of 1990–1991 caused more pain.

As interest rates declined substantially in 1993 and 1994 investors again reached for higher returns. They began to buy junk bonds again. The buying narrowed the spreads again between Treasury bonds and junk bonds. On BB-rated bonds the return averaged about 2.6 percent more than on Treasury bonds. Junk bonds provide high returns as compared to investment-grade bonds. High rewards accompany high risk. At times like this you have to decide whether you are being compensated for taking the extra risk. One way to make this decision is to consider the number of extra dollars you would receive each year from an investment in junk bonds as compared to an investment in Treasury bonds.

Tip

Bear in mind that the ratings by the major rating agencies are good predictors of the likelihood of default risk. Martin S. Fridson, the chief high-yield strategist at Merrill Lynch, has stated that Moody's and Standard & Poor's have accurately gauged aggregate default risk. He has found that the lower the ratings were, the greater the likelihood of bankruptcy. Though there are many bottom fishers, even the most careful are bound to get burned.

Evaluating Ratings on High-Yield Bonds

The ratings of corporate bonds are very tightly structured for the highest grade bonds. The qualifications for a triple-A bond are very clear and very narrow. As the ratings get lower, the parameters become wider. At the double-B level two companies can be rated the same. They may both fall within the same standards. What may differentiate them is that the *momentum for change* is different for the two bonds. The momentum for change can be underestimated or change speed after the rating. The double-B rating is a good indicator of a default possibility if change is going in the wrong direction.

The rating agencies are slow to upgrade a bond from double-B status to an investment grade of triple-B. When a bond is upgraded, there is usually a jump in value. Pension funds and mutual funds seek out new issues to include in their portfolios. Funds frequently have restrictions so that they must purchase all or a percentage of their bonds with a minimum investment-grade rating. There also may be restrictions on the percentage of their portfolio that any bond issue can represent. Once the rating agency upgrades a bond to investment grade there are many more prospective buyers due to the dearth of investment-grade bonds. The price spreads are lower for the better investment-grade bonds.

The yield on junk bonds is mainly affected by credit issues. The price of junk bonds generally does not respond to the movement of interest rates in the same way as better credits. Treasury yields might change, but yields on junk bonds may not move or will move only fractionally. Only investment-grade corporate bonds move in relation to the Treasury yield curve. Traders value junk bonds principally on price discovery. This is logical since the principal risk of junk bonds is not interest rate risk but the risk of default. As the prospects of the company improve and the risk of default is reduced, the value of the bond will increase.

The high returns on junk bonds accurately reflect the thin market for these bonds that makes them expensive to trade. If you are an odd-lot buyer, you might do well as long as you can hold your bonds until they come due. Individual investors should buy new issues and actively traded issues to hold until maturity.

Some people make a lot of money trading junk bonds. These are frequently individuals who are retired and have time to really follow the bankruptcy proceedings. They make a bet on the reorganization. Some of the participants in the bankruptcy just want to get out. A lot of bonds trade at the bottom of a bankruptcy. At that time, the bonds trade at 10 cents to 15 cents on the dollar. If the bet pays off, there can be a return of 40 cents to 50 cents on the dollar. This is not for the faint of heart. This is not for the average person. Distressed investing is very difficult.

Corporations used to go into bankruptcy because they were overleveraged. The business was essentially sound. There were many assets. Now when a business goes bankrupt, it is more likely an empty shell. For example, a typewriter manufacturer suddenly finds that it is a technological dinosaur. It has no core business. It has no legs. Reorganization will not solve its operating problems. In contrast a company like Schwinn was overleveraged as a result of a leveraged buyout, but it was selling bicycles at a record pace. It had positive momentum. To buy bonds of a corporation with positive momentum, the buyer must figure out if there is a business there. Nobody knows the price, not even the dealer. Anyone who can acquire the information can be in the game.

High-Yield Corporate Bond Funds

If you anticipate selling your bonds and still want to gamble on junk bonds, purchase a high-yield bond fund. The funds have the research capabilities to investigate the issues and the size to provide for liquidity in the event of redemptions. In times of crisis, the junk bond funds that reach for the highest returns may have the most loses because they will find it difficult to sell the lowest-rated junk bonds. This will expose them to possible problems if the fund experiences large redemptions.

You may buy these funds for the yield, but you may lose capital. The net asset value of the funds may not be accurate. The bonds are priced daily based on a price matrix rather than on actual trades provided by traders. This can result in a nasty surprise, as happened with funds holding mortgage securities and derivatives. The market had moved, but the matrix was not adjusted quickly enough to keep abreast of the changes. This is true of all bonds, but especially true of below-investment-grade bonds. Since they may not trade for days or weeks, the prices are based on a series of guesses.

Buying high-yield funds might be part of a strategy. For example, if you expect interest rates to rise, the high-yield sector might be better than long-term Treasuries because the maturities in the high-yield funds are about 7 years. There would be greater volatility in the Treasury bond fund holding 30-year bonds than in the high-yield fund with an average maturity of 7 years. In the high-yield fund, however, you have to deal with the possibility of defaults.

In any bond fund, stay away from funds that churn (or frequently buy and sell the same) bonds. A lot of trading will not produce better results. Churning is a very expensive activity. The fund would get whacked on the spreads between the buy and the sell.

Look at the portfolio. If it is overweighted with a lot of small issues, then it is not as strong as a portfolio with fewer large name issuers. Absolute size of the revenues and assets is a big factor in the outcome of a bankruptcy. There are more assets to sell to satisfy the debts. The smaller issuer has fewer options and the situation becomes dicey more quickly. Always buy the bonds of the bigger revenue issuer. Credit analysts take size into account when formulating a rating. The rating companies recognize the strength in the larger issuer.

A Review of Calls and Sinking Funds

A call is the right of the issuer to redeem or call in the entire amount of bonds outstanding prior to maturity of the bonds. Most corporate issues have one or more calls. There are generally more calls in corporate bonds than in municipal bonds. The reason for a call is to allow the issuer to refinance its debt at a lower interest rate. This is exactly what the bondholders do not want. If interest rates have declined and the issuer calls in the bonds, the investor has to reinvest in another bond at a lower rate. If interest rates go up, the issuer will not call in the bond. Thus, if there are onerous call provisions, it is heads the issuer wins or tails the investor loses. Bonds with lots of calls should pay more yield to the investor.

Tip_____

A bond that has a stated call is usually callable every six months thereafter until maturity. Although the broker tells you that the bond has a call on June 15, 2000, you may not be told that the next call is December 15, 2000, and every six months thereafter.

Many corporate bonds as well as municipal bonds are subject to a sinking fund that requires the corporation to retire a specified portion of a bond issue in specified years at par. Sinking funds reduce default risk because some bonds are retired each year rather than all the bonds being retired at once. Also, if bond prices have declined below the face value, the investor may receive an above-market price for her bonds because the issuer must redeem a specified number of bonds at their face value.

The disadvantage of a sinking fund is that the issuer might call your bonds when their market value is above their face value. This would result in you having to reinvest at a lower interest rate. When there is a sinking fund you cannot make an accurate yield-to-maturity calculation, since you don't know the call date of the bonds. Brokers will price the bonds to their average life, the point at which half the bonds will have been called away.

If calls and sinking funds concern you, buy discount bonds that sell below their face value. In this case, if there is a call, you will not lose any principal and might make a capital gain. A possible disadvantage of this strategy is that there is a smaller coupon and a reduced cashflow. This is not a problem if you don't want current income.

Special Types of Corporate Bonds

Zero-Coupon Bonds

Zero-coupon corporate bonds sell at a deep discount to their face value. Zero-coupon means the bond pays no current income. At maturity you would receive the face value of the bond. Zero-coupon corporate bonds are desirable for a tax-sheltered account because your money is fully invested until you need it; they are not such a good idea for your taxable personal account. Each year the IRS requires you to pay taxes on the imputed income from the zero-coupon bond even though you did not receive any current cash.

Put Bonds

A put feature enables the investor to sell the bond back to the issuer at the bond's face value at one or more predetermined dates prior to the bond's maturity. The purpose of a put feature is to protect the investor from a rise in interest rates. If interest rates go up, the value of bonds decline. If the bond has a put feature, the owner can sell the bond back to the issuer without losing any principal even if interest rates rise. Put features are attractive to investors in an inflationary environment. However, every feature has its cost. If the investor gets a put feature, the issuer pays less in yield on the bond.

Floating-Rate Bonds

Issuers reset the interest rate periodically on floating-rate bonds. The purpose of the floating rate is to protect the investor against a rise in interest rates and keep the bond from falling below its face value. In a typical example a bank might issue a floating-rate bond and reset the interest every six months at a rate 1 percent above a six-month Treasury bill. Floating-rate notes have not always protected the investor from rising interest rates. Money-market funds are frequent purchasers of floating-rate bonds. Some are actually long-term bonds that sell with a weekly rate reset.

Bonds with a 100-Year Maturity

Many bonds have a maximum maturity of 35 to 40 years. Even more frequently, bonds mature between 5 and 10 years. Every so often, an issuer is able to sell 100-year bonds. A recent incident was the sale of 100-year bonds by the Walt Disney Company.

Investors who buy 100-year bonds to put away for future generations have great faith in the stability of the U.S. financial system. They must also have great faith in the good fortune of both a company and the industrial sector of which it is a part. The Santa Fe Railroad issued 30-year bonds in 1881, which were finally paid off 114 years later.

The railroad bond initially looked like a great investment. The railroads were doing a booming business opening up new lands. As the number of rail lines increased, so did the competition. The Santa Fe company hit hard economic times as its business declined. In 1889, the company went through a reorganization, and the bondholders were given 100-year bonds paying 4 percent in place of their 6 percent 30-year bonds. Due to bad economic management, the company had to reorganize yet again. Bondholders were issued another 4 percent 100-year certificate maturing in 1995, as partial payment, and an "adjustment bond" on which interest income could be deferred indefinitely. In fact, in 1896 the issuer deferred interest payments for a year, paid 3 percent for 1897, and then paid 4 percent from 1898 until the present. The adjustment bonds of 1889 are comparable to the preferred shares being sold by corporations today in that they both include the option to defer interest payments. The fortunes of these bonds continued to rise and fall with the fluctuation in the economic strength of the Santa Fe Railroad and the fluctuation of the interest rates.

Inflation ate away at the value of the initial investment in Santa Fe bonds. In 1995 the bond investor received the equivalent of seven cents for every dollar invested in 1881. There were many fluctuations in value in the intervening years. It finally paid off at $1000 per bond. We can only hope that the Disney investors have better long-term success.

Checklist of What to Look for When You Buy Corporate Bonds

If you are buying individual corporate bonds, you need to rely on your broker to gather the relevant information on each proposed purchase. The items that you should consider and/or discuss with your broker include the following:

- Compare the yield on the corporate bonds to the yield on Treasury bonds with a similar maturity date. If the yield on the corporate bond is not at least one-half of one percent (0.5 percent) more than the Treasury bond, strongly consider forgoing the extra yield and buying Treasury bonds.

- Purchase the bonds directly from the broker or from the bond exchange. The broker earns a commission for bonds bought on the exchange because she is functioning as a true broker. She brings together a buyer and a seller and earns a fee for this service. The disclosed commission is as big or bigger than the spread the broker makes on a bond transaction from the firm's inventory.

- Buy new issue bonds if you can get them. The price will be more comparable to institutional trades.

- Identify how many debt issues are senior to the bond issue that you propose to purchase. Senior bonds are secured debt. Debt which is subordinated to the senior securities are junior lien bonds. Junior lien bonds may be secured or unsecured. Debentures are junior to all secured debt.

- Buy corporate bonds that are rated single-A or better by either Moody's or Standard & Poor's. If you buy lower-rated bonds you have a greater chance of a default.

- Ask the broker for both the bid and the asked price of any bond that you are considering buying. A wide spread of 4 percent or more between the bid and the asked prices will warn you that you may have trouble reselling the bonds quickly at a favorable price. A wide spread might also be an indication that the corporation is having financial difficulties or that the corporation is having some other current problem.

- Consider buying a mutual fund if you need to sell the bond before it comes due.

- Ask your broker to provide you with basic information about the company before you buy the bond. This is the same information that the broker would give to a buyer of the corporation's stock.
- Check out the calls or sinking fund provisions. If you have a fax machine ask for a printout from Bloomberg or the J. J. Kenny services.
- Ask whether there is any protection against event risk.
- Unless you are willing to trade your bonds, buy bonds coming due within 12 years to minimize unknown future risks.

PART 3

Bond Funds and Unit Investment Trusts

11

Off the Shelf: Open-Ended and Closed-End Funds and Unit Investment Trusts

If you are seeking to place the burden of bond selection on professional shoulders and purchase a diversified portfolio of bonds, there are three product choices:

- Open-ended bond funds (funds)
- Closed-end bond funds
- Unit investment trusts (trusts)

Each of these investments comes in many varieties. All are sold by brokers. Shares of certain bond funds can be purchased directly from the fund companies. There are many differences in composition of each product, depending upon how the organizers constructed the portfolios.

The difference between a trust and a fund is that the trust buys and holds a fixed portfolio and the fund does not. Once a trust is formed, no additional bonds can be bought. The trust manager does have the option of selling bonds out of the portfolio.

Open-ended bond funds and closed-end bond funds do not hold a fixed portfolio. The managers of the fund can and do trade the portfolio, seeking out good opportunities in the bond market and selling bonds which have appreciated or have negative possibilities. An open-ended bond fund is not of a set size. Investors can buy new shares or sell the old ones back to the fund. When open-ended funds receive new cash from investors, they generally use it to buy additional bonds for the fund or build up a cash reserve. When investors redeem their shares, they sell their fund shares back to the fund for cash. If the fund does not have enough cash, the fund will sell some of its bonds to raise enough cash to satisfy the request of the selling shareholder.

The closed-end funds can also buy and sell bonds held by the fund. However, the closed-end fund is of a fixed size and has a set number of shares. In order for a investor to buy shares, another investor has to be willing to sell her shares. Similarly, in order for a shareholder of a closed-end fund to sell her shares, she must sell them to another investor. The closed-end fund will not buy back the shares. This is the major distinction between open-ended funds and closed-end funds. The shares of the closed-end fund are generally listed on the New York Stock Exchange or one of the other exchanges where they are traded in the same way that stocks are traded. You pay your broker a commission for buying or selling the closed-end shares.

Open-Ended Bond Funds

Bond funds are by far the most popular choice among investors. Their diversity and liquidity make them hard to beat. A fund can invest the majority of its money predominantly in one kind of bond, such as Treasury bonds, or can have a more diverse portfolio. The range of possible types of bond funds is daunting at times, but knowable. Most bond funds fall into one of the following categories: money-market funds, Treasury bond funds, corporate bond funds, global funds, high-yield funds, mortgage pass-through security funds, and municipal bond funds. Bond funds enable the shareholders to own undivided pieces of many different bonds, giving a degree of diversification otherwise available only to bond buyers with large sums of money.

Tip_____

Minimum investments for bond funds range from $1000 to as much as $50,000.

Bond funds pass all their interest income and their trading gains and losses on to their shareholders. Investors in municipal bond funds do not have to pay federal income taxes on the interest income from the municipal bonds. Some municipal bond funds are exempt partially or totally from state and local taxes as well. Investors in bond funds must pay income taxes on the interest from bonds that are not tax exempt. Shareholders of all bond funds must pay taxes on the net capital gains. Investors in Treasury bond funds do not have to pay state and local taxes on the interest income from the Treasury bonds held by the fund, if the interest income is exempt within their state.

If you own shares in a municipal bond fund, you will receive a statement each year detailing the percentage of bonds owned by the fund which are issued by each state. Thus, if you are a New York resident and 10 percent of the fund's bonds are New York issues, you would be able to exclude 10 percent of the income of the fund from your New York income tax return.

How to Judge the Value of Your Fund

The net asset value (NAV) tells you what one share in the fund is worth. The NAV is made up of the sum of the values of all of the bonds in the fund's portfolio, divided by the number of shares outstanding. The NAV changes day-to-day as the bonds are "marked to market." That means that every day the bonds are repriced to reflect the current market conditions.

Assume that a new fund is started with a capitalization of $1 million. The type of securities to be purchased depends on the nature of the fund. In this case, the fund is a general market municipal bond fund. The manager of the fund purchases the following bonds with the $1 million:

$250,000 State of Pennsylvania general obligation bonds

$250,000 Texas State general obligation bonds

$250,000 New York State Power Authority bonds

$250,000 Dade County, Florida, bonds

The fund manager decides that the price of one share will be $10. Thus, the fund initially would have 100,000 shares available for sale. The minimum investment is $1000. Each shareholder must buy a minimum of 100 shares. Investors hear about the fund from media advertisements. In no time, the existing shares are sold and more investors are clamoring to purchase shares in the tax-free income fund. This is not a problem. As new money flows into the fund, the fund manager buys more bonds in the marketplace. As long as money flows into the fund, the fund increases its holdings and the number of shares for sale.

If you were one of those original investors, you might suddenly decide that you need your money back. Is this a problem? The fund manager receives your request for redemption, and he repays you with some of the new deposits he receives instead of buying more bonds. If there are more investors redeeming shares than buying them, the manager will sell some bonds and use the cash to satisfy your request.

Your claim on the fund is not for your original $10 per share investment, but for the net asset value of the shares on the day that you redeem them. Assume you own 100 shares of the fund and the value of a share rose to $11. If you decided to redeem your shares, you would have made 10 percent on your original $1000 investment. A $1000 investment would be valued at $1100. In another scenario, assume that you were sold the fund based on its good past performance. After you purchased your fund shares, interest rates rose, and the value of your investment dropped to $900, or $9 per share. Just because the price at one time had been $11 per share, there is no assurance that it will rise to that level again. *In bond funds, share price fluctuates with the movement of interest rates.*

Tip_____

Past performance of a fund is no indicator of future performance.

The bonds in the fund are priced daily by a pricing service. Since the shares have no fixed maturity, a yield-to-maturity is not meaningful. When funds state a yield, it is usually a current yield based on the amount of interest income per share divided by the net asset value. In order to make the funds comparable, the SEC mandated that every fund compute a standardized yield known as the SEC 30-day yield. This yield is composed of dividend income (assuming semiannual compounding of the income) and portfolio expenses. It is the best measure available for comparing one bond fund to another.

The SEC 30-day yield calculation does not take into account sales charges you might pay to acquire the fund or brokerage trading commissions. Some funds, called no-load funds, have no sales charges at all. The best performing bond funds generally do not actively trade their portfolios.

Tip_____

*The bond fund's "Statement of Additional Information" is the place
to look for information about portfolio turnover. The prospectus contains
information about sales charges.*

If you want to compare the performance of one bond fund to another
over the period of a year, use *total return*. Total return consists of whatever dividends you earn from the fund, plus or minus the change in the
net asset value of the fund. A one-year period is required to give you an
accurate portrayal of total return performance. When comparing one
fund to another, information about *cumulative total return* for periods
longer than one year can often be misleading because the same time
periods may not be used by each fund.

Tip_____

*To know what your fund is doing on a day-to-day basis, use the net
asset value. To compare bond funds use the SEC 30-day yield reported
by the funds. Year-to-year comparisons are based on the total return
of the fund.*

How Funds Can Look Alike
but Be Different

Some funds publish total return figures that make them appear to be
premier performers. However, a closer examination of the bonds that
the fund holds may show that there are undesirable reasons for the stel-
lar performance.

- *Greater security diversity.* Broadly titled funds use terms like *government* to allow the fund to invest in a greater range of securities that
  are of lower quality than Treasury bonds. A government fund sounds
  as good as a federal agency or Treasury fund, but it is not.

- *Longer maturities.* Two "intermediate" funds can produce different
  results because the average maturity of one is 4 years and the other is
  10 years. A 10-year bond exposes you to greater losses if interest rates
  rise.

- *High monthly payments.* Investors living off their income prefer a
  steady and predictable stream of income. Funds accomplish this by
  retaining cash when interest rates are high and adding principal to

the monthly income payments when interest rates decline. In doing this, they are sacrificing principal to maintain higher income levels. This reduces the share price.

- *Lower-quality bonds.* Most funds require that 65 percent of the bonds in the fund reflect the title of the fund. With the other 35 percent they have more discretion.

- *Fee reductions.* Some funds temporarily reduce their fees for a period of time to enhance their performance. When more investors come into the fund, attracted by the high performance, the fund raises its fees again.

Ways to Purchase Bond Funds

You can purchase bond funds from brokers, bankers, or directly from the funds themselves. If you purchase the fund from a broker or a banker, there is a fee called a *load.* These funds are called load funds. The purpose of the load is to provide compensation for the broker or banker to sell the fund. If you do the research yourself, you can buy no-load funds directly from a number of fund companies. You cut out the distributor and save the fee. There is no evidence that, over the long term, load funds perform any better than no-load funds. In fact, when you subtract the cost of the load, it is more difficult for load funds to outperform no-load funds.

Investors who feel very insecure about the right fund to buy follow the advice of brokers. Many brokers sell funds that are proprietary products of their employer, like the Landmark funds from Citibank or the proprietary funds of Merrill Lynch, Smith Barney, and Dean Witter, among others. Proprietary products are created, managed, and maintained by a particular bank or brokerage house. For example, if you decided to transfer your assets held in Smith Barney funds to Merrill Lynch, you would have to liquidate your Smith Barney funds so the assets could transfer as cash. Some brokers market funds that are created by other fund companies like AIM, Nuveen, and Van Kampen Merritt. Thus, a Merrill Lynch or Smith Barney broker could sell any of these nonproprietary products.

Many funds are sold through advertisements in newspapers and magazines. The best advertisement for a fund is a reporter's evaluation that shows the fund has produced superior returns. The newspapers, magazines, and media companies that specialize in evaluating the funds report on the best buys. Interested investors find the funds with the best historical performances by reviewing the analyses of fund performance. They can track the daily activity of the fund in the financial press.

Some funds sell on the basis of performance and word of mouth. Brokers may not necessarily sell these funds. The investor has to ferret them out by reading the financial newspapers and magazines. For bond funds in particular these are generally the no-load funds.

The media rates the best known no-load bond-fund families as top performers. Vanguard consistently tops the list by keeping its fees the lowest in the industry, forcing all other fund families to tame their fees. According to *Forbes'* August 28, 1995, "Annual Fund Survey," the following bond-fund families ranked highest in more than one category: Vanguard, Benham, T. Rowe Price, Dreyfus, Bernstein, Fidelity, Scudder, USAA, and Fidelity's Spartan Funds.[1] This ranking was adjusted for the effect of risks and costs on overall return. These are all no-load funds. Information about each of these funds is available by mail directly from the fund. Chapter 15 has a listing of some no-load bond funds.

The Check Is in the Mail?

Do you feel comfortable writing a check for $500, $1000, or more and putting it in the mail to the mutual fund company? Are you concerned about what may happen to it?

Years ago, before mutual funds appeared on the scene, the first and perhaps the only financial institution many people ever dealt with was a bank. The bank was the symbol of safety and security. Banks were impressive structures built of stone, with large windows and fancy floors. Massive and solid were words associated with them. As a result of FDIC insurance, the banks were the cornerstone of respectability and safety.

Maintaining real estate costs money. The depositors paid dearly to support the banks' large overhead. They accepted minimal interest for the use of their money because there were no alternatives for the average depositor. As competition for funds increased, investors became more adventurous and selective. Brokerage houses at first imitated the banks

---

[1]"Best Buys," *Forbes*, August 28, 1995, pp. 134–136.

at downtown headquarters, but then found less costly space in office parks and shopping malls. Competition has forced the banks to join them. Locally, there is now a bank with no store front in the corner of our supermarket. It is a small open space that does business seven days a week. When it first opened, a bank employee helped us find some grocery items!

In comparison, mutual funds sold by mail have comparatively little overhead. Instead of branch offices on every corner, they may have only one headquarters fielding calls from investors and handling account information and transactions. You call the toll-free 800 number and talk to someone who sends out information and answers your questions. You fill out the papers, enclose your check, and put it in the mail. Back comes an account statement that indicates you bought shares in a your specified fund. Some of the funds provide services 24 hours a day.

You may be accustomed to the corner bank or broker, where you can make your deposits and say hello to the teller. If so, buying shares in a faraway mutual fund is probably not very appealing, even if you would make more money. However, banks refer to people who make a few transactions a week at the bank as "transaction hounds." The banks lose money on people who eat up the time of their staff on small transactions. Banks are trying to encourage people to use the automatic teller machines. If automation removes the personal element from your financial activities, you might as well make more money by investing in funds by mail.

Putting a personal check in the mail with a mutual-fund deposit slip is simple. Like a bank deposit slip, it has your name and account number imprinted on it. You just need to fill in the amount of the deposit. If it gets lost, which is an unlikely occurrence, you could write another check. If you want to deposit a check that you receive from someone else, make a copy of the check before you mail it to protect against loss.

Tip_____

You decide. Do you want a higher yield that comes from investing in a fund by mail, or do you want a lesser yield to help your bank and broker pay overhead?

If you are not comfortable with sending checks in the mail, then you could choose a mutual fund company or a brokerage house with a branch office near you. The banks are also getting into the mutual fund business in an effort to keep assets from fleeing to higher interest rates elsewhere.

Information Provided by Funds about Themselves

If you want to know what you are buying, ask to see the following information available from funds and then read it:

- Prospectus
- Fund profiles
- Annual and semiannual reports
- Statement of additional information

The SEC requires that the fund sponsor reveal a great deal about the fund and its plans in the prospectus. The prospectus defines the rules of investing in the fund and outlines the risks.

Investors don't like to read prospectuses, so funds keep making them simpler. The newest effort to simplify fund information is to write fund "profiles." The best that can be said about the profiles is that they will save lots of trees and that more people might read them. The fund profiles highlight fund performance, fees, and risk on one or two pages. While it is better than reading nothing, it will not provide you with the in-depth understanding that the prospectus, the annual report, and the statement of additional information will.

At your request, the fund will send you an annual or semiannual report that lists all the securities held by the fund at the time of the printing. If there is anything unusual it will be listed here.

If you really want to know what the risks are and what the managers can do, ask for Part B of the prospectus, also called the Statement of Additional Information. It states exactly how the managers can invest the funds and describes the risks of each type of investment. It tells you what your management fees pay for. It includes the data on fund trading. It is worth a one-time read. Unless you specifically ask for it, you will not receive Part B.

Fund Fees

Bond funds are subject to a variety of fees. Possible fees on bond funds include:

- Front-end load
- Sales load on reinvested dividends
- Deferred sales charge (back-end load)

- Redemption charge
- Exchange fee
- Frequent transaction charges
- 12b-1 fee
- Management fee
- Shareholder accounting costs

A front-end load can cost the investor as much as 5 percent of his investment. The load charged usually declines when larger sums of money are invested at one time. Many investors avoid front-end loads. In order to appear more competitive with funds that do not charge such a fee, funds have started instituting a deferred sales charge instead of a front-end load. The deferred sales charge, or back-end load, can be as high as 6 percent and decline each year you hold the fund to 0 percent in the seventh year.

When a fund has a front-end load, there may also be charges for the investment of any new investments. This sales charge will probably affect any reinvested dividends. You need to ask the question or review the sales literature to find out.

A deferred sales charge or a back-end load is sometimes more palatable to investors. With this provision the charge is only paid when the investor exits a fund. There may be a sliding scale, with higher exit fees for earlier departures. You cannot avoid paying the fees by departing prematurely if you invest in a fund with back-end loads because the annual charges are higher than similar funds without back-end loads.

Another type of charge is a redemption charge. A fund that is very actively traded, whether a load fund or no-load fund, might institute this charge in order to discourage active trading of the fund. The SEC 30-day yield does not take these fees into account, but the annual total return computation factors them in.

Exchange fees result when you decide that you would like to invest in a different fund within the same fund family. Some funds will allow you to transfer your money without charge and others charge an additional fee.

Some funds have frequent transaction charges. Even no-load funds may institute these fees to discourage the market timers. The market timers often subscribe to newsletters telling them when to sell the shares in one fund and purchase shares in another in order to get the best total return. When there are many market timers moving their money around, all targeting specific funds, it can have a serious effect on the funds' overall performance. The fund managers instituted the frequent transaction fees to make market timing less attractive.

All funds have operating fees and management fees. The management fee is a fee shareholders pay to have the management company manage their investments. Vanguard is unique in that it is the only mutual fund company that is owned by its shareholders. This is one of the reasons that Vanguard is able to keep its management fees the lowest in the industry.

A reasonable level for these fees is 0.75 percent. Some fund managers will temporarily waive these fees in order to make their funds appear more attractive. The plan is to gradually increase the fees after investors have settled into the fund. Fees on balanced funds that include both bonds and stocks have higher fees, ranging from 1 percent to 1.5 percent.

The 12b-1 fee in an amount up to 0.25 percent is another type of fee that is found in some no-load funds. A fee of more than 0.25 percent classifies the fund as either a low-load or load fund. The SEC initially approved this fee as a way to help no-load funds carry the costs of advertising for new shareholders. However, some billion-dollar funds still charge this fee! The SEC approved the 12b-1 fee believing that if a fund reached a critical size then the overall costs for shareholders would diminish. This fee may be very costly because it is an annual charge. Every year the shareholder has to pay this fee. Some bond funds charge a load or deferred sales charge and the 12b-1 fee as well.

Some funds have instituted two classes of shares for the same fund. The class A shares might have a front-end load and no 12b-1 fees. The class B shares might have a 12b-1 fee and redemption charges for a total higher annual cost. Before you invest, take an extra moment to be clear about what you are purchasing. Some funds have three or four classes of shares.

Bond fund performance is determined in large part by the maturity of the bonds in the portfolio. Unlike stock funds that have a possibility of a large capital gain, a bond fund's yield is more predictable. Bonds in the same maturity and asset class pay about the same yield. Therefore, more than 0.75 percent annual costs weigh very heavily on the fund's performance.

The total fees charged by bond funds, without including loads, varies dramatically. Alliance Income Builder-A, a global fund, has the highest charges. The charges include $2.25 per $100 of NAV and, in addition, a load of $4.25 per $100. Compare that to the Vanguard Muni Bond-Intermediate fund that charges $.21 per $100 of NAV and has no load. That means that the Alliance Income Builder-A fund charges 10 times more to run its fund than the Vanguard fund. In addition, the Alliance Income Builder-A has a $4.25 load. Most taxable bond funds and municipal bond funds charge between $.50 and $1.00 per $100 of NAV. The impact of high total expenses is dramatic. If a bond fund is earning $7.00 per $100 and its total charges are $1.00 per $100 of NAV, then you are paying almost 15 percent of your earnings to the fund! If there is a load on top of this, the fund management company, in effect, has become your partner, while you take all the risk. Fees weigh especially heavy on bond funds. They are a major factor in overall performance.

Special Features and Services of Funds

Funds offer services that can simplify the management of your assets. The special services offered by the funds include:

- Professional management
- Monthly income payments
- Automatic reinvestment of dividends
- Annual statement of all transactions for tax-return filing
- Check writing or wire redemption

Funds promise a professionally managed portfolio. In some funds this means that portfolios are actively traded. In other funds, professional management means buying good quality bonds at the right price with minimal trading. The second strategy reduces trading costs that are passed on to the shareholder. Unfortunately, successful trading results in capital gains that are subject to tax.

A shareholder can request monthly or quarterly distributions. These payments will consist only of income or of a mix of income and return of principal. The shareholder can determine the size and frequency of distributions but not the mix. The mix is determined by the amount of the shareholder's interest payments and the fund's overall profitability.

If you do not need your share of the fund's income distributed to you, the fund will automatically reinvest the dividends in additional shares. There is no cost for automatic reinvestment unless a load fund specifies a charge for reinvestment.

Tip_____

Brokerage houses have automatic sweep accounts that transfer any uninvested cash in your brokerage account into a money-market account until further notice. The uninvested cash earns interest in the money-

market account even when the investor has not had time to think about what to do next.

A very important fund service is keeping track of all purchases and redemptions of fund shares. The fund management summarizes your transactions in an end-of-year statement that you can use to prepare your income tax returns. Every time there is a redemption or sale of a share, there is a reportable transaction for tax purposes. (This rule does not apply to money-market funds.) Every time you sell one fund and purchase another, for example, that is a taxable event unless you hold the fund in a tax-deferred pension or IRA account. At the end of every year, the fund reports to you all income, including taxable income, tax-exempt income, and capital gains. Banks and brokers use Form 1099 to report income to shareholders. A fund files a copy of this form with the IRS.

You can write checks on your mutual fund. There is usually a high minimum amount per check because the funds do not want to be used for daily check-writing. You can also wire money from your fund. These privileges require written approval and usually a *signature guarantee,* a stamp signifying that a local bank or brokerage house verifies your signature. This is different than a notary seal.

Closed-End Funds

Closed-end funds are different investment vehicles from open-ended funds. As such, the closed-end funds have their own advantages and disadvantages. A closed-end fund is created with a fixed number of shares. The sponsor of the closed-end fund sells these fixed number of shares through underwriters at an initial public offering in the same way that underwriters would sell a new issue of common stock of a typical business corporation. After the initial public offering, the sponsor of the closed-end fund has no legal obligation to either issue additional shares or purchase the outstanding shares held by shareholders. By contrast, an open-ended fund will sell additional shares and redeem existing shares on the request of shareholders.

In an open-ended fund a shareholder can redeem his shares at any time and receive the net asset value of his shares from the fund. In a closed-end fund a shareholder can only sell his shares on a stock exchange to another investor. While the price that the shareholder will receive for his closed-end fund may reflect the net asset value of the fund, the share price will be set on the stock exchange based upon the supply and demand for shares. Thus, the price that a shareholder will receive for his shares may be significantly higher or lower than the closed-end fund's net asset value.

Closed-end funds and open-ended funds have many similarities as well. Both have a diversified portfolio of bonds continually managed by a professional manager. Both types of funds offer many choices of specialized bond portfolios, such as Treasury bonds, foreign bonds, and junk bonds, as well as a choice of varying maturities. A closed-end fund, like an open-ended fund, never matures because bonds are continually bought and sold.

Let's look at an example of how and why a closed-end fund is formed. Newco, a fund sponsor, has a great new idea for a new financial product. It wants to raise $100 million to buy corporate bonds of Hong Kong companies. The fund will be called the "Hong Kong Bond Fund." Newco contacts J. P. Morgan, a well-known underwriter of foreign stocks and bonds, to serve as underwriter for the public offering of the shares of the Hong Kong Bond Fund. J. P. Morgan undertakes the sale of the fund's shares and raises the required $100 million. For its efforts, J. P. Morgan earns a fee of $7 million (7 percent of the public offering). Thus, the fund's shareholders only have $93 million working for them. After the underwriting the shares of the Hong Kong Bond Fund are listed on the New York Stock Exchange and trade like any other stock. The price of the stock will vary based on the supply and demand for the shares. The manager of the fund receives the $93 million cash and over a period of time purchases a portfolio of Hong Kong corporate bonds. These bonds will be very speculative for two reasons. First, the bonds are traded in the Hong Kong currency rather than in dollars. Second, the bonds are not readily marketable because there are not many traders or buyers for them.

Because of the speculative nature of the Hong Kong Bond Fund's portfolio, including the fact that the bonds are not readily salable, Newco does not want to use an open-ended fund. Newco's fear is that if the market for these bonds declines significantly, many shareholders may want to redeem their shares at the same time. Since the bonds are not readily marketable because there is a thin trading market for them, the investment manager may not be able to meet large redemption orders in a timely fashion. The result might be a financial panic in the shares. For specialty markets such as the one selected by the Hong Kong Bond Fund, a closed-end fund is ideal. The sponsor, once having sold the shares to the public, does not have to stand ready to repurchase them.

The closed-end fund vehicle provides the shareholders of the Hong Kong Bond Fund with a number of advantages as well. First, the shareholders do not have to worry that the fund will go out of business at a big loss because too many shareholders want to redeem their shares at the same time. Second, if the investment manager successfully increases the value of the bond portfolio, the value of the shareholders' stock will go up. Other investors will perceive the enhanced value of the shares and will agree to pay a premium to get into this great new fund. Third, the investment manager can invest all of the fund's cash in Hong Kong bonds and does not need to keep cash on hand to satisfy a possible rash of redemptions. The manager knows he has a stable amount of cash to invest. Fourth, the investment manager does not have to worry about investing a large amount of additional money from new shareholders who want to get in on this great investment. Since there is not a large amount of superior corporate bonds available in Hong Kong, the new money would dilute the great investment opportunity that the initial investors have.

We have painted the best case for closed-end bond funds. There are many drawbacks as well. Closed-end funds frequently sell at a discount to their new issue price and daily net asset value. When they are newly issued they sell at a premium. If you purchase a closed-end fund at the time of its public issue, it is more than likely that you will face an immediate loss. Since it is likely that the fund will soon be selling at a discount, you might as well purchase a closed-end fund on the open market at a cheaper price after the public offering.

Remember in the above example how J. P. Morgan took 7 percent of the cash raised as its underwriting fee. That 7 percent came directly out of the pocket of the initial investors. Those investors thus lost 7 percent before any trading took place. This is comparable to the new car premium. When you drive the new car out of the showroom it immediately declines in value.

It is well documented that after the initial public offering of closed-end funds, the price of a share generally declines. As we can see in the case of the Hong Kong Bond Fund only 93 percent of the money raised was invested. The net asset value of the fund declined by 7 percent and that decline is often reflected in a decline in the fund's price on the New York Stock Exchange. Finally, if you buy at the public offering, you will not know what bonds the fund will buy. The manager does not have funds to buy the bonds until the completion of the public offering when the cash comes in. Thus, you won't know some key facts about the fund's portfolio: the quality of the bonds, the maturity of the bonds, and the yield of the portfolio. It may take many months for the fund to become fully invested. During this time the fund will be invested in low-yielding cash equivalents.

Tip_____

If you want to buy a closed-end fund, a good time to buy is when the price of the shares has moved significantly below the portfolio's net asset value. This may result in an above-average return.

   If you are unhappy with your open-ended fund, you can sell it immediately at the current net asset value of the fund's portfolio. However, with a closed-end fund, you must find another investor to buy your shares and you might receive a lot less than the portfolio's net asset value. Sometimes the broker who sold you the shares may purchase the shares from you as a principal with a large discount. This is a particular worry if you buy shares of a relatively small closed-end fund that is thinly traded. The broker can profit by making a spread as a principal in the transaction and a commission as broker in the transaction.

Tip_____

When a broker trades as principal, the broker cannot give you objective advice. The broker will profit when you buy and when you sell.
Though you may trade your bonds on the New York Stock Exchange, the broker is likely to be on the other side of the trade.

Leveraged Closed-End Funds

Some closed-end funds have an added risk because they are leveraged. This means that the fund borrows money to buy additional bonds. One popular way to leverage the closed-end fund's portfolio is to issue preferred stock and use that cash to buy additional long-term bonds. The strategy here is that the return to the common shareholders will increase more than the cost of the dividends paid on the preferred stock.

   This produces good returns in a rallying market when interest rates are falling, but sharpens the decline as well. In 1994, the closed-end funds fell in net asset value by 10 percent on average, twice the loss of comparable open-ended funds that do not leverage. In 1995, closed-end funds still had not recovered and were selling at discounts up to 20 percent, or 80 cents on the dollar. Many companies issued closed-end American funds containing Mexican, Canadian, and U.S. bonds. When Mexico's economy suffered severe financial spasms, these funds lost money. Whether these funds are a bargain or not depends on whether the fund can recover its losses and the appeal of closed-end funds improves. Whether you can sell the fund at a better price when you are ready to exit is always questionable.

The leveraged closed-end fund may have to cut its quarterly dividend if the costs of borrowing rise high enough. The earnings of the fund may not be enough to cover both the costs of borrowing and the payment of the dividend. This is what happened to the Van Kampen Merritt Select Sector Municipal Trust and the Nuveen Insured Premium Income Municipal Fund among others.[2]

Most closed-end funds are smaller than the well-managed premier open-ended funds. The result is that costs and management fees of the closed-end funds may be proportionately larger and may unduly reduce the net income to the shareholders. Being smaller than the open-ended funds, the closed-end fund has less money available to attract the best managers.

Some closed-end funds are targeted to terminate at a specific maturity date so they will appear to be more like a bond with a final maturity. Targeted means only that they might end at the target date or somewhat later. The bonds in the fund do not all have the same maturity date. There are no guarantees that the fund will retire and pay out par for the bonds. Funds containing zero-coupon bonds are more likely to be able to pay par than those with income-producing bonds. However, if the fund money is invested in zero-coupon bonds it is not earning current income for you now. If the fund manager sees that the fund may not be able to meet its target, it will cut dividends in order to have cash for the final payments. Unlike a bond, the dividends are not guaranteed—nor is the return of your principal.

Unit Investment Trusts

Unit investment trusts are portfolios of bonds representing 10 to 12 bond issues. Once formed, the trust does not change size. The bonds are not traded. Generally, bonds may neither be bought into the trust nor sold out of the trust once the trust is formed. However, the trustee may protect the owners of the trust by selling a bond if there is serious quality deterioration. The trust ends when all the bonds have either matured or been called away or the sponsor decides to terminate it.

---

[2]Reed Ablest, "Bargain Prices in Bonds, Again: How Low Can the Discounts Go on Municipal Funds,"*The New York Times,* June 4, 1995, p. 7.

The sole purpose of the unit investment trust is to purchase and hold bonds for the sole benefit of the investors. All income from the trust, after expenses, must be distributed to the investors. This usually means that there is a monthly payout of the income and any returned principal.

Tip_____

A minimum unit of a unit investment trust is $1000.

It is important to be aware of the difference between interest income and returned principal. The broker reports this information on the brokerage statement under the title of Regular Account Activity. The interest income is indicated as "dividend received," and the principal is marked "principal payment." If the investor spends the principal payments, there will be no principal to reinvest when the unit investment trust dissolves. The principal payments can vary in size. It is easy to view these sums as income and use them for daily expenses.

The return of the principal usually occurs when interest rates have bottomed. That is when issuers call their bonds. This is not the time you want to have your money returned for reinvestment. On the other hand, if you are living on a fixed retirement income and need an increased cashflow, the unexpected return of your principal may be a fortuitous occurrence.

Each return of principal is considered a taxable event. Unlike the end-of-the-year statements from the open-ended mutual funds, the unit investment trust companies provide no help in calculating your taxes. You are supposed to calculate the profit or loss for each bit of principal returned based upon your own records.

Unit investment trusts are packaged by Nuveen, Van Kampen Merritt, and many of the big brokerage houses. They are not as popular now as they were in the 1980s when interest rates were 8 percent and higher.

Costs of Owning a Unit Investment Trust

Unit investment trusts sell at the *public offering price*. The minimum unit is $1000. This price is based upon the value of the bonds in the portfolio divided by the number of portfolio units. Investors can purchase unit investment trusts only through brokers.

Since unit investment trusts are typically a buy-and-hold investment, sponsors do not provide prices unless you call and ask. They are not listed in the daily or weekly papers. Unlike the other funds, their annual statements do not have to have an outside audit. This has led to some problems in the past. In 1993, the SEC accused Merrill Lynch of miscalculating the net asset value of a unit investment trust over a period of time. Without admitting any wrongdoing, Merrill Lynch agreed to pay unit holders around $30 million.[3]

Unit investment trust owners, like owners of other funds, must compensate the management of the trust. The annual management fee on unit investment trusts is very low, generally about $1.50 per $1000. There may be other fees and charges that are paid by the trusts and its investors under unusual circumstances. All unit investment trusts have front-end loads to compensate the broker for his sales effort. The loads have ranged between 3 percent and 6 percent. With a 6 percent load, for every $100 invested, you put only $94 to work; the remaining $6 goes to the broker.

Tip

Trusts are not frequently traded. Due to limited competition, the trust sponsors are able to maintain a fat spread between the bid or purchase price of the units and the ask or sale price.

If you decide to sell your trust, it is generally sold through a broker back to the sponsor of the unit investment trust. The sponsor is not legally obligated to repurchase your shares. The sale price of the trust is based on the net asset value of the bonds in the trust minus a spread, the profit the brokerage house makes. The spreads will vary. A typical 5 percent spread means that you will have to pay $50 per $1000 bond to sell your units. In effect, this is a back-end redemption charge if you need to sell.

Brokers sell unit investment trusts on the basis of their high current returns. However, this high yield is often the result of premium bonds in the portfolio. Often the bonds only provide a high yield for a short time because they have early call provisions. Some bonds may have questionable credit quality because some brokerage firms use the unit investment trusts as burial grounds for bonds that they can't profitably sell to their retail or institutional customers.

[3]Amy Feldman, "Unit Investment Traps," ed. Jason Zweig, *Forbes*, September 25, 1995, p. 210.

A major problem with unit investment trusts is their lack of liquidity. As stated above, the only real buyer is the broker who sold you the trust and that buyer has no legal obligation to repurchase the trust units from you. If there is a repurchase, the price is often unreasonably low.

Off-the-Shelf

Investors seeking to place money with a minimum of effort can purchase the ready-made portfolios of bonds. Unit investment trusts, closed-end funds, and open-ended mutual funds provide three alternatives for placing small amounts of money.

Open-ended funds allow instant access to cash, though the fund managers try to discourage market timers who move in and out of the funds with great frequency. The funds are structured to look like an individual bond. If you like U.S. Treasury bonds, there are U.S. Treasury bond funds. If you want your money back in three years, there is a short-term fund to fill the bill. The costs and risks of the bond funds vary widely depending on whether they are sold by a no-load bond fund with annual management costs or sold through brokers who, in addition, charge some kind of fee or load to earn their money.

Closed-end funds look like a stock because they trade on the New York Stock Exchange. This appeals to many people who like to be able to look in the newspaper on the day designated for reporting the activity of these funds. Closed-end funds can usually be bought at a discount to the net asset value of the fund. That means if the trading value of the fund shares appreciates so it more closely reflects the NAV, you might be getting a bargain. If you need to sell, which most people do at some time, closed-end funds might be difficult to sell at a good price. The fund managers may use leverage to boost the fund's return, adding an element of risk not found in many open-ended funds.

Unit investment trusts are advertised as a good place to park long-term money that you will not need to use for a long time. The minimum ongoing management fees are very small because there is no management. This keeps the costs of investing down. Unit investment trusts are investments that you put in a drawer and forget about because the costs of selling them are relatively high. Information about the value of the trust is available only from the broker. The interest income will come in regularly along with irregular amounts of principal that have to be reported on your tax return.

Off-the Shelf versus a Tailor-Made Portfolio

Weigh the purchase of any investment product against the purchase of individual bonds contained in the products themselves. Packaged products by their nature, whether in the grocery store or in the bond market, are apt to contain hidden ingredients that make their products less appealing. These fillers are not necessarily good for you or your long-term health.

Only individual bonds come due at a specified date. This is a simple statement but a very important one. It takes the market risk out of investing in bonds if you can hold your bonds to maturity. Bonds can be purchased in maturities from 1 year to 30 years and every year in between. They can be purchased to meet your individual maturity requirements. If you can hold your bonds to maturity, you do not have to be concerned with the fluctuation of their value in the marketplace. Unit investment trusts may hold long-term bonds with early call dates so that their due date is uncertain. Neither open-ended mutual funds nor closed-end funds ever come due. New bonds are always being bought to replace the maturing ones to keep the average duration of the portfolio in the advertised maturity range. The action is like the waves on the beach, where grains of sand are thrown against the shore and new ones are retrieved. The energy of the ocean never ceases. If you have to sell your funds when interest rates have risen, you will suffer a loss to your principal. The fluctuation of interest rates is perpetual. The waves continue to crash against the beach.

With individual bonds, you can control the possibility of bonds being called away early by purchasing bonds that are noncallable. Premium callable bonds are purchased in unit investment trusts because it boosts the monthly income. These bonds can come with relatively short calls. If a premium bond is called prematurely, then the owner of the bond takes a loss.

Noncallable bonds are the most desirable and eagerly sought after by trust departments who manage the money for the richest people in the country. You can simply choose not to buy callable bonds unless you feel you have been adequately compensated for the possibility of having them called away. Noncallable bonds are available to you just for the asking.

Whether you buy callable or noncallable bonds, your principal is returned to you in one lump sum. If you are concerned about reinvesting your principal and not spending it, this is important. The return of your principal in unit investment trusts is in dribs and drabs. For open-ended or closed-end funds, you can either redeem or sell all or only some of your shares.

After the initial purchasing costs of buying your own individual bonds, there are no other costs of holding your own bonds unless you choose a specialty brokerage account. That means a one-time cost for the purchase with no continuing costs. If the cost of a fund is 0.75 percent per year, and the yield on the fund is 5 percent, then you will earn 4.25 percent each year. At maturity your principal is returned to you. There are no redemption fees or exit fees.

If you purchase individual bonds you can choose the type and quality of bonds you want. Bond portfolios constructed by experts must compensate for the annual fees, the loads, and the exit fees where they exist. Therefore, the fund managers are apt to buy bonds that would not meet your specifications if you were buying them yourself in order to boost the yield of the fund. The higher the costs, the more risks the manager must take to compensate and overcome these costs.

Tax reporting for individual bonds is quite simple. There is a buy and a sell price for the bond. You will get a capital gains statement at the end of the year if a closed-end fund has made trading gains. The losses are not passed through. In open-ended mutual funds every time you reinvest your dividends or redeem your shares, this counts as a buy or sell. The taxes must be computed for each transaction. Mutual fund companies try to simplify the process for you by producing a detailed end-of-the-year statement.

Do you find the endless variety of bonds confusing? This is often the reason for buying prepackaged products. Someone else does the thinking and the investor only has to make one decision. Individual bonds require more thought initially. If you follow the rule that "simple things are best" and choose to purchase only those bonds with clear and simple descriptions, you will dispel a lot of the areas for confusion.

However you choose to own bonds, whether by buying individual bonds, open-ended mutual funds, closed-end funds, or unit investment trusts, they will be the workhorses of your portfolio. Bonds will pump out an annual income that will provide a cushion for life. For further information about particular bond funds see Chap. 14.

12

Bond Funds: Every Person's Answer to Investing

If you are a housewife, a pipefitter, a lawyer, a doctor, or anyone else with many responsibilities and interests other than managing money, open-ended bond funds become the shining light simplifying the question: "What should I do with my money?" You know that you should do something, but dealing with money means taking risks with investing— all uncharted waters for many people.

So the financial wizards created open-ended mutual funds. Mutual funds are not an entirely new idea. They existed in the 1920s and were one of the reasons that the stock market crash of 1929 took on such massive proportions. At that time, mutual funds were allowed to invest in other mutual funds. Thus, if one of the chain links broke, all the interlocking funds were weakened and suffered as well. To prevent a replay of that history, mutual funds are not allowed to purchase more than 3 percent of another U.S.-based mutual fund.

As in the past, investors have flocked to funds because they seem to simplify the investment process. Satisfying every investment whim or desire, mutual funds have diversified and mushroomed. Like rabbits in a lettuce patch, they have proliferated rampantly across the landscape. Now you can choose among 6500 contestants for your money. Bond funds represent one segment of the market. Every major mutual fund family includes bond funds.

Yes, mutual funds have families too. Like heads of households, the managers who head the funds define how the fund will be run. They define the rules and regulations, within the context of guidelines set by the SEC, and decide on what kinds of securities will be included within the portfolio, what quantities are desirable, and what the trading strategies will be. Every fund must spell out its game plan in its *prospectus*, the document sent to every investor which describes the fund's activity limits and procedures.

Tip_____

You will simplify your life without reducing any investment opportunities if you invest in only one or two fund families.

Managers compete with other fund managers to produce the best results. "My fund family is better than yours, and my fund is better than yours," they declare. Like peacocks trying to attract the attention of pea-hens, they flash their feathers through the major analytical services that track the fund's records and loudly broadcast their quarterly successes to the media hoping to attract more investors to their fold. Any attempts to unnaturally paint their feathers with the fake psychedelic colors of above-average higher yields immediately attracts the attention of the other peacocks, who call in the financial news reporters to cover the story and reveal the impostor. However, it takes time for the stories to disseminate, and unwitting investors flock to the above-average yields resulting from risky investments or investment strategies.

Sometimes the peacock takes a bath to make his feathers brighter. By waving fund fees temporarily, the yield on the fund rises vis-à-vis other funds. Some fund families make it a policy to keep their fees low. The Vanguard Group became an industry leader by keeping its fees the lowest in the entire fund industry. T. Rowe Price and the Benham Group, among others, have moderated their fees as well.

"Fees are not everything!" scream the other peacocks. "What about superior management? We train and groom our fund managers with greater care!" shouts one. "Our fund is smaller and therefore more nimble in declining markets," declares another. And so the competition continues among all the purveyors of the fund families. They come in many flavors, and it is up to you if you want plain vanilla or the more exotic Cherry Garcia.

Money-Market
Mutual Funds

The keystone of bond funds is the money-market fund. The higher yields on money-market funds lure money from the safety of bank certificates of deposit and savings accounts insured by the FDIC into a fund family. The money-market funds invest in high-grade short-term securities. They maintain the value of the fund at $1 per share, though the yield will fluctuate and the maturities of the securities will vary within prescribed limits. The $1 per share valuation is based on the high quality of the securities in the fund and a commitment of the money-market fund's parent corporation to sustain the share value. There is no formal guarantee. The theory is that the short-term nature of the instruments in the funds creates great liquidity. The securities will come due within a very short period of time. In cases where the fund was holding securities which soured, those securities were promptly purchased by the parent corporation in order to maintain the $1 per share commitment. There has, to date, never been a major money-market fund whose share value has continued to sell below the $1 per share minimum.

Money-market funds come in a number of varieties. There are funds which invest in *commercial paper,* unsecured short-term promissory notes issued by the most credit-worthy corporations, and negotiable CDs issued by large banks. Other kinds of allowable investments include Treasury bills, federal agency debt, and various derivatives. The money-market mutual funds are sorted by the degree of risk and the subsequent pickup in yield they offer.

The money-market funds which invest in commercial paper issued by corporations do not announce that information in their titles. They may be called "Cash Reserves," "Money Market," or "Ready Assets." Their lure is the higher returns they offer. The funds that only contain Treasury and federal agency paper are pleased to announce that in their titles

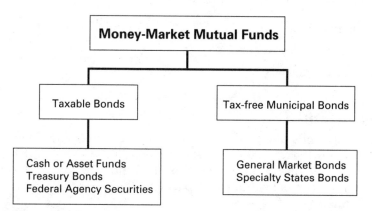

Figure 12-1. Kinds of money-market funds.

because investors seeking safety first will choose them. It is always important to check the annual report to see if Treasury or agency paper is all the fund is holding. The fund manager may have the right to invest a portion of the assets in higher-yielding, riskier investments.

Tip_____

Remember that cash flows to the highest yield unless you evaluate the risks.

Any time you open a brokerage account, you should request that the uninvested cash be automatically transferred into a money-market fund to earn interest while you decide what else to do with your money. Investors are willing to pay extra to have excess cash swept into the money market. The frequency of the sweep, whether it is done daily, weekly, or biweekly, varies from one institution to another. Banks are now also offering money-market funds, though they are not considered a bank deposit and do not usually have an automatic sweep. Money-market funds bought through the bank are not insured by the FDIC. Fund families not connected to either banks or brokerage houses also have money-market funds.

Money-market funds are considered a key asset of any fund family. Money that flows into the money-market fund will often percolate into other funds sponsored by the fund family.

Sorting Bond Funds

Bond funds can be grouped together based on:

- Length of maturity
- Type, quality, and risk of assets
- Taxability of the securities

Bond Fund Maturities

Bond funds hold bonds of either short (1–5 years), intermediate (5–10 years), or long maturities (10–30 years). As a general rule, the shorter the maturity, the less fluctuation in the value of the fund. The longer the maturity, the more the bond fund will pay, and the more the fund's value will fluctuate.

In almost all cases you will earn more income from a long-term bond fund than from a short-term bond fund. In addition, if interest rates drop, a long-term bond fund will appreciate more than a short-term bond fund. However, if interest rates rise the value of a long-term bond fund will fall significantly more than a short-term bond fund. (See Table 12-1.)

For example, assume you own a bond with a 7 percent coupon that matures in 5 years. If interest rates increased by 3 percent, your bond would lose 12 percent of its value. By comparison, if a 7 percent coupon bond had a 20-year life, your bond would lose 26 percent of its value. Of course, the loss in value is only temporary. If you hold these bonds until maturity, you would receive the face value of the bonds. Remember, bond funds never come due. Thus, a rise in interest rates is more serious if you own a bond fund than if you own an individual bond.

The decision to invest in a short-, intermediate-, or long-term bond fund is based on how you view the direction of interest rates and what market risks you wish to take with your principal. Since you can sell your fund at any time, you do not have to purchase a short-term fund with an eye to getting your money back sooner. You might think that if the fund is a substitute for a CD, then you should leave your money in a short-term bond fund. However, remember that your CD will mature and you will get your principal returned. The short-term bond fund never matures, and the return of your principal is not guaranteed. However, the short-term bond fund does give you a higher return and immediate access to your cash.

If your intention is to ride out the waves of interest rate fluctuations in an effort to achieve the maximum return over a long period of time, then a long-term bond fund might be right for you. In a falling interest-

Table 12-1. Total Return Volatility—One-Day Total Return

Instantaneous rate change	5-year bond (7% coupon)	20-year bond (7% coupon)
+3%	−12%	−26%
+2	−8	−18
+1	−4	−10
0	0	0
−1	+4	+12
−2	+9	+25
−3	+13	+41

SOURCE: John C. Bogle, *Bogle on Mutual Funds: New Perspectives of the Intelligent Investor,* New York: Irwin Professional Publishing, 1994, p. 40.

rate environment, you get the highest total return from this kind of fund. If interest rates are fairly stable, you will benefit from being in a long-term bond fund. Unfortunately, it is usually hindsight that reveals the stability of interest rates. If you find yourself in a period of rising interest rates, then a long-term bond fund is a miserable place to be.

Tip_____

Bond funds never come due. Your principal is always at risk. Bonds do come due and you will get your money back at maturity.

Type and Quality of Assets

Classifying bond funds by type and quality of assets held touches another set of considerations demanding your attention. Bond funds hold either taxable or tax-exempt bonds.

Taxable Bond Funds

The varieties of taxable bond funds are very great from a credit point of view. There are very safe funds which hold Treasury bonds, agency bonds, and GNMA bonds. There are the so-called high-yield funds

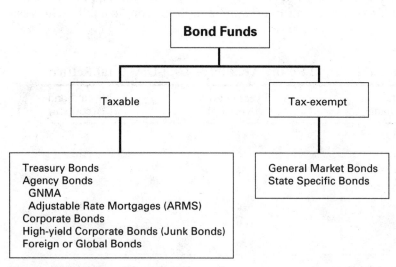

Figure 12-2. Types of bond funds.

which hold junk bonds. There are funds which fall within these two extremes which hold well-rated corporate bonds. Foreign bonds might be very speculative or very safe.

Fund Title: What Does It Mean— Treasury, Government, and Federal Bond Funds?

How do some Treasury bond funds or government bond funds perform so much better than others? Don't they all own the same kind of bonds? The answer is "no"; if they did, they would have similar returns. The major differences would be fees and trading success. Some government bond funds have high fees and expenses. In order to overcome these costs, they aggressively trade their portfolios and use derivatives. Other government bond funds that are not so well known want to distinguish themselves from the pack. They engage in speculative investments.

Looking at the title of a fund does not give you sufficient information about what kinds of securities the fund is holding. Sixty-five percent of all securities a fund holds must reflect the title of the fund. Thus, if the fund is a Treasury bond fund, then Treasury bonds must represent 65 percent of the portfolio. The remaining 35 percent might be in cash, agency securities, zero-coupon bonds, or derivative securities tied to Treasuries.

Funds using the word *government* or *federal* in their titles are permitted to hold a mix of bonds, including agency bonds and corporate bonds. Corporate bonds are included in bond funds called "federal" or "government" in order to boost their yield. If a fund specifies a maturity range or a quality range, then 65 percent of the bonds in the fund must meet that criteria. The remainder of the bonds can be of lower quality or of a longer maturity than specified. Putnam Federal Income Trust and Prudential U.S. Government Fund both are permitted to hold 20 percent of their funds in corporate bonds. Fidelity's Spartan Long-Term Government Bond Fund may hold foreign obligations.

Some of the agency securities may not be backed by the U.S. government. The value of zero-coupon Treasury bonds fluctuates widely with the movement of interest rates. Although Treasury bonds have the best credit quality, zero-coupon Treasury bonds will lose substantial market value in a sharply rising interest-rate market.

Investment-grade corporate bond funds' portfolios will vary greatly with the emphasis on credit quality. The only way you are going to know what the corporate bond fund actually holds is to review the fund's portfolio, which is found in the fund's semiannual and annual reports. As you review the holdings, remember that though a corporation's stock may be listed as a "buy," the credit quality of the company can affect the payment of interest on the bonds.

Some government and federal funds suffered big losses in 1994 due to concentrations of untested securities derived from Collateralized Mortgage Obligations (CMOs). These securities are included in a portfolio in order to raise the overall yield. CMOs dice and slice mortgage-backed securities into sections in an effort to make prepayment and redemption more predictable. The earlier tranches have fairly predictable maturities, but the later ones are almost unknowable and are tellingly called "kitchen sink bonds." They contain the leftovers from the development of other CMOs. In addition to these, there are many other products derived from the basic pass-through securities.

In July 1994, PaineWebber Group said it would spend $180 million to buy two CMO issues from its troubled Short-Term U.S. Government Securities fund that had fallen more than 7 percent—more than other funds in its class. The reason for the steep decline in the value of the bonds was a sharp rise in interest rates followed by an evaporation of potential purchasers for the kitchen sink bonds, which represented 25 percent of the portfolio. The kitchen sink bonds are so complex that trying to understand how they will function under different interest-rate scenarios is a mind-numbing task even for the rocket scientists who created them.

PaineWebber wasn't the only firm suffering from the realization that its fairly recent offspring had an unusual dark side. Piper Jaffray, among others, was also a big loser through its Institutional Government Income Portfolio fund. In 1993 it posted a gain of almost 16 percent—earning top ratings from both Morningstar, Inc., and Value Line Mutual Fund Survey. The use of derivatives, which proved to be a successful strategy since 1989, turned with a vengeance in 1994 to show a 23.3 percent loss in July 1994, coming down from its December 1993 high. In a show of support, Piper Jaffray pumped in $10 million, predicting that when interest rates turned around, so would the value of the portfolio. Other funds suffered similar losses.

As a result of these and other unexpected problems, Standard & Poor's has specified an "r" rating to indicate that there might be more than a credit risk on a bond. Even triple-A rated bonds which have a derivative structure might be given an "r." If you review a fund's annual report where all the securities are listed, you can look for the "r" as a sign of potential risk, and possibly, of larger-than-expected gain.

After these losses were publicized, owners of bond funds started calling their fund companies with a single message—get rid of the derivatives. Some derivatives are used to speculate and possibly give the fund a competitive edge by increasing the yield. Other derivative products are used as a hedge against the movement of interest rates or currency in a global fund. The hedges are not risky, just expensive.

When one bond fund performs significantly better than another, there are objective reasons for this result. In order to get better performance, the manager must do one of the following:

- Reduce the fund's fees.
- Lower credit quality.
- Increase the life of the portfolio.
- Trade vigorously.
- Use derivatives.

All of those actions, except reducing fees, create additional risk to the portfolio in future years. Before you invest, review the portfolio to see why the superior performance resulted and then determine whether you want to take the additional risk. There are no undervalued bonds in the same way as there are undervalued stocks.

Tip_____

The keys to consistently better performing bond funds are lower fees and a buy-and-hold strategy.

International and Global Bond Funds

International bond funds invest only in foreign bonds. Global bond funds invest in U.S. as well as foreign bonds. The purpose of investing in foreign bonds is to increase your diversity of investments. The theory is that risky investments will increase your overall return if properly diversified. Investments are properly diversified if one category of investment declines when the other increases. This had been the case with foreign stocks and bonds. They moved counter to U.S. stocks and bonds. When U.S. stocks and bonds declined, foreign stocks and bonds tended to increase. However, recent studies have shown that U.S. and foreign stocks and bonds are moving more in step with each other. If your foreign bonds do not move counter to your U.S. holdings then you are left not only with more risk, but also no rationale for the investment.

In addition to credit risk, foreign bonds are subject to currency risk.

This means that when you invest in foreign bonds you are betting that the U.S. dollar will decline against the currency in which the foreign bonds are denominated.

The bond fund manager may have called the interest rate turns correctly, but an increase in the value of the U.S. dollar will send the value of the fund plummeting. Furthermore, foreign governments are known to repudiate their debts, which will leave you holding an empty sack. If the stars are in alignment, you may make much more from foreign bond funds than from other bond funds.

Some fund sponsors offer short-term global portfolios. These funds are sometimes promoted as being as safe as money-market funds, while providing a higher return. They have proved neither safer nor more profitable. Short-term is supposed to indicate that the shorter maturity is less risky than bonds in the same category. Unfortunately, the shorter maturity cannot protect against currency fluctuations. Global bond funds also have higher costs of operation due to the purchase of hedges to protect against currency fluctuation and more frequent trading of the portfolio. These funds are not for the retired looking for a little extra income.

Caveat Emptor

The reward is related to the risk entailed.

If you review the August 1995 issue of *Forbes* for its summary of the performance of global bond funds, you will find many more newly created funds among them than for other fund categories. When a fund does not perform well, the dog is put to death or merged into another fund. The new fund starts with a clean record and, it is hoped, produces better results.

International and foreign funds have much higher fees than similar bond funds, with the average annual expense of $1.31 per $100. Their exposure to currency risk is the same as it is for global stock funds, without any of the upside that stock funds provide.

Despite the high fees, if your intention is to invest in non-dollar-denominated bonds, then we recommend that you purchase foreign or global bond funds. Individual bonds in this category are difficult to evaluate and purchase at a good price. They entail substantial foreign currency risk and will be costly to sell if the currency moved against you. These bonds will also complicate your tax return preparation because they are subject to foreign taxes.

GNMA Funds

There are many mortgage funds which hold a whole variety of mortgage pass-through securities. Most of these funds are too difficult to analyze because of the variety of their holdings. In addition, many of them are risky because they hold CMOs and derivatives. Our recommendation is if you are interested in a mortgage pass-through securities fund, you should buy a GNMA fund which only holds GNMA pass-through securities.

GNMAs are attractive investments. They often provide a higher return than Treasury bonds. In addition, the principal of the GNMA securities is guaranteed by the government so that there is no credit risk. (Of course there is always market risk.)

Purchasing GNMA funds is a better way to invest in GNMAs than purchasing individual GNMAs. Individual GNMAs must be purchased in minimum amounts of $25,000. Each individual GNMA security will perform in a unique way, based upon the particular mortgages that it holds. Unless you have a great deal of money to invest in GNMAs, you will not get a diversified portfolio. A GNMA fund will provide all of the following: diversification, a smoother cashflow, a way to reinvest the income received from the GNMAs, and a way to invest with a minimum amount of only $1000 to $3000, depending upon the fund.

GNMAs and GNMA funds have a number of negative features as well. They are volatile when interest rates are moving rapidly, either up or down. They don't perform as well as long-term bonds when interest rates drop substantially. GNMAs perform better than long-term Treasuries when interest rates move within a narrow range.

We recommend the Vanguard GNMA Fund for a number of reasons. It was the best performing fund for the period 1985 to 1994 with a total return of 9.5 percent per year. It is a no-load fund and, in addition, has the lowest annual expenses at $0.30 per $100. Two other excellent-performing no-load GNMA funds with relatively low annual expenses are Benham GNMA Income Fund and T. Rowe Price GNMA Fund.

ARM Funds

An ARM fund principally holds adjustable rate mortgages. Most of these mortgages are guaranteed by a federal agency. The interest rate for the adjustable rate mortgages is reset periodically based on the movement of short-term Treasury securities. All of this would appear to indicate a conservative fund. However, you must look closely at the ARM-fund portfolio before you invest because many of them also include risky CMOs and derivatives in their portfolios to increase the portfolio's yield.

ARM funds were conceived as a safe place to park short-term money. The goal of an ARM fund is to yield more than money-market funds while at the same time being less volatile than longer-term bond funds. The volatility was supposed to be reduced because the interest rates on the adjustable rate mortgages were reset periodically. Until 1993, ARM funds worked as promised. However, in that year ARM funds returned 2 percent less than short-term bond funds. In 1994 the ARM funds performed much worse than money-market funds. While the money-market funds were up from 3 percent to 5 percent for the year, the average ARM fund lost 2.2 percent and some lost 20 percent.

Investment-Grade Bond Funds

There are a large number of investment-grade bond funds. Investment grade means that at least 65 percent of the fund's assets are in investment-grade securities issues. Investment grade means that the rating of the bonds is triple-B or higher. (This is the fourth-highest rating.) Thus, within the investment-grade category fall all U.S. government bonds, all agency bonds, all mortgage pass-through securities backed by the government or a government agency, and all corporate bonds rated triple-B or higher. These funds all hold taxable bonds. The investment-grade bond funds are generally divided into the three categories of short-term, medium-term, and long-term. Short-term means the portfolio has a dollar-weighted average maturity of five years or less. Medium-term means 5 to 10 years, and long-term means more than 10 years.

The shorter the maturities of the bonds in the fund, the less volatile will be the price of the fund. Short-term bonds are less vulnerable to interest-rate risk, making them more suitable for investors who have a low tolerance for risk to their principal. Thus, the most volatile fund would be the long-term fund and the least volatile would be the short-term fund.

Some investment-grade bond funds invest the bulk of their money in the top two credit ratings of triple-A and double-A. Others invest the bulk of their money in the two lowest ratings of investment-grade bonds which are triple-B and single-A. Some investment-grade bond funds are authorized to invest up to 35 percent of their portfolio in junk bonds.

Investment-grade bond funds are good vehicles for pension investments because their high yield is not subject to tax in pension plans or IRAs. In choosing one or more funds for your pension plan, consider both the average life of the fund and the credit risk in the portfolio. If you are seeking less volatility, purchase short- and intermediate-term funds. *Forbes'* August 28, 1995, "Best Buys" picked investment-grade bond funds managed by Vanguard, Fidelity, Bernstein, USAA, and T. Rowe Price, among others. All are no-load funds.

High-Yield Bond Funds

High-yield bond funds can be divided into those with high interest-rate risk and those with high credit risk. Long-term zero-coupon bond funds exemplify those funds with a high interest-rate risk. The value of the fund rises dramatically when interest rates fall and declines in value with equal rapidity when interest rates rise.

Target maturity funds containing zero-coupon bonds with a stated maturity date are not as targeted as they may first appear. The bonds in the fund do not all have the same maturity and will not mature in the same year. Around the target date, the bonds are sold and the fund is liquidated. Though they sound like a bond, they do not mirror the structure of a bond. These funds are not for the faint of heart.

If your intention is to bet that the movement of interest rates will be downward, then you would maximize your return by investing in a fund holding long-term zero-coupon bonds. Benham Target Maturities Trust invests in Treasury STRIPS, zero-coupon bonds issued by the Treasury. Since they pay no interest until maturity, the effect of interest-rate fluctuations is intensified. Before you choose a fund, you must clarify your objectives.

High-yield bond funds with a high credit risk are sometimes called "junk-bond funds" because they invest in low-rated bonds that are highly speculative. Before the surge in mergers and acquisitions in the 1980s, the high-yield bonds were issued by companies which had fallen on hard times. Though there were cashflow problems, a company had basic assets which could be sold, giving credence to the idea that if a cash crunch led to a bond default, the company would be able to reorganize itself and resume paying its debts. Currently, high-yield bonds are more likely issued by a company increasing its debt to stave off a leveraged buyout, or by a company that increases its debt in order to have the cash to buy out another company. Another kind of junk-bond issuer is the technological dinosaur. The products it sells are out of date, and there are no key assets to be sold. These types of bonds make the high-yield funds of today more vulnerable than past high-yield funds.

In 1995, the high-yield bonds paid about 3 percent more than U.S.

Treasuries. However, during the 1990–1991 recession, junk bonds paid as much as 10 percent more than Treasury bonds. That extra yield is not all gravy, however, because the investor has to anticipate possible losses. Junk-bond funds also diversify their holdings into higher-grade corporate bonds, foreign bonds, and Treasuries. The quality mix of a fund will either increase or reduce the credit risks and the ensuing yields.

Investments in junk-bond funds are an aggressive, high-risk investment. An investor should have a well-diversified portfolio and be prepared to lose money. These funds are only good for speculation. In 1989 and 1990 junk-bond investors suffered heavy losses as the market for junk bonds evaporated. Heavy fund redemptions resulting from the substantial drop in value led to further declines as traders had to sell bonds in a saturated market to raise cash. In the worst of the funds, an investment of $10,000 would have dwindled to $2500 by the end of 1990. This was followed by a major rally in 1991, but many of the funds had folded before the upturn.

Some high-yield bond funds focus on the best quality below investment-grade paper. *Forbes* points out that Vanguard Fixed Income High-Yield and Nicholas Income funds focus on the best bonds in this category, while Federated High-Yield Trust and Dean Witter High-Yield securities tend to buy the more precarious issues.

Tax-Exempt Municipal Bond Funds

Tax-exempt municipal bond funds might be *general-market* bond funds that hold bonds from all parts of the country or *single-state* bond funds that hold bonds primarily from one state. They may focus on a particular market sector. The fund may purchase revenue bonds supported by electric utilities, sewer authorities, hospital, or general obligation bonds. General-market funds have more options than single-state bond funds.

Within the municipal market there are also bonds and bond funds which are insured. Here too the quality of the bonds held in the funds may vary. Tax-exempt insured municipal bond funds must invest 65 percent or more of their assets in bond issues that have insurance for the payment of principal and interest. The insurance is issued by bond insurance companies. Insurance does not protect against market or interest-rate risk. Insurance does not come free. To increase the yield on the fund, portfolio managers are allowed to balance the insured bonds with bonds having lower investment grades and higher yield.

Like taxable bond funds, municipal bond funds can be divided into short-, intermediate-, and long-term funds. One fund called short-term may not have exactly the same maturity as another fund using the same term. Each fund may also lengthen or shorten its maturities depending upon how the fund manager reads the market.

Most insured bond funds hold bonds with longer maturities. T. Rowe Price has introduced Tax-Free Insured Intermediate Fund to fill a different niche. Now you can buy insured bond funds in both intermediate and long maturities.

The bonds in both the taxable and tax-free funds are rated primarily by Moody's and Standard & Poor's. The ratings indicate the amount of credit risk you are assuming when you purchase the funds.

Single-state funds arose in response to high taxes imposed by a state on bonds issued outside of the state's boundaries. By imposing that tax, the state insures a market for its bonds and thus helps to keep down the borrowing costs of all the issuers within the state.

While it is very appealing to have all your income exempt from state and local taxes, it is not always the wisest way to proceed. Diversification of assets provides protection. An investor should own a general-market fund for at least some of his assets. In 1995, Orange County, California, defaulted on taxable notes and short-term tax-exempt certificates of participation. The single-state funds owning California bonds had to scramble to try to protect the value of the funds in the wake of the Orange County bankruptcy. Though the fund families supported or bailed out the short-term and money-market funds holding the defaulted California paper, there was no legal obligation for them to do so.

Though insurance adds extra protection to single-state portfolios, it does not come free. Single-state portfolios yield less due to the scarcity of bonds within high-tax states in particular. If you now add another level of cost for insurance coverage, then your total return is further reduced.

The states with the highest taxes on income are New York, California, and Massachusetts. Single-state bond funds for these states provide a definite tax advantage. However, single-state funds have proliferated for many more states. There are even single-state funds for states with no taxes on out-of-state bond income, like North Dakota and Texas. If you purchase a single-state fund for a state that does not charge taxes on out-of-state bonds, you pay higher expenses for the tailored portfolio, you sacrifice the diversification provided by a national portfolio, and you lose the opportunity to obtain the higher yields available in a general-market fund. If you have to pay more to own a single-state tax-exempt bond fund than to own a general-market bond fund, you must evaluate if the cost justifies the benefit you receive. If you do not live in a high-tax state, single-state funds are not for you.

Tip_____

Unlike in other markets, it is possible for the odd-lot municipal bond investor to earn more investing in individual bonds rather than funds if he can buy and hold the bonds to maturity.

Diversified Income Funds

This class of funds combines investments in stocks and bonds into one fund. These funds can either try to increase your principal by allocating a greater percentage of holdings to stock (capital appreciation fund), emphasize principal safety by having a larger percentage of bonds in the portfolio (income-oriented fund), or vary the percentages as the market fluctuates. This last category of funds tries to answer the omnipresent question of whether you should have more or less money in a particular market segment. The discretion is left in the hands of the money manager.

For investors seeking what appears to be the easy way out, the cost is high to purchase a mix of stocks and bonds. For a straight bond fund you can expect to pay 0.5 percent to 0.75 percent in annual charges. For an income-oriented fund the charge might be 1 percent; for a capital appreciation fund, 1.2 percent; and for an allocation fund, 1.5 percent. The greater the equity component, the higher the cost.

Some fund families offer allocation services that distribute your money into bond funds and stock funds. Vanguard's STAR fund and T. Rowe Price's Spectrum Income and Growth funds are available for no additional charge beyond the fees on the funds into which the money is placed. They can keep their fees low because they are making the allocations of your money into their own sector funds.

Wrap accounts charge an annual fee to allocate your money into funds within different fund families. The allocation services offered by Vanguard and T. Rowe Price are serious competition for wrap accounts which charge a 1 percent to 2 percent fee in addition to the funds' fees. Wrap accounts also require a minimum $100,000 investment, while minimum investment requirements in most funds are modest.

Commonly Asked Questions
When Picking a Fund

There is much to know about investing. People sometimes feel that their questions are "dumb" and therefore do not deserve timely consideration. The questions seem so simple that the questioners feel they should know the answers. This is not the case. There are no dumb questions when you are dealing with a source of security for you and your family. The following are some of the questions investors who have gone before you have asked.

How reliable are the records of fund performance?   Though computer searches may tell you which funds were the best performers in the past, they won't tell you how a fund will do in the future. The perspective of a fund's track record can be modified by starting a new fund when the old one didn't perform well, or by blending the old one into an ongoing fund. A fund may advertise the periods of its best performance, which may not be comparable to the time frames of other funds you are considering. It is important that the time frame is the same for an accurate comparison.

Why is one fund yielding more than another in the same maturity category and class?   Bonds of similar quality, maturity, and source yield a similar amount. An above-average 30-day yield on a bond fund might indicate that the bonds in the higher-yielding fund have investments with longer maturities or higher risk than others in the same class, or have bonds with adverse features, such as early calls or derivatives. Higher yields in one of two comparable funds may also be the result of lower fees and transaction costs which allow more income to be passed on to the shareholders.

Is preservation of principal or higher income more important? Bond portfolios in the same class can be managed so as to pay out more income currently at the risk to principal or managed so as to pay out less income in order to preserve capital. Bonds issued at times of high interest rates are bound to be called as soon as their call provisions allow it. If these bonds were purchased at a premium for the purpose of goosing up the 12-month dividend yield, then part of the income you are receiving from the bond fund is actually a return of your principal. If you are a long-term bond-fund holder, this will eventually be to your detriment as those high-coupon bonds are replaced with lower-coupon bonds.

Why do some fund prices gyrate more than others?   The stability of the fund price is based upon the quality of the bonds in the portfolio. Higher-quality, full-coupon bonds are more likely to hold their value in a volatile market. When the fund manager has to sell bonds into the open market to meet redemptions, those bonds will fetch a better price. Funds with a high percentage of high-grade bonds with fewer special features will perform more evenly over the years. The risk of default, though small by most standards, still exists. If a fund reaches for yield by incorporating a large percentage of lower-grade bonds or derivatives, it exposes the investor to undue risk.

How do the maturities of the bond fund affect fund price?   Within a given income class, bond funds holding bonds with longer maturities will lose value more quickly in a rising interest-rate market and perform better when interest rates are declining. Bonds with shorter maturities will preserve their value better in a rising interest-rate scenario than when interest rates fall. Long-term bond funds yield more than shorter-term bond funds but are generally more volatile.

Won't my fund perform better if it is actively and frequently traded?   Bond funds which are actively traded will throw off capital gains and losses as the management seeks a high total return. Trading commissions are charged to the fund but are not included under the heading of general operating costs. Active trading increases operating expenses without necessarily improving the bottom line in bond funds. Seek out funds which adopt a buy-and-hold regime, only selling under special circumstances.

Why should I be so concerned about fund expenses?   The expenses of the fund can seriously eat into the return. If the bonds in the fund yield 7 percent and the fund charges 1 percent in annual expenses, almost 15 percent of your income is eaten up in fees. The gains must be reported for tax purposes on the shareholders' tax returns. Bond funds sometimes wave most of the fees with a start-up fund. This would give the impression that the fund has exceptional performance. Money floods into the fund, and then the fees are reinstated. The yield is reduced subsequently when the fees are reinstated. The fund is betting that lethargy will keep the investor in the fund even though the yield has dropped. The careful shopper will pay attention to the notices of policy change enclosed with his statements, and check for fee changes in funds where fees have been waived.

Are the approaches to managing the fund what I would do if I had the time and know-how?   The management has an investment philosophy which guides its decision. There may be a manager who is a star performer, or a stable team that has produced predictable results over a long period of time. With bond funds especially, today's shooting star may be tomorrow's black hole.

Can I know by the fund title what types of securities the fund is holding?   Look beyond the title of the fund to see what kinds of securities are actually included in the portfolio. The special features of a bond fund may be its undoing. Generally only 65 percent of the securities in a fund must be reflected in the fund title. You should find out what is included in the other 35 percent by reviewing the fund's annual report.

Should I be concerned about derivatives in the bond fund? Derivatives are imaginative creations derived from bonds. They can be used either to hedge a portfolio or to speculate. Hedging takes a bit out of the bottom line, and speculation substantially increases risk. Ask yourself why you are investing in a particular fund. Safe-sounding Treasury or government bond funds may include derivatives which increase the riskiness of the portfolio. A Treasury bond fund holding zero-coupon bonds is going to be more volatile than its peers—and as far from a staid, safe investment as the lamb is from the lion.

What is the primary difference between a bond and a bond fund? *Bond funds never mature. They never come due.* If interest rates go up, the value of the bond fund will decline. As in a stock fund, you may never get your principal back. Bonds have a fixed due date at which time you will get back the face value, unless the bond is in default.

Is there any way to keep track of funds purchased at different fund families?   Charles Schwab & Company's OneSource program was the first program to help you deal with the administrative nightmare of tracking funds purchased at different fund families. The investor can shop among 358 funds from 45 families without paying any loads or transactions fee. However, there is no free lunch. Charles Schwab charges 0.25 percent to 0.35 percent of assets collected through OneSource to funds participating in its program, and currently has about $18 billion in assets.[1] So far the participating funds have not yet passed on this fee to the fund shareholders. There is also a special fee for people defined as market timers, as described in Chap. 11.

Jack White Mutual Fund Network and Fidelity Funds Network have successfully followed Schwab's lead. Not all fund families participate in each of these services, so the flow of money among the funds is not as fluid as it might be.

---

[1]Carole Gould, "Fees Rise at Charles Schwab,"*The New York Times,* June 4, 1995, p. 7.

Other brokerage houses are sprouting services that appear to imitate the more successful programs. Be sure to compare the fees, and remember that brokerage advice is not disinterested in the outcome if the broker makes a commission for his service.

How Should I Judge the Performance of My Funds?   The best way to compare your funds' performance is against indexes published by major brokerage houses which track them, such as those published by Lehman Brothers, Salomon Brothers, or First Boston. There are indexes for short-, intermediate-, and long-term bonds. There are also special indexes for municipal and Treasury bonds of the varying maturities. In making a comparison, it is important to be clear that the index and the fund contain the same maturity span and the same type of bond. If the maturity structure or type of investment does not match exactly, then the comparison will either produce better or worse results than actually exist.

You could also compare the performance of your fund to other funds in the same asset and maturity class. Fund performance is listed in the *Wall Street Journal* and *The New York Times*, as well as in other papers that publish a business section on a daily or weekly basis. The annual surveys published by the financial magazines will also provide you with benchmark information.

The most accurate comparison is the total return figure for the period of one year. To find out how your fund is doing you can call the fund for the total return number, or you can calculate it using your monthly statements. The total return number may also be listed in the semiannual or annual report.

For our recommendations on what fund families you might consider buying, see Chap. 15.

PART 4
The Experts

13

How to Work with Brokers and Financial Advisers

A full-service broker sells stocks, bonds, annuities, mutual funds, unit investment trusts, and most other available investment products. There are many full-service firms. The larger ones are household names, such as Merrill Lynch, Smith Barney, and Prudential. Like their larger cousins, smaller firms, such as Gruntal & Co., W. H. Newbold's, and Janney Montgomery Scott, carry an inventory of bonds or will go to "the street" and buy them for you from another brokerage house. In the latter case the broker is acting as your adviser and the broker's firm is used to execute your bond transactions. Some brokers at the full-service firms have an excellent understanding of bonds. Other brokers are primarily interested in selling other investments and have only a rudimentary knowledge about bonds or bond funds.

Some investors like the comfort level of dealing with only one person for all their investment needs and having all their money in one place. Through a full-service broker, you can purchase bond funds sold by other fund companies or proprietary products sold only by them. If you decide to buy proprietary products of the brokerage house, such as home-grown bond funds, and later decide to affiliate with another broker, you will be faced with an issue to resolve. If you decide to transfer your assets to another brokerage house, you will have to sell those proprietary products and buy others. Selling an investment at a gain generates taxable income. Thus, you will have to pay taxes on your gain or take a loss if you want to move your assets.

Brokers at specialty bond houses are extremely knowledgeable about the bonds that their firm actively trades. These brokers can be great sources of information, but they may not want to spend the time with you if you are not considered a significant customer. The specialty bond firms carry an inventory of bonds and will also shop the market to find what you are looking for. They can quickly give you the particulars on any bond about which you express an interest. The specialty bond houses, called boutiques, specialize in municipal bonds. You can often get excellent selections from these firms. They may also produce insightful research on the areas on which they focus. Roosevelt & Cross is an example of a municipal bond firm focusing on bonds issued in New York, Connecticut, and Rhode Island. This firm produces fine research reports for its clients.

Discount brokers are trained to take your orders, but they don't provide a lot of information. That is why they can operate more cheaply than their full-service counterparts. Using a discount broker may be fine when you are ordering 100 shares of IBM but not as good when you need to know the particulars about a bond you are purchasing. Discount brokers don't carry an inventory of bonds. If you use their services to purchase bonds, you will be burdened with an additional spread plus a fee for the transaction.

You might also invest in bonds by buying one or more no-load mutual funds which only hold bonds. The funds' agents take orders, send out the prospectuses, and answer questions. You basically have to make up your own mind which fund is suitable for your needs. Mutual funds usually have many types of bond funds. For example there are short-, intermediate-, and long-term Treasury bond funds, corporate bond funds, municipal bond funds, and mortgage pass-through funds. One specific type of mutual fund, called an allocation account, provides an automatic asset allocation service for investors. You invest your money in the fund, and the fund manager then allocates the fund's assets between stocks and bonds. You pay extra for this service.

If you have a substantial bond portfolio, you might hire an investment adviser to manage your bond portfolio for a fee. Which manager you might retain depends in part on the size of your portfolio. Investment advisers work in two ways. Most investment advisers only run discretionary accounts. This means that they alone make all the specific investment decisions as to which bonds to purchase within the general scope of your stated objectives. Hedge-fund managers work this way. The other way for an investment adviser to work is to run a nondiscretionary account. This means that the manager seeks your consent before each bond is bought or sold.

How to Work with a Broker

Brokers are individuals. They have individual personalities. Some will be more helpful to you than others. Brokers have conflicts of interest. They are riding three horses. They are employed by the brokerage firm. They are working for themselves. They must also work for you if they hope to keep you as a client.

You must decide if you like the ideas the broker gives you. Tell the broker what your goals are and ask him to discuss with you various possibilities for achieving those goals. Do this well before you are prepared to make an investment so you can consider his recommendations. You do not wish to be hurried into taking actions which don't support your goals.

Find a broker whose basic philosophy aligns with yours or one who at least respects your perspective. He or she should know when to call you. The broker should inform you when bonds come due or when there are substantial amounts of cash in your account. She should inform you about what is happening in the marketplace when you talk together. He must have the patience to answer your questions. There is no such thing as a dumb question. She must not make you feel that your questions are out of place. The broker should not push investments on you that do not support your investment objectives. If he tells you about a new product, you should ask him about how he is compensated if you purchase the product. Always remember that a broker, however good-hearted, only makes money by moving the merchandise and generating transactions.

There are a number of basic questions to think about in selecting a broker and a brokerage firm. There are also basic questions in determining the suitability of particular investments. Gathering the information to answer these questions is a useful exercise.

Items to Consider

What is the level of risk of the investments proposed by the broker? Can you determine the level of risk from the information provided to you by the broker? There is an old expression that certain investments are sold rather than bought. This means that you would not buy the investment yourself unless someone pushed it very hard. It is acknowledged on Wall Street that the return on an investment is always proportionate to the risk involved. Thus, if a broker provides you with an investment with a large upside, you and he must work hard to determine what the risks are and whether you want to step up to these risks. If you have a situation with a large upside without a description of the risks, you only have half of the story. If your broker often describes exciting high-return investments and is light on a description of the risks, you may be heading for trouble. Insist on a full description of the risks or find another broker.

Sometimes you will be offered a new product created by the so-called rocket scientists who are employed to create new financial products. Many of the creators of these products were, in fact, former rocket scientists with a high degree of mathematical expertise. Some of these new products are called derivatives. Some are constructed theoretically to minimize certain risks and others for market speculation. However, when tested in the real world of market trading they often crash and burn. For example, in the 1980s a derivative called portfolio insurance was created. This product was supposed to hedge against a stock market decline. When all of the traders got comfortable with the new product, the stock market crash of 1987 occurred. The product not only did not work, but some think it contributed to the crash. If you can't understand how an investment works and why it should work, think twice before investing in it. If you get the sense that the broker doesn't really understand it either, you have two reasons not to invest.

Is the proposed investment a so-called proprietary product of the brokerage firm? Such a product is produced by and sold only by one particular brokerage firm. Does the broker always push the proprietary products? For example, many of the large full-service brokerage firms have created their own mutual funds. These are all load funds which might have a 4 percent up-front sales fee in addition to the usual management fee. In addition, the selling broker might also get special incentives to sell these funds. All of this might be all right if the proprietary fund is a top-performing fund with a substantial track record. However, they are often poorly performing funds, and you might do much better in other funds which are no-load to boot, i.e., have no up-front sales charge. The weight of fees sits especially hard on bond funds.

Does your broker have a special expertise and interest in bonds? We have found that most brokers specialize in stocks and stock funds since that is where they can make the largest fees. Very often if you buy a bond, that money is then "locked up" for 10 or 15 years with no further opportunity for trading and the generation of commissions. If your broker is to be your adviser in bonds, make sure that he knows about bonds, and that bonds are a large part of his business.

You should gather information. Your purpose in gathering information is to find out more about investing. Even more importantly, you need to find out about the broker who is going to help you invest the money. You need to consider the level of risk in the investments proposed. Are these new-age investments just off the shelf of the wizard, which are not understandable to the average investor? Are the products all proprietary products of the brokerage house? Are the investments packaged into funds, trusts, and closed-end funds? Does the broker know about bonds? Is that part of his business? Does he seem knowledgeable?

Writing down the information you receive from the broker is only part of the work you need to do. Request prospectuses for funds and the offering statements for new bonds. This is Boring reading with a capital "B," but it is the best way you will learn about particular issuers or products. It is the only way that you will learn if the information you are being given is complete. The brokers usually do not read the prospectuses, but work off of sales information sheets.

In a 1995 Florida case, the SEC found Prudential Securities guilty of convincing average investors to invest in tax-sheltered limited partnerships that were dangerous to their financial well-being. Limited partnerships invest in assets such as real estate and oil and gas. They are usually sold to wealthy individuals as special investments open only to select clients. To induce customers to purchase these partnership interests, Prudential provided brokers with sales literature and other information that was found to be misleading. Some of the sales literature even said that these were safe alternatives to certificates of deposit for retirement accounts, pension funds, and other conservative investments. The SEC found Prudential guilty and directed the company to set aside funds to cover client losses. The clients actually invested $8 billion in 700 limited partnerships.

Many investors have bought limited partnership interests from brokers other than Prudential. Prudential stepped over the line in their sales tactics. If the yield on an investment is high enough, then greed often overcomes fear and a person's judgment may be clouded. This is especially the case when the investors feel that they need the extra income to pay for living expenses. Securities yielding much more than usual carry greater risk and a greater possibility of loss.

Investors around the country were buying the limited partnerships. Though Prudential got nailed for providing misinformation, many non-Prudential customers have had to take substantial financial losses on limited partnerships. Each decade provides another product which takes in gullible clients. In the 1980s the tax shelter boondoggle turned out to be the real estate limited partnership. No one wanted to believe that the deals could be other than splendid. Advisers who said that the risks outweighed the rewards only resulted in losing clients. If "Smart Guy" was buying, then it had to be a great deal. Saying it wasn't so was like pointing out that the emperor had on no clothes.

If investors had read the prospectus, the risk section would have clearly spelled out the dangers. It was just inconceivable that if Smart Guy was investing in the limited partnerships, they weren't safe. Even when the prospectuses were read, they were not believed. Believe them!

While you are gathering information, you should listen carefully to everything that is said. You should speak to more than one broker. In that way, you will begin to get a feel for the differences among them. Listening requires that after you present your situation, you encourage the broker to speak. Ask about market trends. Ask about his activities. What kinds of investments have other clients been purchasing? How does he evaluate those investments? Are they short-term or long-term investments? What are his time horizons for an investment?

While you are listening, take notes. Have a notepad or a notebook in which you write down your conversations. It may be easier to take a call wherever you are, but it is important to have a file in one location. You can set up a file folder to keep a record of your conversations. When you review your notes, see if you remember who took the time to listen to your situation. Who responded to your questions and tried to tailor his responses to your concerns?

Learn to use abbreviations in your writing. It takes too long to spell everything out. If you can develop your own shorthand, it will be useful for you. When brokers give bond information they speak very fast. They do this because the good deals often go quickly. They need to provide you with the information as quickly as possible. While it is true that attractive offerings often fly out the window, it is most important that you do not make rash decisions. If a hot product is sold before you can catch your breath, another one will come along later.

Listen first and make your decisions later. Don't make snap decisions. Unless you are very sure that this is the investment for you, make it a practice to hang up the phone and call back. That will save you from becoming the owner of something you regret later. By listening first, you will begin to clarify the issues. You will get a sense of what kinds of products the broker sells. You will know if the broker takes an interest in bonds or is just saying that to make a sale. You should spend more time picking out a bond or other investment than picking out a shirt.

Gathering information will either help you develop a rapport with the broker, or you will discover that there is no chemistry between you. Why do you want a rapport? Finding good bonds requires work. You have to work to find a broker who will work with you. The broker has to be interested enough in your situation to work for you. She has to review the offering sheets and call you with bonds that she thinks are suitable for you. If there is a chemistry between you and the broker, you are more likely to get good service. Your broker is more likely to find a good product for you. She is less likely to sell you a dud if she has a personal interest in your situation. There is a fine balance between interest in the client and getting the extra commission by selling a bond with a bigger spread.

The brokerage houses recognize this conflict and try to weight the advantages in their own favor. Many firms offer incentives to top selling brokers—trips to resorts across the country or extra bonuses for selling particular products. The broker is not there for fun but to earn a living.

Recognizing the broker's conflict of interest does not mean that you have an adversarial relationship with the broker. Your objective should be to create a harmonious relationship. You want the broker to feel that you enjoy talking to him and that the advice offered is certainly considered.

It is easier for a broker to assist you if you are an educated investor. A good way to get a fix on the bond market is to ask for recent new bond issue scales. The new issue scales reveal where the larger blocks of bonds are trading. You might be able to get a better yield on the secondary market, or you might not. The new issue scales help you keep your perspective in the face of daily price changes.

If you feel that you are being pushed into an investment, you might follow the pattern described earlier. Say that you will consider the offering but you have to hang up and think it over. When you call back you can play good guy–bad guy. Say you have considered the investment, but your spouse or partner does not want it. It is never you who is rejecting the offerings, but it is the other person in your house who doesn't like the investment situation.

Another tactic you might consider using is that you have limited authority. Since the purchase is made jointly, both parties have to agree. Or you may claim that though you purchase the investments in your name, it is a decision which affects the entire family and you have to consult. The broker will not be happy with such a statement. He knows that it means that you might not make the purchase, and he will lose a sale. If he is a fast-talking broker, he will try to close the purchase as quickly as possible. Whatever reason you give, find a way not to feel hurried. If the situation doesn't feel good, don't do it.

Remember that brokers are often trained with scripts to learn how to most effectively close a sale. A script is a dialogue between the broker and the prospect. All good cold callers learn how to deal with different twists in the conversation by practicing with scripts. For example, if you told the broker that you need to think about the bonds, the response might be that the bonds will disappear in a minute, so you have to act immediately. The broker is not going to want you to talk to your spouse or hang up and think about the trade. The broker wants to close the transaction. Some brokers are more high-pressure than others. Find one that makes you feel comfortable.

Think "win-win." If you get an investment that pleases you, the broker will be happy because she made some money. In this sense both broker and client win. It is not a "win-win" situation if the broker sells you something that is going to make you unhappy. To make sure about your purchase you need to know the questions to ask, and you need to know what to do with the answers that you get.

Taking information in an orderly manner will prevent you from getting into conflict situations. Many brokers announce that they are recording conversations. Some brokers claim that they use the recordings to help train new staff, which may be so. Ultimately though, if there is a conflict later, the recordings will be used to clarify whether the investor's claims of misinformation or incomplete information are justified.

If a bond has been misrepresented, then the broker should cancel the trade. This occurs sometimes because the complete description of the bond is not given. Sometimes the brokers gather information about bonds from two or three sources. If you were only slightly interested, you might have only gotten partial information. After consideration, you may decide that the bonds offered sound like a good deal. You think you might like to purchase the bonds. When you call back, it is now necessary to make sure that you have a complete description. Giving the broker the benefit of the doubt, he might not revisit one of the computer screens if you say you are ready to buy. He is interested in closing the sale. It is necessary that you make sure that the checklist of information you need to know is complete. Read back the information you have as a way of confirming the details of your purchase. When the confirmation comes, then you will know for sure if you missed anything.

The best way to protect yourself is to get a faxed copy of the confirmation as soon as it is printed. If you do not own a fax machine, find a place in your neighborhood that receives faxes. If that is too complicated, be sure to review the confirmation as soon as it comes. The information you need on any bond is as follows:

- Rating
- Face amount
- Complete description, including the sources of revenue for revenue bonds
- Bond series, e.g., Series A
- The dated date—the date the bonds were issued
- Maturity date
- Call dates, including the yield to the first call
- Yield-to-maturity and price
- Extraordinary call features and sinking fund information, if any
- CUSIP number
- Settlement date

Individuals are being forced into the role of investor whether they like it or not as more direct contribution plans, such as 401(k) plans and IRAs, take the place of traditional pension plans. Now the individuals must make investment decisions that formerly were left to pension managers. You are being asked to make decisions about how to manage your money for 30 or 40 years so that you will preserve capital and protect your investments against inflation. You have to do that in your spare time.

How to Find a Broker

There are thousands of brokers who would like your business. How do you find the right one for you?

The first step is to decide whether the broker is working at the type of firm with which you want to do business. If you want a broker to help you with your stocks and bonds and you want the broker to provide you with stock research, you probably want a full-service broker.

If you want a broker to help you only with bonds, you have two general choices: a full-service broker or a specialty bond house. You might use both choices. It is well known that if you make your own stock selections, you can save on commissions if you use a discount broker to buy stock. However, don't be misled. When you are buying and selling bonds, there is no such thing as a discount broker. You purchase the bonds directly from the broker who owns the bonds. The broker's fee is earned in the form of a spread, the difference between what the broker pays for the bonds and the price at which he sells them to you. Since there is no commission involved, there can be no discount on the commission. The discount broker does not hold an inventory of bonds. He buys them from a dealer and marks them up for sale to you. In addition, some discount brokers charge a fee.

The best broker is one who has a large bond inventory of the kinds of bonds that you want. You might ask the broker to send you a printout of all of the kinds of bonds that you are interested in. For example, if you live in Pennsylvania and want to buy Pennsylvania municipal bonds, you might ask for a printout of the firm's Pennsylvania municipal bond inventory. If they have little or no inventory, you might consider finding another firm.

If you are buying corporate bonds, a large inventory of corporate bonds might be found at Bear, Stearns; Smith Barney; or Merrill Lynch. If your broker owns the bonds you will probably do better than if your broker has to go to another firm to purchase the bonds. However, a large inventory is not a guarantee of good prices. You might also review offerings from a number of brokers to find the right bonds at the best price.

The next step is to speak to a number of friends, family, and business associates to get a recommendation for a bond broker at the kind of firm that you decided upon. After you get a few names, you should speak to them in depth to find out what experience they have with bonds and what their philosophy is. If you are a buy-and-hold type of investor, you might not be comfortable with a broker who encourages his customers to trade their bonds. Some brokers are very conservative and will always encourage you to buy only Treasury bonds. Other brokers will encourage you to buy junk bonds. You must determine what types of bonds are in line with your investment objectives and what broker will provide the necessary research and advice to you to help you achieve your goals and objectives.

If you wish to do more due diligence on the broker, you could call your State Division of Securities, e.g., the attorney general in New York State, and ask for a CRD printout on the broker. This printout will give you information on his record, including whether the broker has been reprimanded in the past.

Is Your Broker Also Your Financial Planner?

Many brokers also act as financial planners. They may have independent offices, but they are affiliated with a specific brokerage house and do all their trades through a specific broker; or they may be housed at the brokerage house of your choice.

Commission-based financial planners make money when they sell products. These products may be offered by the broker with which they are affiliated or by one of the many independent fund families. They may not charge a fee for meeting with you, but they then make a commission on the products they sell to you. Many investors prefer this arrangement because they do not see the extra money leaving their pockets. The charges are not clearly out in the open. You may incur commission charges on the reinvestment of dividends. If you pay commissions for your funds, every time you decide to move from one fund to another you will generate more commissions. Some broker-planners encourage too much trading to increase their fees.

All commission-based planners have a conflict of interest. The more they sell, the more they make. The highest commissions are often on the worst products for you. These pay the highest commissions because they are the most difficult to sell.

Though there are many types of investments and many variations of each type of investment, if you stick with plain vanilla investments you will vastly simplify your work. In the realm of bonds and bond funds, this book is an excellent guide to helping you make simple investment choices.

If you decide to invest in funds, there are many no-load mutual funds from which to choose that do not require an investment adviser or a broker. You merely call the fund, get the prospectuses and the annual report, and look them over. The investment magazines and services provide ongoing evaluations. If you deal with a reputable no-load firm or fund family, your money will generally be well managed (see Chap. 15). That does not mean that the funds are going to hit home runs. Remember that when a fund manager or an account manager hits a home run it is because he has decided to take big risks. The joy of the investment kill could quickly pale if he made the wrong decision. The bigger the gains, the bigger the risks that were taken.

There are only a few outstanding players. John Train in his two books *The Money Masters* and *The New Money Masters* details how those players made money. Every single one of them did something different. There is no one way to make money. If someone has the skill and the luck and is successful, why is he going to let you in on his secret? He will probably be too busy making money for himself to deal with you.

Fee-Only Planners

Fee-only planners generally charge an hourly fee. They help you plan your investment strategies. A fee-only planner does not make money from commissions or financial products. Some planners wear two hats, charging an hourly fee and also collecting commissions on products sold. A fee-only planner can help you evaluate your investments based upon your needs and objectives. If you are a procrastinator, always putting off dealing with your financial matters, a planner can get you focused. If you are indecisive and can't seem to make a decision about what to do, a planner can hold your hand and help you decide. If you don't like thinking about or dealing with money, a planner can take the sting and the emotions out of dealing with money. A good planner can help you to prioritize your goals and help to define them if they are not clear. A good planner is like a good therapist: there to help you clarify your situation and to move you forward without taking advantage of your need for support.

A good planner does not have a conflict of interest. A client is sometimes given the choice of paying a fee only or paying no fee and letting the planner make the difference through the commissions. Many investors choose the latter alternative because they want to reduce the counseling fee. This is penny-wise and pound-foolish. If you have to pay for it one way or the other, it is cleaner to just pay a one-time fee and avoid the conflict of interest of product-based fees. The savvy investor wants to know what the charges are.

If you have a lot of money and you want someone to supervise your assets, then you might hire a discretionary or nondiscretionary investment adviser, also called an asset allocator. He will also create a financial plan for you. Some charge a percentage of your assets under management. Some only manage money in mutual funds, and others manage other investments as well. Some fund families have begun offering asset allocation programs within the family to investors as well.

Whichever type of broker or financial adviser you choose, being aware of the possible ways conflict of interest can hurt you will go a long way in preventing you from falling into investment traps. If you look for the conflicts of interest, you can better evaluate the advice you are given.

14

The Search for Knowledge and Information Sources

Buy the rumor, sell the news.
WALL STREET SAYING

"I saw the news today, oh boy!"   BEATLES

Investors want to make "correct" investment decisions. We all want certainty. We want to know that the person giving us advice *knows*, and can tell us what to do in a very uncertain world to protect ourselves from the dangers to our investments.

You might read the financial section of the newspapers, financial magazines, and even books like this one to gain detailed knowledge about your investments. However, it may seem that the more you read, the more difficult the decisions become.

Why is this? One reason is that everyone refers to and defers to the "experts." There are experts on all subjects. We always rely on experts to help us deal with technical matters. If investing is a technical matter, why is there a problem? Let's just find the experts and let them tell us what to do.

One problem is there seems to be an endless number of very qualified experts who are easy to find. They appear everywhere: on TV and radio, in newspapers and magazines. They have all kinds of different titles and degrees. Some are economists; some are authors; some manage billions of dollars. If you don't find an expert, don't worry. Many of the so-called experts will find you. Some are brokers who cold-call you at dinnertime to begin a "relationship"; some are accountants; and some are financial planners. They all know exactly what you should do with your money and they are certain of their advice.

While each expert is sure of his advice, the experts' advice is conflicting. One great expert says that bond prices have nowhere to go but up, and another equally qualified expert expresses grave concern about a severe drop in bond prices. It also seems that the worst advice comes when most of the experts agree on something.

Why is there such a conflict of opinion from the experts? We believe that the answer is that each category of experts really does have significant knowledge about the subject. However, the basic questions are too complex to solve with any degree of consistency.

Economists would have us believe that the economic data that rains down upon us day after day represents meaningful hard facts; that the unemployment figures or the industrial production numbers really sway the marketplace and determine what will happen on a particular day. However, all the experts won't interpret the numbers in the same way, since they may take into account other extraneous factors. More than likely, the experts see that something happened, and then they look for why it happened. The culture of the financial world is like other cultures of the world. It is about intangible, ambiguous, unstable, and often contradictory stories that people tell each other as they try to make sense of the actions of the marketplace.

Interest Rates Are Going Where? This Must Be the Time to Buy

When purchasing bonds, one question always in the mind of the buyer is whether this is the right time to be buying bonds. Are interest rates rising, and the value of my newly purchased bonds declining, or are interest rates falling? If you buy bonds at the wrong time, you may have paper losses. If you don't buy bonds now, but leave your money in a low-yielding savings account, you still lose money. You could have made much more if you purchased a bond. You kept your money liquid, but lost the incremental amount or the *opportunity cost* of your money.

A news reporter asked a great financier the usual question: "In what direction will the stock market move in the next year?" The financier thought for a moment and gave this advice: "The market will move in a sawtooth pattern."

Bonds also move in a sawtooth and unpredictable pattern. The market players try to predict the highs and lows based upon an endless stream of economic data. This includes the rise or fall of unemployment insurance claims, the inflation rate, the Consumer Price Index (CPI), the Producer Price Index (PPI), and housing starts. The traders anticipate the timing of this information and try to build their expectations of the rates into their prices before the announcements.

Also of concern are the actions of the Federal Reserve Bank in trying to control the supply of money in circulation. One tool often discussed is the Federal Reserve's plans for the discount rate. This is the rate of interest that the Fed charges banks when they borrow. When the rate is lower, the banks are able to borrow more, putting more money into circulation. This enables businesses to borrow at lower rates, increasing economic activity. Raising the discount rate makes borrowing more expensive, reduces borrowing, and drains money from the economy. The Federal Reserve meets monthly and usually announces discount-rate changes after those meetings. During the month, the Fed may sell Treasury bonds to drain cash from the economy or may purchase Treasury bonds to increase the money supply. When the Fed raises rates or buys Treasuries, the market interprets these actions as anti-inflationary measures. When the Fed sells Treasuries, it tends to drive up interest rates and increase borrowing costs for corporations and individuals. As interest rates rise, bonds become more attractive to buyers, drawing money out of the stock market.

Any significant economic action, whether national or international, has an impact on the financial markets. What is usually not clear is what that reaction will be. Talk of changes in the tax code, government spending, the deficit, the value of the dollar in relation to the other major currencies, the balance of payments, and a host of other factors bombard the reader. The herd waits to see which way to run.

Should you expect that if you read all of the papers and gather all the information you will know if you should buy or sell? Even the most respected soothsayers miss the mark. Some years ago Henry Kaufman was a senior partner at Salomon Brothers, a major bond house. He competed with Albert Wojnilower of First Boston for the title of most knowledgeable pundit on interest rates. Together they were known as Dr. Gloom and Dr. Doom. They were quoted daily in the newspapers, and investors hung on every word. Mr. Kaufman's December forecast became a media event, broadcast from the Waldorf Astoria. He was so well regarded that the *Wall Street Journal* researched and recorded every call that Mr. Kaufman ever made on the direction of interest rates. The startling finding of the study was that Mr. Kaufman correctly called the direction of interest rates 50 percent of the time!

Today, with the widespread use of computers and the proliferation of information sources, the chief economists at brokerage houses do not have the same hold on public attention. Superstars like Bear, Stearns's Wayne Angell burn with an intense brilliance so long as they can accurately predict interest rates, but they lose their luster when their forecasting accuracy diminishes. Angell was the first former governor of the Federal Reserve Board to ever take a chief economist job on Wall Street. His initial predictions were so accurate that Congress investigated whether he was getting insider information from his old buddies at the Federal Reserve. When he spoke, the markets reacted. In January 1995, he was indecisive about whether the Fed would raise interest rates. Angell forecast a rate increase, changed his mind, and then changed it again, correctly predicting that the Fed would raise interest rates. The flip-flop was all that was needed for the markets to discount his advice. The traders were no longer sure that his judgment was predictive of future events. He went from angel to ordinary person in only a few months. If his prognostications hit the mark again, then he will shoot back into the heavenly firmament.

The function of the chief economists at the brokerage houses is to lend an aura of learning and knowledge to what otherwise might be viewed as a high-class poker game. It is their job to paint the canvas with all the economic complexities combined into an intelligible portrait. For special clients, they present seminars and telephone conferences. The brokerage houses broadcast their messages of economic trends to give a semblance of understanding and security to the investment process. They provide the nail on which to hang your hat. Their overview is essential in that it provides a context for understanding.

It is hard to accept that no one can predict the movement of the stock or bond markets. Many years ago we chatted with a writer for *The New York Times* who wrote the daily stock market column. His column explained why the market went up or down the previous day. We asked him how he went about writing this column. He seemed surprised by the question because he thought the procedure was as easy as it was obvious. There are always about 10 factors that are currently discussed by the economists and market experts. Five of the factors are positive and five are negative. When the market goes up, you point to the positive factors. When the market goes down, you point to the negative factors. "How else would you write this column!" he declared. After the fact it is much easier to draw a clear picture of why things happen; being able to predict what will happen before the fact is more difficult. This does not prevent people from trying to beat the market and guess interest rates. Hope springs eternal.

Even the traders who are in the market every day get burned. In December 1994 interest rates hit a peak, resulting in huge losses for traders and bond funds. When interest rates go up, bond prices drop. The peak was followed by a long slide of declining interest rates and rising bond prices. Traders eager to recoup their massive 1994 losses loaded up on long-term Treasury bonds that they planned to unload when they saw the rally bottom out.

Many traders were so sure that bond prices had peaked that they placed a bet that bond prices would decline by *shorting* Treasuries. A *short position* entails selling bonds you don't own in anticipation of buying them back at cheaper prices later. One trader was so sure the market was turning that he made a classic mistake. He placed his bets and went on vacation. Upon his return he was met by a market that had continued to rally, and he had to purchase the bonds at higher prices! Since he was a trader, he thought he could read the market and could figure out what would happen. The economic indicators failed to guide the traders to a correct reading of the market. Traders did well if they simply recognized the downward flow and went with the flow despite the views of the economists and the economic indicators.

Many traders were caught by the rapid slowing of the economy in early 1995, the wild gyrations of the dollar, stratagems of the mortgage market, and the fearful buying of professional investors. The old paradigm thinking about the dollar resulted in unexpected consequences. The value of the dollar dropped precipitously against the Japanese yen and the German deutsche mark in May and June 1995. The usual result of such a decline in the dollar is that U.S. bond yields rise because of the fear of U.S. inflation. Foreign money is expected to flee the falling dollar. This time the result was different. Foreign central banks intervened on the dollar's behalf by buying dollars and parking their dollars in long-term U.S. Treasury bonds. Usually this money is put into short-term Treasury bills. This time the money bought long-term Treasuries, taking advantage of the comparatively rich U.S. yields.

The economic indicators of industrial production, home-building, and payroll jobs showed declines, indicating an economic slowdown. This should have resulted in a drop in interest rates.

Joseph Spiers of *Fortune* magazine described what happened next. "In a bolt, bears became bulls. This crush on the buy side—like rush-hour commuters cramming onto a train—caused bond yields to tilt to the lower side of 7 percent triggering a second unexpected wave of buyers."[1] The owners of mortgage-backed securities feared that the drop in interest rates would allow homeowners to refinance their mortgages. If they did refinance, then the higher-yielding mortgage bonds would be redeemed much faster than expected. To keep the yields on their portfolios up, fund managers purchased 5- to 10-year Treasuries, further fueling the market rally.

On June 21, 1995, the 30-year Treasury bond yielded 6.47 percent. There was talk of the Federal Reserve cutting short-term interest rates. It seemed clear that the economy was slowing, and a recession might be looming. Then on June 23, 1995, came the report of durable goods orders (cars, chairs, airplanes, etc.) for the month of May. Unexpectedly, they were up 2.5 percent, indicating that the economy was much stronger than expected. The price of long-term Treasury bonds dropped significantly, and yields were up more than half a point on that day.

You can look at the history of interest rates and know when interest rates are historically high and low. The last time the 30-year Treasury bond was below 6.7 percent was in 1975.[2] In mid-1995, the interest rate on 30-year Treasury bonds was 6.54 percent. Since 1975, 6.54 percent has been an historically low rate. However, 6.54 percent is historically a high rate for the years 1922 to 1975, with only a few exceptions. The fluctuation of interest rates cannot be predicted. Compared to the 3 percent long-term yield in Tokyo, however, that 6.54 percent U.S. rate sparkles. When compared to *real returns,* the amount of return you receive after inflation, even these seemingly low rates are historically high.

What can we learn from the above stories? Interest rates move in a sawtooth pattern, and it is difficult to call the turn. If the experts can't do it, who can? It is said that correctly calling the direction of interest rates is even more difficult than predicting the direction of the stock market. Hope springs eternal.

The Flood of Information

If we can't predict the direction of interest rates, why do we have the endless articles and discussions about this subject? Investors are hungry for any information that may give them an edge in making their investment decisions. Brokers pay rocket scientists megabucks to figure out the angles. As long as there is hope for a huge score, there will be information

---

[1]Joseph Spiers, "Inside the Big Bond Rally," *Fortune,* July 10, 1995, p. 66.
[2]Roger Lowenstein, "Intrinsic Value," *Wall Street Journal,* June 1, 1995, p. 1.

buyers. This information is a salable product that sells through newspapers, magazines, TV, radio, and now on the on-line computer networks. It makes a lot of money. It doesn't seem to matter to investors that much of the information is inaccurate, misleading, contradictory, and frequently changing. It is a straw in the wind. If you read the media carefully, you can find something to support any position you wish to take.

For example, the headline news of the *Philadelphia Inquirer* on Tuesday, July 4, 1995, reported that "New reports see economy weakening: Personal income and construction spending fell in May. That puts more pressure on the Fed to cut interest rates." On the same date, *The New York Times* published a contradictory article on page 49 entitled "Rise in Consumer Spending May Rule Out Fed Rate Cut."

There were four economic indicators announced on Monday, July 3, 1995. Spending by consumers showed unexpected strength in May, considerably faster than April's increase of one-tenth of one percent, reported *The New York Times*. The *Times* viewed this indicator as the most important one. The *Philadelphia Inquirer* focused on the drop in Americans' personal income, a scaling back of construction spending, and a contraction of the manufacturing sector. Both articles mentioned all the measures. They chose to weight the information differently. Despite the differences in the headlines, both articles concluded that no one had any idea what the Fed action would be at the next Federal Open Market Committee meeting the following Wednesday and Thursday. Though the barrage of information might influence your feelings about the direction of interest rates, in fact you cannot really know which way they are headed.

Investors seek certitude. That is, they want to feel that the experts advising them *know* what they should do to protect themselves from the dangers of investing. "Anyone who underestimates the power of a falling dollar to drive our interest rates higher will have their head handed to them on a platter," shouted one newsletter writer.[3] In June 1995, in the face of a falling dollar, interest rates continued to decline. The newsletter author was correct in stating a relationship between interest rates and the dollar that existed in the past. Unfortunately, the predictable pattern became unpredictably different. As Jim Grant reminds us in his book *Minding Mr. Market*, markets are unpredictable. Just as a consensus is reached on the future course of events, something unexpected may happen. Grant reminds us that what people know is the past and the present. It is comforting to anticipate that the future will follow patterns with which we are familiar. However, anticipating that often brings unsatisfying results.

---

[3]Martin Weiss's *Safe Money Report* as reported in *The Bull & the Bear*, May 1995, p. 44.

What to Do If You Know
That You Don't Know

Tolstoy in his epic novel *War and Peace* laid out two alternative views of history. The first alternative is that history moves in a circular path and thus repeats itself in regular cycles. The second alternative is that history is linear and continually moves forward without substantial repetition.

If you believe that history is circular and will repeat itself, you will find comfort and knowledge in historical facts. One historical fact is that for the past 65 years the stock market has averaged a gain of about 10 percent a year, while long-term Treasury bonds have averaged a gain of about 5 percent a year. If you believe that history repeats itself endlessly, you may be persuaded that stocks will always outperform bonds and therefore you should invest the bulk of your money in stocks.

If you believe that history is linear, you may be interested in what has happened in the past but not persuaded that the past is always prologue to the future. In this case you will not automatically conclude that because stocks outperformed bonds in the past they will surely outperform them again in the future. A consideration of risk and your own personal situation is also important.

A savvy reader will want to know how the experts computed 10 percent stock gains and 5 percent bond gains. Lawrence Siegel, managing director of Ibbotson Associates Inc., a Chicago research firm, calculated how fees and taxes reduced the stated returns on stocks and bonds. The period he selected was 1926 to 1992.[4] The picture is not pretty.

Their analysis initially supported the general knowledge that both stocks and bonds made money and stocks outperform bonds over a long period of time. However, the real lesson does not become clear until you factor in what those raw returns leave out, reductions that must be made in the real world for trading costs, management fees, and taxes. The raw numbers do not include any of these items. The Ibbotson data showed that if the gains in both stocks and bonds were adjusted for inflation, transaction fees, and taxes most of the gains evaporated. Instead of riding a racing bike, the investor was really trying to cross the finish line on a stationary bike. In addition, their analysis did not take into account the effect of the impact of state and local taxes or the higher current fees for trading stocks and bonds.

Does this mean you should shove your money under the mattress? Unfortunately, you must invest your money. If you don't invest, even modest inflation will eat away at the value of your dollars.

---

[4]Barbara Donnelly, "Why Taxes and Fees Are Killing You," *Smart Money*, April 15, 1992, p. 53.

Many of the outcomes that we thought were certain to occur have not occurred. The world is changing rapidly and changing *more* rapidly all the time. No one could have predicted that within a short period of time all of the following would occur:

- In the international scene:
  The Berlin Wall fell.
  The Soviet Union dissolved.
  The Arabs and Israelis made substantial progress toward peace.
  Japan rose quickly toward economic dominance.
  China, while still a communist country, moved toward being a major economic power and may shortly become *the* major economic power.

- In business:
  Microsoft successfully challenged IBM in software.
  Middle managers were no longer needed.
  The U.S. dollar slid 20 percent against the yen in a short period of time.
  Moody's considers downgrading the debt of the U.S. government.
  The American health industry is transformed, leading to hospital consolidations and the rise of the health maintenance organizations.
  Utilities, which had enjoyed monopolistic control of electricity, face competition from "free wheeling," forcing a lowering of electric rates.
  Major tax reforms are proposed.
  Banks consolidate their services and merge with other banks to hopefully gain a competitive edge.
  Stocks are offered for sale on the Internet as an Initial Public Offering (IPO), bypassing the traditional brokerage channels.

In this rapidly changing world can we validly accept the fact that stocks will always outperform bonds? From the earlier analysis it is not even clear that they did so in a real-world environment, factoring in taxes and transaction fees that you would pay. Finally, stocks and bonds are not the only investments to consider. In an inflationary environment, neither stocks nor bonds perform well. If there is substantial inflation, investors should consider investments in tangibles. Tangibles include investments in art, antiques, real estate, gold, and commodities. Remember how well these investments performed from 1975 to 1983, a time of high inflation.

Market Strategies

Socrates said that he was the smartest man in all of ancient Greece because he knew that he knew nothing. Knowing what you don't know is a powerful piece of information. You will be in a good position, especially compared to those who think they know everything. If we admit that neither we nor anyone else can predict the direction of interest rates or bond prices, we now have an important vantage point of knowledge to see what we do know. This knowledge can be used as follows:

- Clarify when you are an investor and when you are speculator. Know when you are making a bet on the direction of interest rates or the movement of the markets.

- Ladder your portfolio by spreading your money over many years. Reinvest the proceeds of bonds which come due every year or two in new bonds. This will achieve an average return over a period of years.

- Purchase long-term bonds with 20- to 30-year maturities with caution. They yield more than shorter-term bonds. If interest rates spike upward, long-term bond prices plummet. In 20 years you'll get your money back. You probably either can't or won't want to hold long-term bonds until they come due to reinvest the principal at higher rates. By contrast, you can hold short-term or intermediate-term bonds to maturity and have reinvestable cash. Bank trustees used to invest trust funds in long-term Treasuries. In the past, that was considered the most conservative approach. That policy lost megabucks for the beneficiaries and got the banks sued.

- Use a *barbell* instead of a ladder if you prefer to lock in longer-term rates. In a barbell, you invest your portfolio by purchasing relatively long-term bonds to capture the higher returns and very short maturities as a way of parking cash for placement later. The barbell may yield more or less than a bond ladder. Whatever you choose to do, it has to be because it will meet your specific economic needs.

- Avoid market timing, i.e., moving money in and out of bonds in response to interest-rate fluctuations. This is best left to traders who move big positions and watch the trading action all day every day. Even successful portfolio managers avoid market timing. Henry B. Spencer is the portfolio manager for Integon Corporation. He manages a $435-million consolidated fixed-income portfolio with a market forecast. Instead of market timing, he invests the cash when it comes in. Spencer stated:

    You get some rich bonds and you get some cheap bonds in terms of the market being high or low. But anytime you buy anything you try to

---

[5]Jon Birger, "Rate Forecasts Not His Forte, But He Gets Results," *The Bond Buyer*, June 30, 1995, p. 6.

buy the most attractive thing in the market at the best yield. . . . Though you may not always get something with particularly high yield, you may get something that's very high quality at a very good price which you can then trade [for] a richer price later on or buy something else that represents value.[5]

Being able to hold a bond until it comes due is a major advantage of bonds as compared to stocks. Consider the stock market investor who has big paper gains and a very low tax basis. If he sells his stock, he will have to pay a big tax on the gain. To avoid paying the taxes he could hold the stock until his death, giving his heirs a step-up in tax basis. If the stock investor lost his job, thereby cutting his expected annual income, this would reduce the rate at which he has to pay taxes. Both of these events are unexpected, but it is precisely the unforeseen that may result in investment opportunities.

In the spring of 1995, every newspaper and magazine article screamed that stocks were at an all-time high and bonds were at an all-time low. High short-term interest rates gave rise to a nearly inverted yield curve, an indicator that the stock jockeys view as an omen of a bear market. Yet stocks continued their unrelenting climb upward. Do you sell out and take your gain?

If the media parade is all marching in unison to the same music, then for sure the institutional investors have already included that information in their market strategies. Once an idea is in print in any publication, it is old news. You have to decide whether you want to lock in your gain by selling your stock and buying bonds. Once interest rates and the stock market change course, the prices of stocks are likely to fall much quicker than the rise in interest rates. What is an acceptable interest rate to reduce your risk of loss of principal in the stock market? Do you want to lock in your stock gain or continue to risk it every day? Each day when you make a decision not to sell, you are in effect making a decision to buy the stock at the current market price. If you would not buy at the current price, then why are you still a stock owner?

Market Timing: Is This for You?

There are two types of bond investors. Those who engage in a buy-and-hold strategy and those who try to time the market. The buy-and-hold investors buy bonds and hold them until they come due, unless there is a personal financial reason for them to sell their bonds. The market timers seek to anticipate interest-rate movements and then capitalize on short-term market swings. As interest rates go down, the price of the bond will go up, and vice versa.

Market timing is a strategy of in-and-out trading. Some brokers think they can guess which way interest rates will go. However, the only thing that the brokers will do for sure is generate fees for the brokerage house. There is little evidence that even the top pros can consistently guess the direction of interest rates. If that is so, what is the prospect that your broker will do any better. A great deal of the hype is based on the myth of frictionless motion that is unrealistic.

The first friction on trading is taxes on the gains. Mark Hulbert is a well-respected financial writer for *Forbes* and the editor of the *Hulbert Financial Digest,* a newsletter that ranks the performance of investment advisory newsletters. In the August 1992 issue of the *AAII Journal,* published by the American Association of Individual Investors, he reported on a study carried out by his newsletter on market timing. Hulbert's conclusion was that successful market timing is difficult enough in a tax-free world and is nearly impossible for an individual who has to pay taxes on his portfolio.

The second friction is trading costs and timely execution. Even if the advice is correct when given, you may be late in getting this good advice and your execution might not result in the most favorable price for your purchase. Warren Buffet, the most successful investor of our time, follows a buy-and-hold strategy in order to avoid transaction costs and taxes on gains. Hulbert has stated that the average investor who frequently trades is almost guaranteed to be less successful than one who follows a buy-and-hold strategy. He suggests that investors "take with a whole spoonful of salt any letter's claim to earth-shattering results for its followers."

Finding the Relevant Information

Investors need information to find out what is happening in the bond market. All the major newspapers will highlight the major economic news:

- Will the Fed raise or lower interest rates?
- In what direction are the leading indicators moving?
- To what rhythm did the stock and bond markets dance today?

- Changes in the closing price or yield of long-term Treasury bonds.
- Major news events affecting the economic markets.
- A listing of bonds traded on the bond exchanges.
- A listing of the current prices of Treasury bills, notes, and bonds.

The Financial Press

The major daily newspapers covering bond news are *The New York Times*, the *Wall Street Journal*, and the *Investor's Business Daily*. They all comment on the major economic news driving the bond markets. They all have information on Treasury bonds and stock exchange bonds. After that, the information diverges.

The *Wall Street Journal* provides a wealth of information on every category of bond each business day. One of the most useful columns is the "Bond Market Data Bank." This table shows the daily, weekly, and monthly price changes for U.S. Treasury bonds, U.S. corporate bonds, tax-exempt bonds, mortgage pass-through securities, guaranteed investment contracts, and international bonds. The index shows the changes for each category of bond. For example, the Lehman Brothers indexes track U.S. Treasury bonds.

A daily table shows the general level of interest rates on all the major categories of debt and key indicators such as the prime rate, federal funds rate, discount rate, and commercial paper rate. The paper provides a municipal bond index that shows the current interest rate and the change for the week in the major categories of municipal bonds. The tables show all of the closing prices for the previous day for (1) Treasury bonds, notes, and bills; (2) government agency and similar issues; and (3) New York Exchange Bonds, Amex Bonds, and NASDAQ convertible debentures. There is an extensive listing of new issues, as well as daily commentary about the credit markets.

The New York Times publishes information similar to that published in the *Wall Street Journal*. In addition, *The New York Times* provides information on active corporate bond issues, federal agency bonds and zero-coupon bonds, money supply, new municipal offerings, and other economic indicators. *The New York Times* also charts municipal bond yields and Treasury bill yields, showing how they have changed over a period of time. The Sunday edition of *The New York Times* has extensive articles and pages of mutual fund quotes.

Investor's Business Daily prints Treasury offerings in the largest typeface and with the widest spacing of the three dailies. That is much appreciated by those of us who are trying to avoid reading glasses.

Barron's is a weekly newspaper, which has a credit markets column written by Dan Forsyth. It also has extensive fund coverage and interesting tidbits about the bond markets that are not found elsewhere.

The *Financial Times* is a London-based paper that focuses on the news and investment stories of Europe. For those interested in foreign bonds, this is an excellent source of information. The *Economist* is a weekly magazine also focusing on world economic news.

Other weekly and monthly financial magazines also have articles about bonds and bond funds. *Smart Money, Worth, Kiplinger's Personal Finance Magazine, Financial World,* and *Money Magazine* address the individual investor's personal financial strategies. What you choose to read depends on your personal taste for the presentation style of the magazine.

Moody's Bond Record and *Standard & Poor's Bond Guide* are monthly publications recording changes in the ratings of bonds. These publications provide summary statistical information on corporate bonds, and ratings for municipal bonds. In addition, there is information on foreign bonds and convertible bonds.

New on the scene from an old-line company is *Moody's Outlook on Municipals.* It is a publication that targets the individual investor. This new publication plans to alert you to important developments that might affect the credit quality of your portfolio. It explains Moody's techniques used to evaluate municipal securities in order to help you become a more knowledgeable investor. It highlights municipal market sectors.

Brokerage houses can be a good source of research information. Most entertaining is the literature written by Jim Lebenthal of Lebenthal & Co., which is included with the bond offerings they mail. Gabriele, Hueglin & Cashman also publishes *News & Offerings,* which contains interesting pieces of information with their bond lists. Smith Barney has a monthly publication called *Municipal Bond Research* that provides excellent insights into trends in the municipal markets. Some regional bond houses, such as Roosevelt & Cross in New York City, do their own analysis of regional credits and write very thorough reviews of situations affecting local municipal bonds. Merrill Lynch publishes *Fixed Income Strategy,* which gives a monthly review of factors affecting all kinds of bonds and includes tables and graphs that Merrill Lynch prepares for its high-net-worth clients.

A newsletter that has stood the test of time is the *California Municipal Bond Advisor,* which focuses, as you might imagine, on the California municipal bond market. There is a lead article on current events, a heavy focus on bonds in trouble, and updates on bonds in default. It is published by Zane Mann in Palm Springs.

Another newsletter that has been around for a while is the *Income Securities Advisor* published by the Bond Investors Association. It focuses on corporate and municipal bonds. Its author, Richard Lehman, is often quoted on major issues affecting the market. Part of the newsletter focuses on bonds in default, municipal bonds on credit watch, new products, interest-rate profiles, and preferred-stock prices. Lehman also publishes a *Defaulted Bonds* newsletter. It provides an in-depth look at both corporate and municipal bond defaults. If you have an interest in a particular defaulted bond, this publisher has a database from which it can produce a customized report.

In some states there are very active state advisory commissions. The California Debt Advisory Commission publishes monthly *Debt Line*, which describes the debt coming to market and considers the major issues concerning California debt. Its focus is primarily to assist state and local agencies on matters of debt issuance. Perhaps more interesting for the individual investor is the annual report, which gives an overview of debt issuance in the state and lists the publications of the commission. Other states, such as Texas, Oregon, Washington, and North Carolina, also have active state agencies, though the function of each agency differs from state to state. These agencies usually operate out of the treasurer's office or the executive office of the state.

Sources of Information on Open-Ended Bond Funds

There are many sources of information about open-ended funds. The foremost publisher in the field is Morningstar, Inc. It publishes biweekly, monthly, and annual reports on the funds. The most frequently published is the *Morningstar Mutual Funds*. Lipper Analytical in conjunction with Standard & Poor's publishes quarterly the *Mutual Fund Profiles*. CDA Investment Technologies publishes a monthly and annual report under the general heading of *CDA/Wiesenberger Mutual Funds Update*. Value Line has also entered the field with its *Value Line Mutual Fund Survey*.

All the major financial magazines publish annual reviews. This includes *BusinessWeek, Financial World, U.S. News & World Report, Money Magazine,* and *Forbes*. In addition to *Forbes*'s extensive August issue each year on funds, its editors also update some information in the February, May, and November issues. *Barron's* and the *Wall Street Journal* publish quarterly reviews, in addition to the daily updates by the financial newspapers.

If you are just starting to gather information, you might try visiting your local library. Many of these publications and others are in the periodicals and the reference sections.

Sources of Information on Closed-End Funds

Information on closed-end funds is available in a Morningstar publication called *Morningstar Closed-End Funds,* which offers a three-month trial subscription for $25. *Forbes* ranks closed-end funds in its August issue. The most complete source of information on closed-end funds is the annual *Encyclopedia of Closed-End Funds,* published by Thomas J. Herzfeld Advisors, Inc., in Miami, Florida.

Computer Searches for Mutual Fund Winners

Computerized Investing is published by the American Association of Individual Investors in Chicago, Illinois. Though most of the information focuses on stock investing, the publication sometimes has articles about bond software or how to find World Wide Web sites. In addition to a monthly publication on financial planning and investing, the AAII also provides an on-line service to evaluate bond-fund performance and annually publishes the *Individual Investor's Guide to Low-Load Mutual Funds.*

There is an ever-proliferating supply of companies eager to help you sort out past mutual-fund performance to find the next winner. The major on-line services, such as CompuServe, Prodigy, America Online, Dow Jones News Retrieval, and others, provide data on over 4000 mutual funds. Some come with software to help you navigate the service, and others leave you to your own devices. Comparing prices for access is difficult, because they all charge in different ways. Some vendors will charge for unlimited access per month, and others will charge for a fixed amount of data. Perhaps the best way to decide what service to use is to decide what information you would like to have. Price out what it would cost you to obtain it on the different services.

Using these sources you can obtain a variety of information by applying various screening devices to the data. The idea is to search for funds that have particular characteristics. Once you select a group of funds, then you can compare their behavior to the fund indexes. The screening can provide information on the relative performance of a specific fund compared to all other funds. The user could graph the performance of a $10,000 investment in several funds over a period of time. Also of interest is how different investment strategies might pan out. For example, you might compare making a single lump-sum payment versus a pattern of systematic investment. The historical patterns and the current value of the fund would result. Finally, the investor might be interested in a detailed description of a particular fund.

The Internet's World Wide Web can be accessed directly, or through the software provided by the on-line services. One site location is NETworth, which is managed by GALT Technologies. It charges companies to list their funds. Investors can search funds by investment type; quality ratings by Morningstar, Inc.; and risk/return ratios. Graphing that illustrates the search criteria is also available. Fidelity Investments has its own site on the Web. Vanguard has its prospectuses and financial advice available on America Online.

Another recent entry into the on-line scene is an on-line endeavor that is called *Bonds on Line*. It is accessed through Microsoft Windows 95. It plans to have articles about municipal bond issues, current prices, and a graphically displayed new-issues calendar depicting new offerings on a state-by-state basis. The service will be supported by brokers. The display of new issues will be accompanied by a geographic list of the broker offices that are selling the bonds. There will be a charge for the municipal bond prices. Software will be available that will function as a bond calculator and a portfolio manager. You will be able to download bond price information into your computer, as you can currently do for stocks.

For those not willing to navigate the on-line services or the Internet, a large database of fund information is available on disk. One possibility is the $40 *Donoghue Online Software*. You can update the information via a modem and read advice provided by the syndicated columnist. Morningstar, Inc., the fund-rating company, publishes *Mutual Funds OnDisc* and *Mutual Fund Expert*. These have impressive systems, but they come with a hefty price tag. The exact costs are dependent on how much information the user wants and the frequency of the updates. On the low-cost end is *Fund Map* issued by the brokerage house Charles Schwab. It contains information on only 20 funds, but it combines the fund information with a retirement planner that tries to assess the user's appetite for risk. It asks hard questions, such as "How many years do you plan to live after retirement?"

Questions, Questions! Do You Have the Questions?

As you can see, there is a slew of information about investing and about bonds and bond funds in particular. The real issue for you is whether you can maintain a focus on your personal objectives and needs which guide your investment decisions. Too often an avalanche of information can bury you or a rush of information can sweep you away. To keep to your objectives, you must stay focused and centered. Asking questions of both yourself and others will increase your effectiveness in problem solving and decision making. Questions provide the opportunity to be self-observant—finding out what are your real objectives and goals. By asking questions, you will have an opportunity to reflect on your current situation and plans, and make corrections in those plans in order to achieve your goals. Dr. Marilee C. Goldberg in her workshop on The Power of Questions,[6] states that first we observe what our situation is by asking questions, and then we evaluate and correct it by asking additional questions. Some of these questions might be helpful to you in guiding your investment decisions. You might ask them of yourself or ask them of someone else.

Dr. Goldberg's questions are general and apply to diverse situations. We have listed them below in italics. Next to them, we have reframed them to apply to investment decisions.

Observation Questions[7]

"What is really going on here?" What kind of investment am I considering buying?

"Is this what I was aiming for?" Is this investment going to help me meet my goals with the minimal amount of risk?

"Am I being objective?" Have I read the material about this investment, or am I being swayed by the personalities of my friends or by a salesperson?

"What prejudice might I have?" Does my family have a history of investing in certain investments? Have I really considered all the alternatives?

"Would others describe this as I do?" What are the other points of view? Have I really evaluated them before making my decision?

"What might I be missing?" Do I have all the facts? Is there any information that has been withheld inadvertently or on purpose?

"Is there anything I am avoiding?" Do I really want to deal with the consequences of my investments?

"Am I being honest?" Have I really evaluated the risks of the different investments I am considering, and have I fully faced the consequences?

---

[6]Dr. Marilee C. Goldberg, *The Power of Questions,* December 9, 1994.
[7]Goldberg, p. 13.

Correction Questions

"Where am I compared to where I want to be?" Have I evaluated my investments on a monthly, quarterly, or yearly basis? Are the investments doing what I hoped they would do?

"What do I need to do to get back on track?" If the investments are not meeting my expectations, how do I want to restructure my portfolio to achieve my goals?

"What's the smallest correction that will work?" Buying and selling costs money. What do I have to do to improve the situation?

"Can I do this myself, or do I need help?" Do I have enough information? Can I be objective about my situation, or do I need an outside person to help me think through the process?

If you use these questions before you take an action, they will help ensure that proper deliberation took place in making the decisions. You will be less swayed by the media and other noise around you, and more likely to achieve your personal objectives.

15

A Simple Guide to Buying Bonds and Bond Funds

Many investors spend more time picking out a shirt than they do selecting a bond. All of us know what to look for in the purchase of a shirt since we have bought many shirts in the past. However, there is a lack of knowledge of how to proceed to buy a bond. This chapter outlines the procedure that we use when we buy bonds for ourselves and our clients.

If you have a basic understanding of bonds, you may have come right to this chapter to see what you can learn that would improve your bond-buying techniques. This is a summary chapter and assumes that you already know basic information about bonds. You can find all of the information and definitions that you need to know elsewhere in this book, including the glossary.

Preparation

Determine the Maturity of the Bond You Want. Review your existing portfolio of investments including your stocks, bonds, and mutual funds that hold stocks and bonds. Then decide upon the maturity of the bond you wish to buy.

We ladder our portfolio of bonds. This means we spread the maturities of bonds over many years. Laddering results in a reduction in your interest-rate risk and reinvestment risk since you will have money to reinvest each year or two as one or more of the bonds come due. For purposes of laddering we consider real estate, stocks, and mutual funds that hold stocks or bonds to be long-term holdings. Thus, if you have these kinds of investments, you will already have the long-end of your ladder completed. To complete the rest of your ladder, you would buy only short-term bonds (maturity of five years or less) or intermediate-term bonds (maturity of 5 to 15 years).

Take all your investments in all investment categories into account when preparing a ladder. Don't forget to add in your pension money, the money in your child's name earmarked for college, the money squirreled away in the cookie jar, and other money pockets. In addition to the maturities of securities, don't forget to consider your need for liquidity.

Find Out What the Yields Are on Newly Issued Bonds. You might be able to negotiate the price of the bond that you are buying. However, to do so you must have a good idea of what is a fair price. The new-issue market is not negotiable, whether you are buying a $10,000 bond or a block of $10 million. Thus, the new-issue price scale that you see in the newspapers will provide some guidance for you as to price. The scale for municipal bonds will be different than the scale for corporate bonds or Treasury bonds. Each is a separate, though related, market.

Compare All Fixed-Income Yields to Treasury Yields. The yield on Treasury bonds is a benchmark for all bonds. Bond professionals always compare the yield on Treasury bonds to the yield on other bonds. Treasury bonds have a number of outstanding features that make them generally the most desirable bonds. Treasuries have the best credit, are the most liquid, and are free of state and local but not federal income tax.

The media widely quotes Treasury bond prices. They are an indication of the direction of interest rates. Each day every major newspaper will print the close-of-the-day Treasury yield-to-maturity and prices for bonds selling with a one-month to a 30-year maturity. There is more easy-to-find information on Treasury bonds than on any other bond.

Traders judge corporate bond yields in relation to Treasury bond yields. If the yield on a corporate bond is not more than one-half of one percent greater than the Treasury bond yield, then the risk of the corporate bond might not justify the reward.

Traders compare how much less municipal bonds yield than Treasury bonds. Municipal bonds yield less because the interest from municipal bonds is free of federal income tax, while the yield from Treasury bonds is subject to federal income tax. Judge all investments on an after-tax basis.

Determine Your Marginal Tax Bracket, i.e., Your Highest Tax Bracket. Your tax bracket will help you determine whether you should buy a taxable bond or a tax-free bond. If you are in the 28 percent bracket or higher, you can benefit from tax-free interest. If you are buying a bond in a tax-deferred account such as a pension, IRA, or 401(k) account, buy taxable bonds. Municipal bonds yield less than taxable bonds and they confer no tax advantage in a tax-deferred account.

Investigation

Once you know what maturity you want and whether the bond will be taxable or tax-free, you are ready for the next step.

General brokers, banks, and specialized bond houses sell bonds. Call one or more of these sellers and ask them if they have bonds that match your needs and wants. You will get the best prices on bonds that the broker has in its inventory. If the broker has to find the bonds in some other seller's inventory, you will compensate two sellers instead of one. Take notes on the yields available.

If your brokers do not have suitable offerings in their inventories, then ask them to look in the Blue List. The Blue List is the broker-to-broker listing of what each of the bond houses is offering to other traders.

Ask your brokers whether there are any new issues slated to come to market in the near future and if there is a preliminary idea of the yields. Review the new-issue offerings in a major financial newspaper because brokers don't generally advertise the bond offerings of the competition. The new-issue syndicate tries to sell all the bonds itself. Only if the syndicate fails, will it sell the bonds to nonparticipating brokers.

Checking Credit Quality

You are now ready to begin to get serious about your specific bond purchase. Your biggest concern about a bond is its credit quality. Will it default after you buy it? How can you simply make a judgment about a bond?

Ask the broker for the rating of the bond. Generally two credit rating agencies evaluate the bonds. The two major credit rating agencies are Moody's and Standard & Poor's. Fitch and Duff and Phelps usually rate corporate bonds. Find out when the issuer last came to market. If the rating is 10 years old, it might be misleading. Also find out whether the rating outlook is stable or changing. For a deeper credit check ask the broker to send you a sample of an offering statement for the kind of bonds in which you might have an interest. These offering statements are long legal documents that will tell you more than you ever want to know about the issuer. There may be more than 100 pages of small print that warn you of every problem known to the human mind. However, offering statements also provide a wealth of information and will give you some comfort once you become familiar with them.

Issues Specific to
Municipal Bonds

Credit enhancements play an important part in the upgrading of the rating of municipal bond issues. Credit enhancements include bond insurance from an insurance company, a letter of credit from a bank, or some other guarantee. Credit enhancements are important and so are the underlying ratings of the bond. You might not buy an uninsured bond rated BB, four notches below AAA, but if the bond is insured by a major insurance company, it has added protection.

The rating agencies give all insured bonds a triple-A rating. If the rating agencies downgrade the insurance company's rating, all the bonds insured by the insurance company will also be downgraded. The marketplace keeps a watchful eye on the activities of its bond insurers. Thirty-eight percent of all new municipal issues are insured. It is useful to note that the market does not consider insured bonds to be as good a credit as a bond that is triple-A in its own right, and neither should you. Thus, you should pay somewhat less for a bond rated triple-A because it is insured.

If you are buying a municipal bond, find out from the broker the source of the funding for the bond. Will real estate taxes be the source of funds to pay the bond's interest and principal? Is it from a toll road, a sewer system, or rent from a municipality? The source will give you a clue as to the bond's security.

If you are buying a revenue bond, ask the broker for the debt service coverage. This is a measure of whether there is presently enough revenue being earned by the issuer to pay interest and principal when due. Coverage that equals two times the debt is good, but less than one-time coverage is a warning signal.

Consider the history of the issuer. Has there been a history of default in that state or area? How did the municipal officials respond to financial difficulties? Was there a willingness to pay by the public and the public officials? For example, New York City defaulted in 1975; however, there was a willingness to cure the default, and the officials agreed upon a solution in two weeks. By comparison, in mid-1995 in Orange County, California, there was not a willingness to pay although the county was clearly wealthy enough.

Remember that every state has different issuers, so it is not possible to provide a specific list of bonds to buy. Also, most bonds are not available at all times. The bond market is more like a Persian-rug market than a supermarket where your favorite foods are available every day. For the novice individual bond buyer, we recommend the following categories:

- *Buy state general obligation bonds.* The rating agencies give most states a single-A or better rating. Even if a state has a low rating, traders favor bonds issued by the states because of the states' large tax base.

- *Buy pre-refunded bonds that have been rerated triple-A because they are backed by Treasury bonds.*

- *Buy school district bonds rated A or better.* In many states, school district bonds by law have the extra support of the state. In many states they are general obligation bonds of the issuing district. Texas has an independent school fund backed by oil revenues.

- *Buy water and sewer bonds rated A or better.* This is an essential service, as long as the service is going to a place where there are already people who need these services. If the water and sewer lines are going to a new area, however, this may not be as good an investment because the new development may not succeed.

- *Buy general obligation bonds of rich local districts and counties rated single-A or better in states that have not passed restrictive measures against taxation.*

- *Buy from different issuers with different insurers.* Diversify your purchases.

Issues Specific to Treasury, Corporate, and Agency Bonds

Your broker can buy Treasury bonds for you on the secondary market or new-issue market. You can also purchase Treasury bonds directly from the Federal Reserve Bank. Corporate bonds and bonds issued by federal agencies are available through your broker.

Bonds sold as part of a new issue will give the retail investor assurance that the price is fair because the price is the same to all buyers.

Be concerned about the bond calls. A slightly higher yield may not be enough compensation for your bonds being recalled when interest rates have dropped.

Be concerned about bond ratings. If the rating of a bond falls from a triple-A to a double-A, it is not likely to have a serious credit problem.

However, if a triple-B rated bond drops one notch, it falls below investment grade. This indicates the company may be in serious financial trouble.

Making a Purchase:
The Mechanics

If you have done all of the above, you are now ready to begin the buying process. When the broker shows you a bond (this is the lingo in the bond business), make sure you get the details concerning the bond. While most brokers sell stocks and bonds, many brokers are less interested and knowledgeable about bonds. In this case, you must make them do their homework before they sell you a bond.

The key to the whole process is to get a complete description of the issuer and the bond you are purchasing. Find out the following:

- *The precise name of the bond.* This will enable you to identify the issuer and evaluate the credit quality as discussed earlier.

- *Call features.* Does the bond have any features that would force you to relinquish the bond before its due date? Such features include an ordinary call provision, an extraordinary call provision, and a sinking fund provision. You should ask about each of these features separately and specifically. For some reason, traders do not routinely disclose extraordinary call features unless you ask about them specifically. If a trader prices a bond to the call, the confirmation should reflect that. A general statement on the confirmation that this bond is subject to call features is not helpful. You can ask for a printout of the call features provided by one of the wire services.

   Unless you know about all the call features, you can't evaluate the yield-to-maturity of the bond since you don't know when it will come due. Remember, all calls are in the interest of the issuer. You will never benefit from a call since calls will happen when interest rates have gone down and you will have to reinvest the bond proceeds at a lower rate. If there is a call feature, ask the broker to compute the yield-to-maturity both to the call date and to the maturity date. Remember that you can't compute a yield to an extraordinary call since you can't determine when it might occur.

- *The bond rating.* What is the underlying rating of the bond and what are its credit enhancements, if any? Is the rating high enough?

Remember, return is always proportionate to the risk. If there is an above-average return, there will always be more risk. Find out what the risk is by asking questions and evaluate it.

- *Maturity date.* Don't count on a call to shorten a maturity date. Some brokers present a call as if this feature will shorten the bond's maturity in your favor. As already explained, a call is never a good thing.

- *Par, premium, and discount.* There are reasons for buying each of these kinds of bonds. Trust departments like par bonds. New-issue bonds often sell at or close to par, and the trust departments can buy the large blocks they require. A deep-discount bond may be a bet that interest rates will fall, or just a convenient way to save for college or retirement. A premium bond is a cushion against the fluctuation of interest rates. If income is your goal, then the premium bond provides the maximum cashflow. Be aware though that some of the interest income is a return of your principal. Some premium bonds have calls. A call might reduce your yield considerably, or it might provide a better yield if you bought the bond priced to its call instead of to maturity.

- *Form of ownership.* If you want to have the bond delivered to you so that you can put it in your safe-deposit box, you must buy a registered bond. More and more bonds are being issued as "book-entry" bonds that must be housed at a brokerage account. Brokers are beginning to lay charges on inactive accounts. If you have book-entry bonds held in an inactive account and must pay annual account charges, check other brokerage houses to see if their fees are lower.

- *Payment for the bonds.* After you place your order for a bond you must pay for it within three days of its purchase. If possible, you want to review the confirmation before you send in your money. You want to make sure that the bond description on the confirmation matches the one told to you. If there is a discrepancy, discuss it with your broker. You may want to request a revised confirmation. To get the confirmation in time, ask the broker to fax it to you if you have access to a fax machine. Otherwise review the confirmation when it comes in.

    Make sure you get the proper amount of payment to the broker within the three-day period. If your payment does not arrive on time, you may receive a Western Union mailgram telling you that your position is in danger of being sold. This is the standard follow-up by the brokerage house if there are insufficient funds in your account. Your broker will call you to advise you of the problem before you receive written notice.

Simple Rules for the New Bond Buyer

Simplify the bond selection process by staying within certain guidelines if possible. You should feel secure in purchasing bonds if you follow the saying: "Simple things are best."

- *Buy "plain vanilla" bonds.* These are clean and simple-to-understand bonds. They are noncallable and have good ratings. The opposite of a plain vanilla bond is a "story bond." A story bond may be complex because of the special terms and provisions of the bond. Another kind of story bond is a bond that seems weak, but which the broker says is really stronger than it looks because of the wonderful story explaining the bond. If you can't understand the story or don't feel comfortable with it, forget the bond, even if it seems to be a good deal.

- *Buy new-issue bonds.* Everyone pays the same price on a new issue, and thus you will get a properly priced bond. However, a proper price is just one aspect of the bond purchase, as discussed earlier. You may often get a better yield from the secondary bond market, though you may not feel as comfortable buying odd lots on the secondary market as buying new issues.

- *Consider buying par bonds.* Par bonds or bonds with only a small premium or discount help you avoid the specific disadvantages of premium and discount bonds.

Bond Fund Families

There are so many different bond funds, how do you decide in which to invest? One way to proceed is to select one or two mutual fund families and buy bond funds offered by these families. There are a number of practical advantages in using families of bond funds rather than selecting five or six different funds from different families. Using a family of funds keeps your paperwork to a minimum. When you trade from one fund to another within a family, you can do it with one phone call. You can also conveniently trade into one or more money-market funds that each fund family has. Your funds may all be presented on one statement. Many fund families give you considerable help with record keeping for tax purposes.

We will recommend nine fund families for your consideration. Our recommendations do not reflect our view that these fund families will outperform other fund families in the future. Each fund family was selected because it meets *all* of the following seven criteria:

- The fund family has a good selection of different kinds of bond funds as well as stock funds.

- Most of the bond funds in the family are no-load funds. We have seen no convincing evidence that load funds will outperform no-load funds. Obviously, a load will reduce the amount of money that you have invested in the fund and thus is likely to reduce your overall return, if all other things are equal.

- The management fees are within a reasonable range. Taken as a whole, Vanguard has the lowest fees.

- Most of the bond funds in the family have been in existence for at least five years.

- The family's funds are of substantial size. The larger size splits the overhead among many investors and enables the fund to afford to hire good managers.

- The funds in the family have performed reasonably well for the past five years. Past performance will not tell you which of the funds will do well in the future. However, why choose a fund that has had a poor past performance when there are so many other choices?

- Initial investment in the fund's family is reasonably low. This is the sole criteria why we did not include the PIMCo funds (1-800-927-4648). For many of the PIMCo funds, the minimum investment is $200,000. PIMCo meets all the other criteria.

The nine fund distributors that meet all of the above criteria are:

Benham Capital Management
1665 Charleston Road
Mountain View, CA 94043
1-800-321-8321

Dreyfus Service Corp.
144 Glenn Curtiss Boulevard
Uniondale, NY 11556
1-800-645-6561

Fidelity Advisor Funds
161 Devonshire Street
Boston, MA 02110
1-800-526-0084

T. Rowe Price Associates
100 East Pratt Street
Baltimore, MD 21202
1-800-638-5660

Scudder Investor Services
PO Box 2291
Boston, MA 02107
1-800-225-2470

SteinRoe Mutual Funds
PO Box 804058
Chicago, IL 60680
1-800-338-2550

Strong/Corneliuson Capital
  Managements
PO Box 2936
Milwaukee, WI 53201
1-800-368-3863

USAA Investment Management Co.
9800 Fredericksburg Road
San Antonio, TX 78288
1-800-382-8722

Vanguard Group of Investment Cos.
PO Box 2600
Valley Forge, PA 19482
1-800-662-7447

There is another way to buy a number of different funds, which has the same flexibility as a fund family. You may use an organization that will do the asset transfers and keep the records when you want to buy funds from different fund families. There is no additional charge for this service. With a single phone call you can buy one fund and sell another. In addition, you get a consolidated account statement and cost-basis accounting to help you prepare your tax returns. There are currently three organizations that offer these services. They are:

- Charles Schwab & Company's OneSource (1-800-266-5623). This was the first of its kind and is the largest with $18 billion in assets in 1995.
- Fidelity Funds Network (1-800-544-8666).
- Jack White Mutual Fund Network (1-800-323-3263).

These services can purchase bonds only from selected fund families. Some of the most popular funds choose to be the sole distributors of their services.

Let the Buyer Be Aware

When interest rates drop sharply, yield-hungry investors begin to look for alternatives. Many investors live on their income, relying on the interest from bonds to support them. When interest rates drop, people living on their interest income begin to look at alternative investments to bolster their sagging bond income.

The foremost traditional alternative is the stock market. Though the current belief is that the stock market can only go up with occasional minor corrections, history has taught us that the stock market is a fickle friend. It can soar like an albatross and then take the predictable dive into the sea. When you have ridden the stock market to the top of the roller coaster, will you have the strength to take your gains and pay the taxes? Are you young enough to wait to recoup your assets if you take a big loss? Is this the safest way to achieve your investment goals?

When interest rates are at the lowest point, the brokerage houses always produce new or slightly altered products that have a higher annual pay-out than bonds. These products may look like a bond. They pay interest monthly or quarterly. The yield on the new products is always higher than current bond yields. It seems like the answer to a prayer.

The new products usually contain features that are not in the best interest of the investor. The broker who is selling them to you may not know, and may not want to know, the less attractive features of the product. After all, it is the job of the broker to sell the products of the brokerage house. It is your function to know the questions to ask when you are deciding what to buy.

If an investor really needs the higher yield, the investor often does not want to hear about the negative aspects of an investment that is being offered. If one broker doesn't provide a product with the higher yield, then the investor will find another that can provide it. It is at times like these that the investor must decide whether to bite the bullet and reduce his or her standard of living, or risk principal in the search for higher yield.

This book provides you with the standards for good income-producing investments. When you encounter bond look-alikes that are going to pay a higher return on a regular monthly or quarterly payout, ask the same questions about them as you would for bonds.

- What is the likelihood that I will get all my principal back?
- How secure are the monthly or quarterly payments?
- What are the call features?
- When does the investment come due?
- How do I exit? Who will be the buyers of this product if I decide to sell?
- What are the fees for buying?
- What are the ongoing fees?
- What are the fees for exiting?
- How many more dollars will I earn per year from this new product compared to a traditional bond or bond fund?
- How secure is the income flow?

Ask these questions of new products if you want to know the answers and are prepared to evaluate the risks to your principal. Reading about all the different types of bonds and bond funds may help you develop additional questions. The biggest question though is always to yourself. Ask yourself: What am I prepared to risk for the additional return?

Glossary

Accrual Bond: A bond whose redemption value automatically increases every six months; for example, U.S. savings bonds and zero-coupon bonds.

Accrued Interest: Interest due the seller of a bond. It is interest which has accumulated since the last interest payment to the date of sale.

Ask Price: The price at which sellers offer to sell bonds to buyers.

Basis: Another word for yield-to-maturity, often found on confirmation slips.

Basis Point: 100 basis points equals 1 percent; used to measure interest rates or yields.

Bearer Bond: A bond that is not registered and has no identification of ownership on its face. A bearer bond is generally owned by the person who possesses it.

Bid Price: The price at which the buyer offers to purchase securities. This is always a lower price than the ask price.

Bond: Written evidence of an issuer's promise to repay a loan to a bond-holder, with interest, at a specified time.

Bond Bank: A special bank established by some states to purchase the bonds that are issued by local government units, using the proceeds from the sale of the bank's own bonds.

Bond Fund (or Fund): An open-ended mutual fund which holds a portfolio of bonds, generally within a stated class, such as municipal bonds, taxable bonds, or Treasury bonds.

Bond Price Volatility: How much the price of a bond varies. Volatility increases with the lengthening of maturities.

Book-Entry Only: A type of bond ownership where evidence of your ownership is found in the confirmation that you receive at purchase and the listing on your monthly brokerage statement. With this form of ownership you cannot get a physical certificate sent to you.

Boutiques: Small specialty houses that deal in a narrow range of bonds; a municipal bond boutique, for example, only trades municipal bonds.

Broker Loan Rate: The interest rate at which a broker lends money to a customer using the customer's stocks and bonds as security. It is generally a low rate of interest because of the good security.

Call Date: A specified time when an issuer can redeem (i.e., repurchase) all or part of a bond issue before its maturity date.

Callable Bonds: Bonds that the issuer can redeem (i.e., repurchase) at its option before the bond's maturity date and at a specified price which is sometimes above its face value. See **Fixed Call** and **Extraordinary Call**.

Cash Flow: The number of current dollars received from an investment during a specified time period.

Certificates of Participation (COP): A document which evidences a debt that is legally less than a bond because there are contingencies that must be met before the debt must be paid, such as when a legislature has to appropriate funds before interest or principal is paid.

Commercial Paper: Unsecured short-term promissory notes issued by the most credit-worthy corporations.

Confirmation: A written document that confirms an oral agreement to buy or sell bonds.

Coupon: The interest rate at which the bond was originally issued. The amount of interest expressed as a percent of the bond's face value (e.g., 6 percent) which the issuer will pay the bondholder annually.

Credit Enhancement: Provides extra protection for the bond investor and thus improves the rating assigned to a particular bond issue. The issuer benefits by receiving lower net borrowing costs.

Credit Watch: A list kept by the rating agencies of bonds that might be upgraded or downgraded in the near future.

Current Yield: The bond coupon or rate divided by the price.

CUSIP Number: An acronym for the Committee on Uniform Security Identification Procedures. A nine-digit industry standard securities identification number that uniquely identifies each bond issue.

Dated Date: The date of issue of a municipal bond. Also used for bond identification.

Debenture: An unsecured bond. In a bankruptcy it is paid after all secured borrowings.

Default: The failure of the issuer to pay any interest or principal payments promptly when due.

Derivative: An investment whose value is based on or derived from an index, interest rate, currency exchange rate, or other asset.

Desk: Traders who are hired to deal in specific types of bonds, such as a Treasury bond desk.

Discount Bond: A bond sold at less than its face value.

Discount Rate: The rate of interest that the Fed charges banks when they borrow.

Distribution Yield: The amount of cash distributed by a bond fund over the past 12 months.

Double-Barreled Bond: A bond secured by the pledge of two or more sources of repayment.

Downshifting: When individuals decide to trade money for time by seeking less demanding or more fulfilling work.

Escrowed Bond: Similar to a **Pre-refunded bond.** The difference is that an escrowed bond is priced to its maturity date.

Extraordinary Call: A call based upon an unanticipated event; for example, housing agency bonds, which are callable anytime if there are unexpended funds or a catastrophe occurs.

Face Amount or Face Value: The par value or the amount that the issuer will pay when the bond matures (i.e., comes due); the amount appearing on the face of the bond.

Fixed Call: A definite date that the bond may be called by the issuer.

Funds, Closed-End: An entity that trades on an exchange. The entity stays the same size. Shareholders must buy and sell their shares on an exchange like a stock. Shareholders cannot sell their shares back to the fund.

Funds, Open-Ended Mutual: A mutual fund where investors can at any time, except in unusual circumstances, purchase new shares from the fund and redeem (sell) their existing shares back to the fund. This fund is not traded on an exchange.

General Market Bonds: Municipal bonds from all parts of the country as opposed to single-state bonds which are bonds from only one state.

General Obligation (GO) Bond: A bond secured by the issuer's full faith, credit, and taxing power. Some GOs are **limited tax general obligation bonds** that can only be paid off with a specified stream of income, rather than from all of the municipality's revenues.

GNMA: Government National Mortgage Association (Ginnie Mae). See **Mortgage Pass-through Securities.**

Guarantee: If certain criteria are met, the promise of the guarantor to pay interest and/or principal of a bond within a defined time limit if the issuer of a bond is unable or unwilling to pay.

Indemnity Bond: An insurance policy to protect the issuer and potential buyers in case a "lost" security is redeemed or sold; also called *surety*.

Industrial Development Bond: A municipal bond generally issued by a state or state agency to construct or purchase industrial facilities which are leased to a private corporation. This bond is secured by the credit of the private corporation rather than by the state or state agency.

Insurance: A guarantee provided by a private insurance company to pay interest and principal in the event of a default.

Interest: The amount of money that is paid by the borrower for the use of the principal that is borrowed.

Issuer: The entity that borrows money and issues bonds as evidence of the debt.

Junk Bonds: High-yield bonds that have ratings below BBB.

Laddering a Portfolio: Purchasing many bonds and spreading the maturities over a number of years. Laddering will reduce the interest-rate risk.

Letter of Credit (LOC): A bank's promise to pay principal or interest or both in the event of a default on a bond during a specified period of time, often 10 years or less and not necessarily for the life of the bond.

Leverage: The use of borrowed funds to achieve higher returns.

Load: A sales charge collected upon the sale of a unit investment trust or the sale or redemption of certain fund shares.

Long First Coupon: An interest payment for more than six months of interest.

Margin Call: A demand from a broker to its customer for additional cash to guarantee performance of an investment position. A margin call results from a lack of money in a margin account, usually resulting from a decline in the value of the investment.

Marked to Market: Repricing of securities in a bond fund to reflect current market prices.

Markup: An amount added to the cost of a bond, including account spread and profit.

Matrix Price: An estimated price or value for a fixed income security. Matrix prices are based on quoted prices for large blocks of securities with similar coupons, ratings, and maturities rather than on specific bids and offers for the security.

Maturity Date: The date when the principal amount of a bond is payable.

Moral Obligation: A feature of municipal bonds which implies that the state will support the bonds in the event of a default, although the state has no legal obligation to do so.

Mortgage Pass-through Securities: Securities which represent an interest in a pool of mortgages of at least $1 million. Investors receive monthly their pro rata shares of principal, interest, and mortgage prepayments received by the pool.

Municipal Bond: A bond issued by a state, a state agency, or a subdivision of a state, such as a city or county; also called *muni*. An **In-State Bond** is sold by an issuer located in the same state as the resident bond owner. This bond is generally not subject to state tax. An **Out-of-State Bond** is sold by an issuer located in a different state than the resident bond owner. This bond is generally subject to state tax.

Net Asset Value: The sum of the values of all the bonds in a portfolio divided by the number of shares outstanding, priced on a daily basis to give the value of one share.

No-Load: No commission is charged to the buyer of the fund. This is only one cost to consider in the purchase of a fund.

Offering Price: The price at which sellers offer to sell bonds to buyers, also called *ask*.

Original Issue Discount (OID): The amount of money a bond sells for below $1000 face value at the time of issuance.

Par Value Bond: A bond sold at a price equal to its face value.

Premium Bond: A bond sold at a price in excess of its face value.

Pre-refunded Bond (pre-ree): U.S. government bonds, U.S. agency bonds, or other such obligations purchased by a municipal issuer and placed in an escrow account at a bank for the sole purpose of meeting the interest and principal requirements of its outstanding municipal bonds. Bonds are priced to the first call date and will be redeemed on that date. See **escrowed bond.**

Primary Market: New issues are sold in the primary market. See **Secondary Market.**

Principal's Market: In a principal's market the broker who sells you the bond is the owner of the bond. The broker is functioning as a principal rather than as a broker. A true broker is a person who brings together a buyer and a seller to earn a fee, called a commission.

Proprietary Products: Financial products which are created at a particular brokerage house and generally sold only there.

Prospectus: A document required by the Securities and Exchange Commission which discloses a huge amount of data about the issuer and the investment, including all of the risks.

Put: A bond feature providing the bondholder with the right to sell the bond back to the issuer at a specified price at a specified time.

Rating: An estimation by a rating agency of an issuer's ability to pay interest and principal when due.

Real Return: The return from the bond after taking inflation into account. The formula to compute real return is: Stated rate for the bond − inflation rate = real return.

Refunding: The exchange of one bond issue for another.

Registered Bond: A bond which is recorded in the name of the bondholder, evidenced by a physical certificate.

Revenue Bond: A municipal bond payable solely from the revenues derived from operating a project acquired or constructed with the proceeds of the bonds.

Risk, Default: See Default.

Risk, Early Call, and Reinvestment: The risk of getting your principal back when interest rates are low and you have to reinvest at that time.

Risk, Event: A significant downgrade of a bond caused by an unexpected event such as a takeover.

Risk, Interest Rate: The risk that interest rates go up and the value of your bond goes down; also called **market risk.**

Risk, Liquidity: The risk that bonds cannot be sold quickly at an attractive price.

Rule of 72: This rule tells you approximately how many years it takes a sum of money to double, by dividing a rate of return into 72. For example, if the rate of return is 7 percent, it takes 10 years for a sum of money to double (7 percent/72 = 10 years).

SEC 30-Day Yield: The SEC mandates that every fund compute this yield so that investors can compare the yield of one fund with another. The yield is composed of dividend income, assumes semiannual compounding, and takes into account expenses.

Secondary Market: The trading market for outstanding bonds and notes which have already been issued. See **Primary Market.**

Secured Bond: A bond that has some form of designated revenue source.

Security Number: The number of a specific bond certificate in a bond issue.

Settlement Date: The date funds are due for payment of a bond purchase. Currently it is three business days after the trade date. Nonpayment by that date might result in late fees.

Short First Coupon: An interest payment for less than six months of interest.

Short Position: A short position entails selling bonds you don't own in anticipation of buying them back at a cheaper price later.

Sinking Fund: A fund set aside by an issuer to retire bonds at or prior to maturity usually through a lottery.

Spread: The difference between the bid and the asked price of a bond; the profit that the brokerage house makes on the sale of a bond. The difference between the yields of bonds sold in different market sectors.

Story Bonds: Bonds that require a long description and explanation (i.e., a story) of where the money is coming from to pay the bond's interest and principal.

Structured Notes: Bonds that are especially sensitive to fluctuations in interest rates.

T-Plus 3: The rule that requires municipal bonds to be paid for within three days of purchase.

Taxable Equivalent Yield: A comparison of the yield on a taxable bond (in your tax bracket) and a tax-free bond to see which is more desirable for you.

Teaser Rate: An initial high interest rate used to attract investors that is lowered after a short period of time.

Total Return: For a fund, the sum of the dividends received plus or minus the change in the net asset value of the fund. Expenses are taken into account as well. Total return = (value of bond at computation date + interest payment − amount paid for bond) ÷ amount paid for bond.

Trade Date: Each date that bonds or funds were purchased. This is the date used in tax reporting.

Trustee: The financial institution responsible for receiving funds and paying out funds for a particular security.

Underwriter: A firm that submits a bid to buy an entire bond issue from an issuer to resell it to the public. It is common for a number of firms to band together as an **underwriting syndicate** to do the underwriting in order to spread the remarketing risk.

Unit Investment Trust (or Trust): A fixed portfolio of bonds usually sold in undivided interests of $1000.

Unit Price: The amount paid for a bond expressed in terms of one hundred, rather than one thousand; for example, 102 means you paid $1020 for each bond.

Volatility: Change in investment value.

When Issued: A bond or security, such as a Treasury bill, that has not been issued yet and is trading in anticipation of its issuance.

Yield Curve: The name given to a line graph that plots the interest rate paid by bonds of similar types but different maturities.

Yield-to-Call: The yield-to-maturity calculation where the call date is substituted for the maturity date.

Yield-to-Maturity: A computation which takes into account the time value of money and the discount or premium on the bond. It is used as the basis for comparing one bond to another.

Yield-to-Maturity after Tax: The yield-to-maturity reduced by the tax on the difference between the purchase price and redemption price on a discount bond.

Yield-to-Worst: The lesser of the yield-to-maturity over the life of the bond or the yield-to-call.

Bibliography

Bogle, John C. *Bogle on Mutual Funds.* New York: Richard D. Irwin, Inc., 1994.

Grant, Jim. *Minding Mr. Market: Ten Years on Wall Street.* New York: Farrar, Strauss & Giroux, 1993.

Lewis, Michael. *Liar's Poker.* New York: Penguin Books, 1990.

Malkiel, Burton G. *A Random Walk Down Wall Street.* New York: W.W. Norton & Co., 1990.

Needleman, Jacob. *Money and the Meaning of Life.* New York: Doubleday & Co., 1991.

Stein, Benjamin. *Financial Passages.* New York: Doubleday & Co., 1985.

Tobias, Andrews. *The Only Other Investment Guide You'll Ever Need.* Toronto: Bantam Books, 1989.

Train, John. *The Money Masters.* New York: Harper & Row, 1980.

_____. *The New Money Masters.* New York: Harper & Row, 1989.

Index

About the Authors

Hildy Richelson, Ph.D., and Stan Richelson, J.D., LL.M, are Registered Investment Advisors, bond traders, and the owners of the Scarsdale Investment Group, Ltd., Blue Bell, PA. They have taught bond investing at Manhattan's New School for Social Research and elsewhere. The Richelsons have appeared on numerous radio talk shows and have been quoted in a wide array of financial publications, including *The Wall Street Journal* and *Money Magazine*. They are the authors of *Income Without Taxes: An Insider's Guide to Tax-Exempt Bonds*.